# WORCESTER PARK AND CUDDINGTON:

# A WALK THROUGH THE CENTURIES

## David Rymill

The Buckwheat Press

Reprinted October 2000


Published by The Buckwheat Press
77 Cromwell Road
Worcester Park, Surrey  KT4 7JR

ISBN 0-9538418-0-4


Printed by Grove Business Services Ltd
Driftway, Woolfords Lane,
Elstead, Godalming, Surrey. GU8 6LL

# Acknowledgements

My greatest debts are those closest to home: my brother Stephen has typed the manuscript with great skill and patience, my father Bob has spent many hours carefully preparing the typescript for publication, and my mother Margaret has not only answered my constant questions about places and people in Worcester Park, but has helped in innumerable practical ways. Nor should I forget that this book would never have been written if my mother's and father's parents had not chosen to move to Worcester Park in 1937 and 1964 respectively.

One of the most enjoyable parts of my research has been the chance to meet many present and former residents who remember Worcester Park across the decades. I must make particular mention of Horace Shrubb, Maurice Upperton and Gerald Woods who have shared with me their vivid memories on more than one occasion, and have helped in other ways with great enthusiasm.

I am very grateful to all those who have allowed me to make use of their recollections, including Terry Aves, Ada Batt, Canon Cornelius Beausang, Lucy Bell-Chambers, Philip Betteridge, Ruth Bissell, Bob and Joy Blake, David and Audrey Blake, Harry Butcher, Ray Child, Stephen Church, Olive Dare, Rosemary Deacon, Jenny Dore, Joyce Fellgett, Jean Harrison-Smith, The Lord Ironside, Jim Jolley, the Revd Leslie Jolly, Canon Idwal Jones, Thelma and Marian Jones, Ron Kinton, Doris Knight, Stan Lumsden, Greta Mallin, Terry Moore, Jim and Margaret Parker, Dorothy Payne, Frank Petley, Dr E H D Phillips, Pam Phillips, Katherine Pollock, Frank Read, Margaret Rymill, Arthur and Peggy Saitch, Mary Samuda, Margaret Trickett and Roger Wilks.

Many of those listed above have also provided illustrations or suggested contacts or improvements. I should also like to thank the many others who have assisted in these ways, including Stan Dare, Nick Gaselee, Major Andrew Gossage, Evelyn Gregory, Nicholas Halsey, Ivor Lindsell, Terry Major-Ball, Robert Mills, Gerald Smith, Cyril Southerby, Joanna Tarbutt, Barbara Webb and Eileen Wilks. I am also grateful to the many archivists and librarians who have provided advice and assistance, especially Kath Shawcross at Sutton Library and my former colleagues at Surrey Record Office (now Surrey History Centre).

The Ordnance Survey maps, and several of the illustrations as indicated, are reproduced by permission of Surrey History Service.

Frith Acknowledgement: The postcards on pages 10, 76 and 140 are reproduced by courtesy of The Francis Frith Collection, Frith's Barn, Teffont, Salisbury, Wiltshire SP3 5QP, tel. 01722 716376. The Francis Frith Collection holds the photographic archive of the Victorian postcard publisher Francis Frith and his successors, containing views of over 4000 towns and villages between 1860 and 1970; mounted and framed reproductions of Frith photographs are available from the Collection.

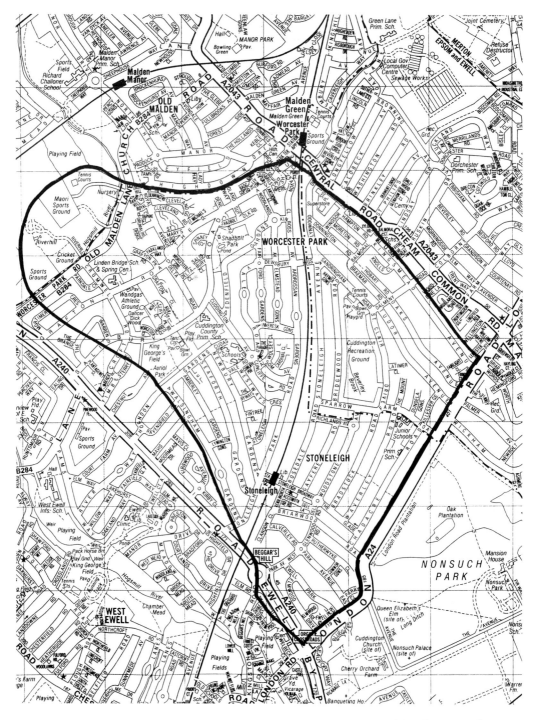

Modern Worcester Park, showing the probable boundary of the Great Park
in the time of the 4<sup>th</sup> Earl of Worcester, c.1610
(In Tudor times the Park extended further towards Old Malden)
The Little Park extended south-east from the London Road to Cheam Road

*[Reproduced by permission of Geographers' A-Z Co. Ltd. Licence No. B0482.*
*This map is based upon Ordnance Survey maps with the permission of the Controller of Her Majesty's*
*Stationery Office. © Crown Copyright 2000]*

# A Walk through the Centuries

## How to use this book

The aim of this book is to present the story of Worcester Park and Cuddington in the form of a continuous circular walk, to be undertaken either on foot or from the comfort of your armchair. Inevitably this geographical format means that episodes will not be covered in date order, so you may wish to begin by reading the introduction, which gives the context.

The walk itself begins at Worcester Park Station where so many people have caught their first glimpse of the locality. It is served by trains from Waterloo and Epsom, and is almost adjacent to the Malden Green bus stops served by the 213 from Kingston and Sutton. The walk, which covers about 8 miles, can be completed in about three hours at a fairly brisk pace, excluding reading time. If you follow the suggested detours to the Banqueting House and Longfellow Road / Green Lane, you will need to allow another 15 to 20 minutes each. As the walk is circular, you can of course start at any point: for instance, beginning at the London Road car park in Nonsuch Park enables you to follow the history of the early Cuddington village and Nonsuch Palace before visiting the estates which have been built on their hinterland.

Further practical points and summaries of various routes start on page 157.

## Introduction

The history of Worcester Park and Cuddington can be summed up in five phases.

The first phase sees Cuddington as a medieval village. Like most villages, its origins are unrecorded. We know that many people would have travelled through the area long before the Anglo Saxons, ranging from the inhabitants of the Iron Age settlement on the Percy Gardens site in Old Malden to the Romans travelling between London and Chichester along Stane Street (roughly the line of the London Road beside Nonsuch Park). In the Anglo-Saxon period, a village was established in the area we now know as Nonsuch Park, and was named, after its founder, as "Cuda's farm", or Cuddington. Like most of the communities between Guildford and Croydon, it developed into a long, thin parish, with its village placed centrally on the geological spring-line, and arable fields and pasture on the chalk downs to the south and the clay to the north. By 1538 it had a stone church, St. Mary's, a manor house with the latest fashion in bay windows, and several well-to-do farmers.

1538 saw an abrupt end to the first phase, when Henry VIII acquired the whole of Cuddington manor, demolished the village and began constructing Nonsuch Palace, designed both as a satellite of Hampton Court for use during hunting trips, and as a symbolic presentation of the Tudor dynasty. The site of the church disappeared beneath the inner courtyard of the palace. Two deer parks were set up within the parish, and the appointment in 1606 of the Earl of Worcester as Keeper of the Great Park, stretching from the London Road through Stoneleigh and over The Avenue to the Hogsmill, inspired its later name of Worcester Park.

During this second phase, Nonsuch's fortunes rose and fell, as it proved popular with Elizabeth I, was given to the Queens of both James I and Charles I, and after the Civil War was used by Government officials evacuated from plague-stricken London. Charles II gave Nonsuch to his mistress Barbara Villiers, who brought the second phase to an end as abrupt as its beginning, by demolishing the palace and selling off the building materials.

A quiet phase now began, which saw Cuddington as a parish without church or village, the other deer park (the Little Park) mainly given up to farming except around the Mansion House, and Worcester Park divided into several farms and troubled only by occasional accidents at the gunpowder mills on the River Hogsmill beside Old Malden Lane.

The fourth phase, heralded by the coming of the Wimbledon-Epsom railway and the opening of Worcester Park station in 1859, began in earnest in 1865, and saw the focus of attention shift from the Nonsuch area to the northern tip of the parish. The Landed Estates Company laid out the area around The Avenue for the construction of a genteel suburb, aimed at professional classes wishing to combine rural surroundings with easy access to City offices. Meanwhile, the British Land Company began developing Longfellow and Washington Roads off what is now Central Road, on the former Cheam Common, and the name Worcester Park advanced across the old park and parish boundary to cover this area as well.

By 1925, development was largely limited to the areas immediately adjoining The Avenue and Central Road, the new churches of St. Mary's Cuddington and St. Philip's Cheam Common having been established at their respective southern ends. In that year, the fifth phase was, like its predecessor, ushered in by the railway: electrification of the line through Worcester Park, followed in 1932 by the opening of Stoneleigh station, made the farmland an attractive proposition to the inter-war developer, and the suburban dream became affordable to a larger proportion of the capital's office workers. By 1939, Worcester Park had taken on its present pattern of Tudor-style avenues, and the largest surviving open space was, ironically, Nonsuch Park, where the medieval population had been most concentrated.

These five stages of development have left the historian with a problem of definition. Worcester Park is a postal district split between three parishes within two dioceses, three boroughs within two administrative counties. Worcester Park station, arguably the focal point of an area which remains popular with commuters, stands close to the point where the three parishes and boroughs meet. The old village of Cuddington lies over a mile outside the present ecclesiastical parish boundary, and the present St. Mary's church stands outside the medieval parish. Worcester Park has, for postal purposes, extended not only over the whole of Cheam Common but also over most of Old Malden.

This leaves us with at least four possible definitions of 'Worcester Park and Cuddington': the medieval parish of Cuddington, the modern ecclesiastical parish which has succeeded it, the Great Park as it existed in the Earl of Worcester's time, and the modern postal district of Worcester Park. The present writer's compromise has been to attempt to cover those areas which are included in any two of these definitions. This means that the more distant parts of the postal district, such as Old Malden village and North Cheam, and the southern part of the medieval parish, from Howell Hill to Banstead Downs, are only mentioned briefly. It is hoped, however, that this will be sufficient to demonstrate the ways in which our common history has been shaped, both by a few major actions of the influential, and by many smaller steps taken, knowingly or unknowingly, by inhabitants down the centuries, ever since a man named Cuda put his spade into the ground and discovered a spring.

## Worcester Park Station

The railway station, opened in 1859, has perhaps had a greater effect on Worcester Park than any other secular building since Nonsuch Palace. It was one of the original stations on the London and South Western Railway's line to Epsom, a branch line from its main London-Wimbledon-Southampton route. Until the opening of the station, no significant development had been undertaken in the area and, indeed, the station was known as 'Old Malden and Worcester Park' until 1862. The arrival of the railway meant that this area of farmland, isolated from shopping facilities and areas of employment, was within half-an-hour's journey from the capital. However, when the proposed Wimbledon-Epsom line was being considered by a Parliamentary committee, the principal argument put forward by Thomas Weeding of Fullbrooks in favour of opening a station was that it would enable local farmers to have chalk brought from Ashtead to improve the soil.[1]

The 1862 timetable shows seven trains in each direction on weekdays, taking between 21 and 31 minutes depending on the number of intermediate stops. The fares from Waterloo for the three classes were 1s 9d, 1s 3d and 10½d. By 1922 an hourly service was provided each weekday, taking 23 - 25 minutes; there were extra services in rush hours: eight up trains were provided between 7.13 and 9.29. Two of these, the 8.33 and 9.29, ran fast from Worcester Park to Waterloo in 19 minutes.

*Extract from November 1862 timetable*

In 1925 the line was electrified. The service was increased to three trains an hour, plus an additional train at 8.33 which ran to Waterloo via East Putney. By 1938 there were

14 up trains between 7.22 and 9.30. Many services ran fast to Waterloo from Motspur Park, where connecting trains for intermediate stations were available.[2]

The original station, shown in the photograph below, complemented the semi-rural aspect of pre-1930s Worcester Park. Councillor E W Sams, writing in The Courtier (the magazine of the Ewell Court Residents' Association) in 1956, described the station as it existed when his family moved to Worcester Park in 1926:

"Many an evening have I stood on Worcester Park station and been entertained by the stationmaster's family singing while someone strummed the piano. Before the station was rebuilt it incorporated the stationmaster's private residence and the room used for this hilarity opened direct on to the platform for all and sundry to look in and, if in the spirit, join in."[3]

*Worcester Park station from the footbridge, postmarked 1907. Notice the signal-box on the down platform, and the siding leading to a goods yard just beyond the up platform*

The present station was constructed between 1935 and 1939 at a cost of nearly £14,000. Its style is an example of the trend towards modernist architecture by the Southern Railway (whose architect at this time was J Robb Scott), also seen on the Chessington line. The use of this style for station architecture had been pioneered on The Underground by Dr Charles Holden during this decade, borrowing from Scandinavian and Dutch designs.[4]

The relationship between the station and the local inhabitants has always been a delicate one: without the railway, they would be unable to reach their places of work and entertainment in London, but the disruption caused by leaves, snow and other problems has probably generated a similar brand of impatience from one generation to another, perhaps providing the office-worker's only outlet for the natural tendency to relate "travellers' tales".

Most local organisations seem to have turned their thoughts to the question of railway services. In 1871 the Cuddington Vestry (the official meeting of parishioners, which was responsible for the secular duties later transferred to the civil parish council as well as ecclesiastical affairs) voted unanimously to send a 'memorial' to the LSWR, stating:

"That your Memorialists are Inhabitant Householders at Worcester Park, and most of them are daily Travellers by your Railway from the Worcester Park Station. That your Memorialists and their families are greatly inconvenienced by the want of an earlier morning train, and a later night train. The present morning train… is not sufficiently early to allow of those Gentlemen wishing to leave London by the 9 oclock express trains on other lines reaching the various stations by that time; and a later train is required to enable your Memorialists and their families to avail themselves of the evening London Entertainments."[5]

Another source of annoyance to regular passengers was the fact that the only means of access to the platform was by Station Approach. This could mean the difference between catching or missing a train in the mornings, and in the evenings resulted in travellers arriving on the down trains having to cross over the footbridge and walk down Station Approach before, in many cases, turning back under the bridge. The desire for a shorter means of access to the up platform, and a direct exit from the down side, was being discussed by the Cheam Ratepayers' Association (later the Cheam and Worcester Park Ratepayers' Association) as early as 1905, and in 1907 the Secretary was directed to write to the LSWR to "express the hope that at no distant date they will be willing to give more prompt facilities for exit on the south side for passengers arriving between 5.30 and 7.30 pm from Waterloo".[6]

Even when they had left the station, the travellers might encounter further problems: one resident described how (as his son recalls) around 1890, when he must have been

*Postcard of Worcester Park station, postmarked 1905*

about ten, "the sport of the boys was to wait behind the hedgerow near the station when the city gentlemen came off the trains to come up to their houses in The Avenue with their stovepipe hats on, they used to try and knock the stovepipe hats off by throwing clods of mud."

*Walk down Station Approach.* Until its demolition in 1999, there was a small building on the right, last occupied by the furniture dealers Perrings, standing on the site of the coal merchants' office shown in the photograph on page 5 when it was run by Millward Bros. The siting of the coal office adjacent to the station was by no means accidental: sidings were provided across the present station car park for ease of unloading into open bunkers. Maurice Upperton recalls that, in the 1920s, the shunting yard was "a hive of activity from five in the morning", when the coal train arrived. "All the horses and carts were lined up, taking their quota of coal, the postmen were there with their barrows for the mail, and the fishmonger was there with a van."

*At the foot of Station Approach we reach…*

# Malden Green

This green, at the southern end of Malden parish, is often named on maps as Lower Green, to distinguish it from Plough or Upper Green which lies further up Malden Road at the junction with Church Road. As the map on page 13 shows, Malden Road – the main road from Kingston to Sutton – runs across the green. A little to the north is Back Green, which runs eastwards to Green Lane (see page 149), and a narrow neck of land formerly connected the two. The railway, however, ran across both Back Green and Lower Green, and the connecting strip of land was separated from the former.

In the late 1940s, the station side of the Green was regularly transformed into a fairground once a year. As Margaret Rymill recalls, "It was quite a big fair, with a Big Wheel and horses on the roundabout and hoop-la and roll-a-penny, and a roundabout with little cars on slopes going up and down."

Behind the green stand the buildings of Malden Green Farm. A farm has stood here since at least the 1620s, and the present farmhouse and barn may date from this time. In the 1840s its land extended to 156 acres, including most of the land between the Beverley Brook and the 1930s development of Malden Green Avenue and Broadmead Avenue, as well as some land between Malden Road and South Lane. In the 1920s the premises housed a shooting school (see Kingshill Avenue, page 147).

In 1932, after building development had begun on the farmland, the farm buildings were bought by Thomas Parker who had previously rented space there for his coal carts. The Parker family had been in Worcester Park for some decades before that: Mr Parker was initially a greengrocer, and Mrs Parker ran a corn chandlery at no. 1 Cheamside, later taken over by Tommy Waite, and then by James Pearson (see Cheamside, page 137). By 1926 the Parkers had moved to Idmiston Road, and Mr Parker had become a coal merchant, with premises in the Station Yard.

In the 1930s the business expanded greatly: in addition to coal, the firm delivered parcels for the Southern Railway, and some garden supplies such as topsoil and turf. A large stock of horses was stabled at the farm, some of which were leased to other companies such as United Dairies and bakeries in the suburbs for use with their own delivery carts. Mr Parker, who died in 1947, was assisted in the running of the business by his sons James, Tom, Charles, Harry and George.

*One of T Parker & Sons' fleet of delivery carts at Malden Green Farm, 1930s*

In 1948 the coal business was sold to Charringtons. Tom and Charles Parker continued to work with horses, and began to specialise in training showjumpers. They enjoyed great success, and their customers included the Dutch royal family. Their brothers Harry and George developed the garden supplies business under the name T Parker and Sons (Turf Management Ltd), supplying grass seed, fertiliser, sand and machinery for sports grounds and golf courses. This business continued to be managed by the family until 1990. A residential development, preserving the farmhouse and the barn, is now planned for the site.[7]

On the other side of Malden Road, beyond the Green, the land now occupied by the Manor Drive estate was in the 19th century run as the home farm for Fullbrooks, Thomas Weeding's mansion off Church Road (near Avondale Avenue). This land was still a meadow in the late 1920s, and Gerald Woods remembers seeing long-haired and long-horned cattle grazing here. This estate was built by Lavender and Farrell, already responsible for developing the Lavender family's own farm at Cheam Common.

Many of the road names reflect the old names of the fields: The Hollands runs through the site of a field shown as 'Hollands' on a map of 1627, and Down Field was one of the common fields, divided into small individual strips of land, and occupying much of the central portion of this area. The modern Highdown runs across two sections of this field shown as Upper and Lower High Down Shot in 1627, while Lady Hay was a small field part of which is now occupied by the Parochial School.[8]

A footpath ran from the back of The Worcester across the meadow, and skirted the gardens of Fullbrooks before emerging on Church Road beside Malden Parochial School. This school was opened in 1864, with a single school-room and school-house, and has been extended on several occasions (in 1896, 1958, 1967 and 1976). Until the opening of Cheam Common Junior Mixed School in 1932, most of the boys from Longfellow Road and Washington Road would transfer to Malden Parochial when they were seven or eight, and many used this footpath each day. Maurice Upperton recalls being puzzled by the sign on the side of the Railway Inn beside the footpath "Flies meet all trains". Mr Upperton vividly remembers his years in the school, around 1920:

"I started with a Miss Philpot: one of my first recollections with her was having to stand out the front and read something I'd written. I had no idea that I was good at writing, or enjoyed writing, but it seemed to give her pleasure and it seemed to give me pleasure. Then one day I discovered in a book there a verse, and this poem so entranced me that I copied it all out, and from that day on I seemed to have an affinity with poetry and writing. Then I went on to a Miss Furmedge: she introduced me to real stories that you could read for yourself, and I got a love of books when I was in her class. Then I went on to Miss White: she was a severe lady but I got on well with her.

"Mr Geary took the last three years, and when I got into his class I seemed to romp on. He was a very good disciplinarian and an excellent Head. The boys loved him: they called him Gaffer. He did all sorts of things that headmasters don't normally do: he ran the football team; if there was an outing he would be in charge of it. When people came to see him on business he would put up the blackboard, and he would write on it 'You are on your honour to behave yourselves until I return': and the school was quiet."

*Using the pedestrian lights, cross over Malden Road and Park Terrace. Walk up Park Terrace for a few feet.* Before we turn into The Avenue, we should notice the buildings in…

# Park Terrace

On the right is the Worcester Park public house. There has been a pub on this site for over 200 years: in 1794 it was referred to as The Cross, and for most of the following century was known as The Red Cross Knight or a variant of this name; the inn sign would perhaps have depicted St. George.

Around 1865 the premises were rebuilt; in response to the increased business brought by the railway they were renamed the Railway Inn.[9] Sir Alexander Harris remembered it, at the turn of the century, as "a substantial inn with good stables and coach-houses."[10] As the population increased rapidly in the inter-war years, this building in turn became insufficient: Frank Read remembers that, when he moved to the area in 1935, "The Worcester was a tavern, and if you did go in there for a glass of beer you had to all stand together and drink at the same time, otherwise you couldn't get your arm up – shoulder to shoulder it was."

The present building dates from the late 1930s, and was clearly designed to attract the middle classes who were moving to the area. Its function rooms became the venue for the annual dinners of a number of local organisations. It was given the name The

Worcester (the word 'Park' was only added around 1996). Arthur and Peggy Saitch recall the regular ballroom dances here in the post-war years. Latterly it has earned a reputation for live music on weekend evenings.

*Postcard (c.1900) showing, from left to right, Alan Woods's butcher's shop and delivery van, and the rest of Park Terrace; Millward & Sons' post office and estate agency; the footpath to Malden Parochial school; and the Railway Inn*

To the left of the Worcester Park, closing off the end of Park Terrace, is a small office block built in the late 1970s on the site of Worcester Park's first Post Office. Thomas Frith Millward was post master by 1874, and in 1899 Millward Bros. were operating as "house agents, coal merchants, stationers, drapers &c" from the premises. From 1902 the Capital & Counties Bank (absorbed into Lloyds in 1918) rented one room from the Millwards, and opened an agency, operated from their Epsom branch, and open in the mornings on two weekdays and Saturdays. In 1922 they concluded a new tenancy agreement, giving them the use of the room from 10 till 1 on weekdays and 10 to 12 on Saturdays for £30 per year, with the right to remain open until 3 pm on weekdays for an additional £8. Increasing business caused the branch to move twice in quick succession: in 1925 two rooms were rented in G W Young's premises on the corner of Brinkley Road and then, probably in 1930, the purpose-built bank on the corner of Green Lane was opened. By this time the manager of the New Malden branch was responsible for Worcester Park, where day-to-day control was in the hands of the Clerk-in-Charge, Mr T H Willoughby. Full branch status was achieved in 1936.[11]

By 1924 Julia Greenwood, who later had a stationer's shop in Park Terrace, was running the Post Office. Maurice Upperton describes her as "the fiercest lady in the village. She had pince-nez and when she looked at you over the top of them you really quavered." By 1926 Sydney Short Smith had taken over both the Post Office and draper's business, while the Millwards continued the estate agency. The Post Office moved to Green Lane in 1939, and the premises, under the name Bank Buildings, were used as offices until they were burnt down.

*Postcard of Park Terrace, postmarked 1952. The shops are still present, but the
Railway Inn has been replaced by The Worcester
[Courtesy The Francis Frith collection]*

The large office building on the left side of Park Terrace was built in the mid-1970s on
the site of a parade of shops that dated back to about 1870. At the left-hand end of the
parade was a butcher's shop, run from about 1898 by Alan Woods. As his nephew
Gerald Woods recalls, Alan was a butcher-grazier, with a farm in Cheam Common
Road near the Drill Inn, and another closer to Cheam, not far from Cheam Church of
England School. His main shop in Park Terrace had a yard and slaughter-house at the
back, and living accommodation on three storeys behind and above the sales area; he
also had a branch shop in Cheamside (now part of Central Road, near the junction
with Longfellow Road).

Until the reorganisation of the junction of The Avenue, Park Terrace and Malden Road,
there was a triangular patch of ground between the main shop and The Avenue. The
maintenance of this patch caused problems after the collapse of the Landed Estates
Company. Eventually Alan Woods undertook to keep it tidy. However, as his nephew
recalls, "My uncle had chestnut paling fences put right the way round there, and they
took it as their own, they called it the Plantation, and they used to sit out there in their
deck-chairs." Eventually Malden Council took possession of the land, removed Mr
Woods's rustic shelter and delivered it to one of his farms.

He seems to have enjoyed a more harmonious relationship with Cheam Parish
Council. For an annual fee of £52 10s he undertook to provide horses for Cheam's
manual fire engine whenever required for call-outs, and for six drills and three test calls.
The horses were to be kept at the farm near the school in Malden Road during the day,
and stabled behind the Prince of Wales public house at night; Mr Woods also had to
provide a driver as part of the agreement, drawn up in 1910.

*Left: Alan Woods's butcher's shop.*
*In front of Henry Dare's fruiterer's and florist's shop*
*is a bicycle which, according to the sign, is on hire*
*from Tom Mearing's Imperial Cycle Works.*
*Above: Alan Woods with his car outside the shop,*
*with the Railway Inn in the background*

Alan Woods cut a memorable figure in Worcester Park. Tom Parker recalled seeing him "wearing a beautifully cut suit, in black and white dog's tooth check, with highly polished boots and gaiters" as he walked round to Cheamside. On one occasion Tom Parker was walking along what is now Central Road "when suddenly a horse and rider burst over the hedge and landed on the pavement near him; it was Alan on his hunter" coming out of the Bean Field between Cheamside and Green Lane. He died in 1925, and his horse-drawn hearse was followed down Malden Road and Old Malden Lane by his roan hunter "complete with saddle and with Alan's riding boots reversed in the stirrups," led by his groom Fred Morgan.[12]

*Turn left into…*

## The Avenue

We are now approaching the Landed Estates Company's development. It appears that the company was set up early in 1865, purchased over 140 acres of land, and laid out The Avenue, Grafton Road and Salisbury Road. Building work commenced, and large detached villas began to appear in The Avenue. Most of them were transferred to the Worcester Park Building Company, probably a subsidiary, which leased them, mainly to professional families.

Although little is certain in the history of these companies, it seems that the principal role in their formation was that of Frederick Chifferiel, a law stationer who owned a substantial office and printing works on the corner of Chancery Lane and Cursitor Street in the centre of London's legal quarter. He lived at The Bungalow (later Ivy Cottage), where Forresters Court now stands. By the time of his death in 1883 the sluggish demand for property in Worcester Park had brought the companies into difficulty, and building had ceased. Three years later, the mortgagees took possession of much of the property, and horses were pastured on much of the land that Mr Chifferiel had intended to make into a large professional community.[13]

It is worth spending a few moments comparing the next two maps, which show this area in 1865/6 and 1894. The earlier map shows The Avenue (or The Great Avenue as it is often shown on pre-war maps) running straight up from the Malden Road. By 1894, however, The Avenue diverts into a curve, and part of the old route has survived as the cul-de-sac known as Park Terrace. This was no minor highway realignment: it took an Act of Parliament to achieve it.

When the Landed Estates Company bought the estate, the only means of access was by a track alongside the railway line. In order to provide their tenants with a more attractive drive, they bought the land on which the Red Cross Knight stood and apparently rebuilt the pub just away from the line of their proposed road. They also agreed an exchange of land with the owner of the intervening field (no. 115 on the map), Thomas Weeding. The agreement had not been settled in writing, however, when Mr Weeding died in 1864. His heir, Thomas Baggallay, who took the name of Weeding, declined to complete the agreement unless better terms were offered. By this time the road had been built, as shown on the 1865-66 map. Mr Weeding began to issue threats, and employed "a man with a board who walked up and down the park stating that it would be closed after a certain date." In the early hours one morning he

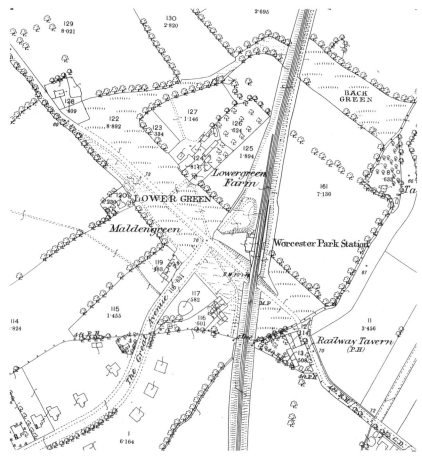

*Ordnance Survey maps of 1865/6 and 1894: during the intervening period*
*The Avenue has been diverted, the shops in Park Terrace have been built, the*
*Railway Tavern has been renamed the Huntsman's Hall, and development*
*has begun in Longfellow Road*

had part of the road dug up and had trees felled and laid across it. By this time the company had begun building a new road, bypassing Mr Weeding's land and Park Terrace in what H G Wells was to call a "consciously elegant curve". Part of the route lay across Malden Green, and approval was sought from Parliament; the bill urged that the inhabitants of the new "houses of a superior class" had to put up with approach routes which were "circuitous and inconvenient". Mr Weeding opposed the bill, on the grounds that his right to pasture animals on the common would be infringed, but his objection was dismissed and the new route was authorised by Parliament in 1871.[14]

*We now enter The Avenue,* passing Chiswell Lodge on the right. This was probably built soon after the re-routing of The Avenue, in order to provide the development with a lodge, a near-essential feature of a country gentleman's estate: an 1874 directory lists William Martin as the Landed Estates Company's lodge-keeper. The late Mrs Puttock, who grew up in the stationmaster's house above the station in the 1900s, could remember the gates to The Avenue, attached to the lodge. Beyond the lodge, and built in a similar style, was Briarwood, which was used as a maternity home from c.1930 down to the 1950s, and an old people's nursing home in the 1960s-70s. Briarwood Court now stands on this site.

The first building on the left is Worcester Park Baptist Church. The main church was opened in 1958, but the story of this congregation goes back to 1890, and begins in Longfellow Road.

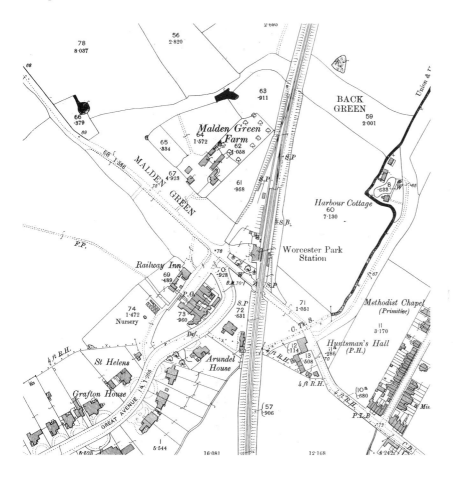

The congregation's founder was Frederick Lewis Baldwin. The year 1875 found him in business in London, where he had been an upholsterer for some years, with an interval in a repertory company in Norfolk, and had then opened a coffee house. By this stage in his life, as he recorded in his memoirs, "I did not know who Jesus Christ was… I am certain that the story of the Cross would have broken my heart at any time. But I never heard it." Then, however, a combination of the simple Gospel preaching of a visiting evangelist at Bow, and the support of an aunt and a friend, brought his struggle for faith to a climax "and in the place of that dreadful darkness, there was light." Within three months, he found himself preaching the Gospel to others.

Some time afterwards, he was staying in Epsom after suffering from over-work, and "one day being taken out for a drive… we arrived at a village, and I exclaimed 'Oh, what a pretty place, it is like being fifty miles away in the country.' 'It is called Worcester Park,' said my brother-in-law, 'it is not much known, but will be bye-and-bye, for it is only twelve miles from London.' … I then saw a solitary shut-up shop. I looked up at once to God, for I felt somehow as if I should like to make this my home." He decided that he should open the shop as a general stores, although he had never been behind a grocer's counter before.

A few days after his arrival, George Snashall invited him to attend the Methodist chapel in Longfellow Road. "Oh, how different it all seemed to be to my London life – only twelve people all told. The singing went wrong… so that I was compelled to lead off and help." He was invited to take over the Sunday School, began with four children, and raised the numbers to forty. Mr Price, the Superintendent Minister, persuaded him to be trained as a local preacher, and he preached both within the Kingston circuit and at mission services for a variety of denominations.

In 1889, however, he resigned from this work, after a friend of his had been, in his opinion, unjustly removed from the list of preachers. With the assent of his friends at the chapel, he decided to start a Bible class in his home; he soon found that forty people wished to attend, and decided to put up an iron building on a piece of land he owned adjoining his house. Part of this land was occupied by a dairy whose walls "were just one single brick thick, and these had twisted in and out in a peculiar and alarming manner." The building had been let as a stable, but Mr Baldwin dreamt how it could be transformed, with blue paint on the walls and doors, and the bulges of the brickwork repaired, into a mission hall. He set to work, covering the brickwork with sugar bags sewed together and faced with varnished oak-paper, and opened the hall on New Year's Day 1890 "with a good, homely, spiritual meeting, but far too crowded. I was rather amused at two or three who brought their own chair, and after using it for the evening, carried it home with them, quite unconcerned, as if it was a customary thing to do."

Mr Baldwin was assisted by John Fiddyment of Cheam Park, who on Good Friday "erected a large tent on the ground outside the stables, for a Gospel service, and we had our first tea meeting in the room… But oh, what a scene. The numbers of people that came… The helpers were completely packed – or rather wedged in – and could only obtain provisions by reaching out at arm's length, from one to the other, over the people's heads. But everybody was so happy."

It was clear, however, that the stuffiness of the stable was beginning to deter other visitors, and Mr Baldwin drew up plans for a permanent hall, although he made it clear publicly that he did not aim to draw people away from their existing places of worship.

The lowest estimate he obtained was £400, but he decided to proceed in faith. On Easter Monday he found two large windows in a builder's yard, and bought them for 16s. At a sale of surplus materials from a development at Raynes Park, he was able to get a quantity of wood for the roof and floor, together with glass, mouldings and nails. "A builder said 'Yes, but how is it that these sales should always just happen at the right time and right place?' – and well might he say so." It even proved possible to buy a three-sided oak-and-mahogany structure that had been a shop counting-house, which would be opened out to partition off one section of the 48 ft hall to make a prayer and enquiry room: this cost him 11s.

The new hall was being built around the old one. The last service in the latter was held on Whit Sunday, and it was demolished the next day. Services began in the new hall the following week, although it had neither roof nor floor. In August the building was finished, and was found to have cost less than £200. Four people had already been converted at services in the half-built structure. The official opening services were held on 12-13 Oct 1890, and by the second anniversary the membership had reached 44.[15]

Maurice Upperton recalls the range of events at the Hall in the 1920s: on Sundays there were Sunday School classes in the morning and afternoon, and services in the morning and evening. "And then for children they ran meetings during the week: there was the Band of Hope, and my own sister started a meeting for girls." Mr Baldwin continued to take the Sunday services, with the help of student pastors and others. He "never forgot that he was on the stage, and when he prayed it was just like a great orator. He was a magnificent figure of a man; he had white hair and a walrus moustache, and people hung on every word he said because he spoke with such inner conviction." His daughter Elizabeth "became the mainspring of the place when her father grew older. She was really dynamic: what she said people jumped and did, but she had a heart of gold, as did Mr Baldwin."

The Mission Hall was lit by gas brackets and heated by a round stove: "I can remember sitting there as a boy and seeing the cast-iron image of the tortoise on the front of this boiler. It was rather a draughty place, with a front door that opened straight into the street, so a red curtain would be drawn just behind the boiler." A smaller hall was built behind the main room, and was used for many of the children's meetings "sitting round on chairs making little circles", although

*Frederick Lewis Baldwin with his wife Anna (centre), daughter Elizabeth Baldwin and son in law Albert Fiddyment (top) and daughter Ada Fiddyment (front), c.1925*

the afternoon Sunday School sometimes occupied both rooms. "There was one tiny room built into the rear hall" where Mr Baldwin established a library, "hundreds of books, from floor to ceiling, which people were able to borrow."

At this time the mission was undenominational. Before his death in 1930, however, Mr Baldwin expressed the wish that it should be attached to Cheam Baptist Church. In 1940 it was reorganised as Worcester Park Baptist Church, and became independent, affiliated to the Baptist Union and London Baptist Association.

By this time, Elm Lodge at the foot of The Avenue had been acquired. This was requisitioned by Surrey County Council for use as a day nursery for children whose mothers worked in munitions factories, and a pre-fabricated building was added. In 1951 the site was released, and the pre-fabricated building (known as the 'Red Cross' hall) was refurbished as a church. Elm Lodge itself provided space for the Sunday School, meeting rooms and a caretaker's flat. The final service at Longfellow Road was held on 29 December, and the congregation reassembled at Elm Lodge to re-commit themselves to Christ. A retired minister, Revd A H Hawkins, took over the leadership of the church. He obtained an additional hall from a friend, Sir Herbert Janes, to accommodate the overflow from the Red Cross hall, and in 1955 began a campaign for a permanent church building adjacent to Elm Lodge. A dual-purpose church / hall was built for £9750, and opened on 4 Jan 1958. It was named the R Wilson Black Memorial, after the father of Sir Cyril Black MP who had supported the fundraising campaign. The congregation now had a facility for baptism by full immersion, which was put into use at the first Sunday service.

This proved to be a time of growth in the congregation. In particular, the young people's fellowship nearly doubled in numbers, and it became common to see young people making up half the attendance at mid-week prayer meetings. The Boys' and Girls' Brigades successfully competed in regional and national events. By the end of 1969, the church's membership exceeded 200.

There have been two building projects since the completion of the church: in 1970 two purpose-built halls, with ancillary rooms and caretaker's flat, replaced Elm Lodge, providing scope for new outreach to the community, and in 1989 the Red Cross Hall and Janes Hall were removed, and replaced with more permanent buildings.

Beyond the Baptist Church, and behind the borough boundary post, stands Purdey Court, built in the mid-1970s on the site of a house previously known as Arundel House or Wavertree, and latterly the home of Dr E H D Phillips, who had served Worcester Park as a G.P. for nearly forty years (with Dr Robinson in Malden Road).

Dr Phillips recalls "When I first went to Worcester Park we had surgeries every day 9-10 am, 6-8 pm with no appointments including Saturdays, and appointments on Sunday mornings. If you got to the surgery between those hours you were seen and they usually ran on in the evenings until 9.30-10, in fact often to nearly 11 pm. Shortly after I arrived I was asked to give an anaesthetic for a dental extraction in a private house in The Avenue. This I did using 'open' chloroform (ie drops from a bottle into a mask). This 'open chloroform' was in 1937 used routinely in confinements needing forceps delivery as it had been in Queen Victoria's day.

"When I first joined the practice there were no such things as penicillin or any antibiotics as we now have them and the sulphonamides or 'M & B tablets' as they came to be referred to. On the few occasions that one managed to get them outside hospital the side effects of the sulphonamides could be very serious. If someone developed pneumonia there was little one could do apart from antifebrile drugs and expectorants combined with careful nursing, and one hoped to ease them over the acute stage when the body's resistance to disease would fight the infecting organism. Now we use antibiotics and are surprised if there is not a marked improvement in 24 hours."

Opposite the end of Purdey Court is the entrance to Orchard Court, built in the early 1930s on the site of the Bungalow Nursery, owned by Henry Dare & Son who also had premises at the top of Central Road and in Lindsay Road. Beyond this, Forresters Court occupies the site of Frederick Chifferiel's house, The Bungalow. The large house at no. 13, Alauna (formerly St. Helen's), is typical of the villas erected in the 1860s.

On the left, we next pass Rushmere Court, which occupies the site of three pairs of large semi-detached houses, originally known as "1-6 Worcester Park". They were built in the late 1860s by the architect Chester Foulsham (of Craven Street, off the Strand), probably with his partner John Giles. Initially the Landed Estates Company's trustees granted Mr Foulsham 99-year leases of the first two pairs, in return for the expense he had incurred in constructing them and a ground rent of £12 on each house; the Company sold nos. 5-6 in 1869, and the freehold of 1-4 (for £1200) in 1870, Foulsham and Giles providing the purchase money in equal shares.

The first pair of houses, St. Andrew's and Woodville, were leased to John Francis Clarke and Mrs Clarke respectively in 1880 and 1882. In due course the two houses were converted into one: Horace Shrubb, a chorister at St. Mary's Church in the 1920s, remembers visiting the house at the end of an evening's carol singing.

*One of the large houses at the bottom of The Avenue, perhaps St. Andrews, where Rushmere Court now stands*
*[Copyright of Surrey History Service, 6348]*

"Two of the senior boys would usually go round and book into these houses – at nine o'clock on Christmas Eve it was always Mrs Clarke we went down to. We used to get invited into the hall in these places, and she had a plate on a table in the hall, and there were all the sixpences in a circle round, and we were given sixpence each."

The second pair of houses were named Elm House and Rushmere, while the third pair were given the names St. John's and Shelocke. Initially John Giles retained St. John's as his own residence. By 1881 Shelocke had become St. John's College, a girls' school which was later run jointly with Lansdowne College next door (see later).

Both these houses later had medical connections. Around the turn of the century St. John's was the home of Lt-Col, later Lt-General Sir Launcelotte Gubbins, who became an army surgeon in 1873. He accompanied the 1st Battalion 5th Fusiliers on the Afghan campaign of 1878, and served in Egypt and Burma during the following decade. In 1894 he became Assistant Director of the Army Medical Service, and was closely involved in its transformation into a royal Corps. He returned to the field in 1899, serving in the Boer War at the relief of Kimberley and the entry into Bloemfontein. After returning to England, he handled the medical arrangements for Edward VII's coronation, and from 1910 to 1914 served as Director-General of the Army Medical Service. After his death, *The Times* paid tribute to "his struggles to combat those maladies which especially affect the soldier abroad, and also for the forward preparation of the medical service in the years immediately preceding the Great War."[16]

In the 1920s the final house (then known as Chesterfield) was the home of Dr Louis Macrory, said[17] to have been the first Worcester Park resident to own a car, and Matron Macrory, who ran a nursing home there. By 1930 both houses were occupied by medical men, Dr Rowat at St. John's and Dr Hamilton Hart at Chesterfield. In 1952 the site of these six houses was sold to Epsom and Ewell Borough Council, and Rushmere Court, with its Dutch-style mansard roofs, was constructed. Its curving drive neatly accentuates the line of The Avenue at this point.

Next on the left is Lansdowne Court, a development of maisonettes in a restrained moderne style (see Timbercroft, page 61) built in about 1935. The name, however, was inherited from the house (arguably the largest of the Victorian houses in Worcester Park) which had stood on the site since the 1860s.

In 1869 the Misses Jane and Eliza Turk, with their sister Mrs Fanny Carter, took a lease of the building, where they opened a ladies' school, known as Lansdowne College. On census night in 1881, there were thirty-two girls boarding in the school, with four governesses and six servants assisting the Misses Turk.

In January of that year, another school, St. John's College, had been opened in the adjacent house with five girls taught by Mrs Mabel Robson, as part of a network of schools devised by Prebendary Joseph Lloyd Brereton.

Canon Brereton, Rector of Little Massingham near King's Lynn, was a pioneer in the field of educational reform. In 1858, whilst serving as a clergyman in Devon, he had founded a 'county school' at West Buckland, the intention being to provide liberal and religious boarding education suitable for sons of farmers within the county, with fees which enabled the venture to be a commercial proposition. He moved to Norfolk in 1867, and continued to promote his 'county' scheme, which he extended to university education, founding Cavendish College at Cambridge in 1873 as a 'county college',

18

with lower fees than the existing colleges. In 1881 he established a scheme for a Graduated County Schools Association, to provide self-supporting schools and colleges for girls and women.

The Association was given the description 'Graduated' because three grades of institutions were planned: junior or 'County' schools serving particular counties, senior or 'Centre' schools serving a whole region, and colleges at universities. Worcester Park was selected as the site for the Southern Centre school. In 1882-83 Lansdowne College was taken over and amalgamated into the St. John's Schools; Miss Eliza Turk stayed on as housemistress. An iron passage was put up linking the two schools, and Canon Brereton later used this as an illustration of his attempts to encourage private enterprise and public resources to be used in co-operation.

The schooling provided at the Worcester Park Centre School, as it became known, was academically rigorous. In the summer of 1884 it was reported that 13 girls had passed the Cambridge Local Junior Examination. A syllabus of c.1886 ranges from Todhunter's edition of Euclid's Geometry to book XI of Vergil's Æneid. A trip to London Zoo would have provided an exhilarating change: Mrs Robson wrote that "I had the greatest difficulty in persuading them to leave the Monkey House even after we paid it a second visit. They rode on the elephant and were quite brave about feeding all the animals." In 1885 there were eleven resident teachers and seven visiting teachers for music, drawing and classics. There were 55 boarders, 14 day girls and two 'governess pupils' (probably student teachers).[18]

Canon Brereton's projects ran into financial difficulties: the Association went into liquidation in 1887, and Cavendish College closed, its buildings being taken over for Homerton College. A year after his death in 1901, however, education was officially organised on a county basis, albeit through the County Councils rather than on the proprietary system.

The Worcester Park school, however, was perhaps more viable than some of the Association's other institutions. Miss Elizabeth Walsh, who had been appointed Headmistress in 1885, took over the lease of Lansdowne herself in 1888.[19] The 1891 census shows Miss Walsh still operating under the name Worcester Park Centre School, and occupying three houses. Also on the premises on census night were a French mistress and five other assistants, thirty-eight pupils, eight domestic servants and a gardener. The pupils, all girls, were mostly aged 12-18. Some had been born as far away as Yorkshire or Cumberland, whilst six had been born in India and two in Trinidad (probably the children of colonial officials or businessmen, who had been sent back to be educated in a less hazardous climate).

By 1926 the premises had been converted into a private hotel, run by a Miss Dodd. Adjacent to the house was a large hall; a postcard from the early years of the 20th century shows this hall, with several rows of individual sloping desks, a curtained stage and, above the stage, a notice urging "Right for right's sake." This hall was presumably less useful for a hotel than for a school, and in 1933 Miss Dodd agreed to let the congregation of St. Mary's use it as a church hall.

On the right, meanwhile, after passing Squirrels Court (on the site of Grafton House) and Mowat Court (on the site of Park House), we come to Kingsley Court. The house which previously stood on this site, known in turn as Park Villa, Bannadon, Dunsdale, The Laurels and Bridstow, was converted into a girls' private school known as…

# Kingsley High School

The school was run by Miss Edith Trott and her sister Miss Lilian. Miss Trott had begun with seven pupils in a single room in a house near Raynes Park Station in 1927. The school grew rapidly and further accommodation in the area was acquired. In January 1934 a branch school was opened in the Malden Institute, which moved in February 1936 to the house in The Avenue. These premises could accommodate over 250 pupils, and the schools were amalgamated here in 1942. The school catered for girls aged 5 to 19, although many took the 11-plus exam. to the local grammar schools. Margaret Rymill (née Batt), a pupil in the 1940s, remembers it as a tall Victorian house, with a conservatory at the side where they hung up their coats, and a cellar which was

*Kingsley High School*

used as an air-raid shelter. The uniform consisted of a gymslip with box-pleats, blouse, tie, and red (latterly navy) blazer. Margaret Trickett (née Davies) adds "The summer uniform was blue and white dresses: these could be floral or a shadow-check, but stripes and dots were forbidden as they might fog the eyes of anyone sitting behind." The school motto was borrowed from the RAF's: "per ardua ad astra: through endeavour to the stars."

Margaret Rymill recalls "Lessons were very formal right from the first day at school, which could be rather bewildering for a timid five year old. We had copy books, with printed writing which we had to copy exactly, difficult for the left-handed among us. In the afternoon the little ones were allowed to play with Plasticine, but still sitting at their desks. We learned French from about six years old, learning the French words for everything on a large picture of a farmyard. We had a percussion band: Miss Lilian played the piano, and we joined in on drums, cymbals, tambourines and triangles. We received a sound education with a number passing 'the scholarship' to grammar schools."

In winter, at mid-morning break, "we had little tin cups with warm milk in, and I used to take a little jar or packet of sugar with me, because I liked it sweet. And first thing in the morning we had our nails inspected to see if they were clean, and if they were clean all the week we had a sweet."

In the back garden was a small playground, and a school hall-cum-gym was built here in about 1945. This was used for "marching – very formal, to music, coming up in twos and dividing and going round; and exercises," as well as for gym lessons, assemblies and singing with Miss Lilian Trott. There were indoor games lessons in the hall, supplemented by tennis in Cuddington Recreation Ground.

Another former pupil recalls that, in the 1930s, the garden "was divided out in little plots and each pupil had a little plot of their own… we grew all sorts of things, or if we wanted to bring a bowl and dig it into the ground and make a little pond we could do."

In the years after the war, school outings were a rarity, but Rosemary Deacon (née Willett) recalls that "In 1953 we went down to Portsmouth on the train, and went over the Victory and along to Southsea – that was a big event."

Margaret Trickett recalls Miss Trott's study, to the right of the front door. "A smell of mantel polish used to hit you as you went in, and she was sitting grandly behind her desk. She was very fond of cats, and whenever you went in there was a cat somewhere in the study. She used to call them by fantastic names. One day in February '52 she came into all the classes, and we stood up – and we stayed standing for her – and she said 'I'm afraid I have some very bad news for you all: I'm afraid the King is dead.' She didn't say much else because she had to go round to all the other classes, and several of us, because she gave her cats such fantastic names, thought she was telling us about the death of her cat, and it was some minutes before we realised what it was all about.

"We used to have, about once a fortnight, a French day, or a French assembly, when she would speak to us in French, and announce all the hymns in French. Looking back I think she had more humour and a lot more understanding than perhaps we all gave her credit for at the time."

*Kingsley High School in June 1950. The staff shown (from left to right) are Miss Bentley, Miss Hillier, Miss Lilian Trott, Miss Edith Trott (headmistress), Miss Brown, Miss Francis, Mrs Lake, Mrs Davies, Mrs Holloway, Mrs Roebuck and Miss Tyler*

*Turn left into…*

# Woodlands Avenue

We shall return to The Avenue later but our route now takes us into the 1930s development known at the time as the Avenue or Cuddington Estate. The bungalow about 50 yards along on the left, Oak Cottage, stands almost above one of the streams of the Beverley Brook (see page 144): this stream used to run behind Rushmere Court and beside the allotments which occupied the land where the northern part of Avon Close now stands.

Mr Frank Read, who moved to a newly-built house in the area in 1935, recalls "I had an allotment on there during the war… the ditch used to go along there and we used to get our water there for watering the plants." When he moved in, Woodlands Avenue had not quite reached its present state: "We used to walk across the fields there to get home sometimes – carry your shoes under your arm when it got wet."

Margaret Trickett, who grew up in Woodlands Avenue, recalls one year when the brook caused more serious flooding: "I remember Mr Reynolds who lived in no. 11 wading up and down outside our house, piggy-backing the slightly older, frailer people coming back from the City: and there was Mr Reynolds, quite a tall chap, and there were the little men in bowler hats being ferried past our house – and then Miss Trott of all people came down with a big umbrella to look at the floods, and she was saying 'Good evening, Mr Davies,' as was her way, and then all of a sudden, 'Oh, aren't your laburnums *magnificent*, I have never *seen*' et cetera et cetera, and the floods were momentarily forgotten while the laburnums were admired."

*Continue as far as the roundabout.* We are now standing in the 'Avenue' or 'Cuddington' estate, which until the 1930s was part of Worcester Park Farm, operated from a farmhouse in Central Road (see page 135), and owned by the Stone family, whose property extended across most of Stoneleigh.

The road down which we have just walked was not, however, originally part of the Stone family's property. In order to realise the development value of this farm, the Stone trustees bought this strip of land for £755 in 1928 from Mr Baldwin, the owner of Oaklands, the next house in the Avenue. Little more than a year later, it began to seem as if the purchase had been unnecessary: in July 1929 Ralph Stone was informed by one of his fellow trustees: "Some of the residents in the immediate neighbourhood of the Avenue are promulgating a scheme to purchase 90 acres... for [the] purpose of a Golf Course."

Nothing came of this scheme, however, and in 1933 a number of plans were submitted to the planning authorities in Epsom for the layout of an estate here, initially by local builders Lavender and Farrell, and then by Atkinson and Marler, the agents responsible for the overall development of most of the Stone family's property.

*At the roundabout, turn right into...*

# Edenfield Gardens

The houses we are now passing were built between 1934 and 1939; the first part of the road was developed on Middle Meadow (to the right) and Upper Meadow (to the left), while most of the houses above the junction with Fairford Gardens stand on Buckwheat Field. During the course of our journey we shall walk along quite a few roads of 1930s houses, and it is worth overcoming our familiarity with the inter-war style to appreciate some of the subtleties used by the builders.

The houses on the 'Avenue' estate generally follow the most common Thirties pattern, using the 'Universal plan' layout with a 'Tudorbethan' exterior evoking the English country cottage. The layout consisted of a sitting-room at the front, with a dining-room behind, and a hall that was sufficiently wide to allow the kitchen to be placed behind it, avoiding the need for the kitchen back-extension common in earlier houses. Upstairs, the principal bedrooms were placed above the reception rooms, with a small third bedroom over the hall, and the bathroom over the kitchen.

Although there were variations to this plan, such as the provision of sliding doors between the living-rooms, or a downstairs cloakroom, the builders relied on their treatment of the façades to make their houses distinctive. Since the 1880s designers of larger houses had been returning to traditional vernacular materials, such as the black-and-white half-timbering of the west Midlands, the tile-hanging of the south east, and the decorative plasterwork of East Anglia. Suburban builders incorporated all these features, mixing half-timbered gables, leaded windows, and walls of red brick or tile to give Londoners the chance to own a cottage within commuting distance of their offices.

The pairs of semi-detached houses on the left side of Edenfield Gardens display a number of features associated with the upper end of the Thirties market: the half-timbering is extended over the whole of the façades, and oak doors with false iron hinges are emphasised by large porches. Nos. 1-3, occupying the prominent corner site, demonstrate a particular concern for authenticity with projecting upper storeys mimicking the 'jetty' of timber-framed buildings, while nos. 5-11 feature the sweeping gable, a vernacular feature re-introduced by C F A Voysey into country-house architecture around the turn of the century, and standardised for the suburban market.

## WORCESTER PARK

| AN IDEAL HOUSE | | IN IDEAL SURROUNDINGS |
|---|---|---|

**DEPOSIT £35** FREEHOLD **FROM 16/7** WEEKLY

**DEPOSITS FROM £30** FREEHOLD **FROM 15/3** WEEKLY

**DEPOSIT £35** FREEHOLD **FROM 16/10** WEEKLY

**FAIRFORD GARDENS.**
Special features—Large 3-ft. Bays in Front Bedroom and Reception Room, Crittall Guaranteed Windows, Tiled Kitchenette and Bathroom, separate w.c., " Easiwork " Kitchen Cabinet, Fitted Plate Rack, Large Airing Cupboard, Divided Coal and Coke Bunker, " Panella " Gas Wall Fires to Bedrooms.

**ARDROSSAN GARDENS.**
Charming strongly built Houses equipped with all modern devices. Situated in ideal residential district. Well served by buses and trains. Waterloo reached in 20 minutes.
**ALL PROPERTIES THREE-BEDROOM TYPE GARAGE SPACE**

**VALE ROAD.**
Attractive well built Houses with Porch Entrance, large " Easiwork " Cabinet and Airing Cupboard fitted, special Cream Wall Tiling to Bathroom and Kitchenette, Separate w.c., Panelled Staircase, Divided Coal and Coke Bunker, Wall Fires fitted to Two First Floor Rooms, and Cupboards where required in Bedrooms.

**EXCELLENT SHOPPING CENTRE AND NUMEROUS SCHOOLS WITHIN EASY REACH**

## NO ROAD OR LEGAL CHARGES

The Estate Office can be reached from Worcester Park Station via The Avenue (first turning on left), or Lynwood Drive (first turning on right).

*Write for full details or, better still, come and visit them this week-end.*

**FROM £620**

**CUDDINGTON ESTATES LTD.**
The Avenue Estate, Fairford Gardens, Worcester Park, Surrey
*Telephone: Derwent 2508      Map Reference, see page 93, square F4*

**TO £700**

*Advertisement from the Homefinder Small Property Guide, 20 March 1937*

*Continue around a left bend as far as the point where Edenfield Gardens bends to the right and Fairford Gardens leads off straight ahead.* The first half of Fairford Gardens was developed with semi-detached chalets, a style which was pioneered by New Ideal Homesteads but taken up by many smaller builders, these ones being built by Bartons of Leatherhead. They were popular with buyers because of their economical layout, with the two reception rooms, study or third bedroom, kitchen and bathroom radiating from the side entrance hall, and a central staircase leading to the two main bedrooms, thus saving much of the space devoted to the hall and landing in the more conventional layout of the 'universal plan'. Frank Read, who chose one of the houses in 1935, recalls "We had a choice of fireplaces, picture-rails if you wanted it, wallpaper all included – I paid £25 deposit and that included road charges and the front garden laid."

At that time, Fairford Gardens continued only for about half its present length, and stopped near the remains of the Forty Acre Pond (named not on account of its own size but after the adjacent meadow). A decade earlier, Gerald Woods recalls, his father used to skate on the pond, and he himself used to "fish for stickleback – take my jar and a bit of cotton with a bent pin on it, and find a worm;" on one occasion "I was there on the bank, squatting down, with the thing immersed in the water, and I was quite unaware that my centre of gravity was going forward, and the next thing I knew was 'splosh', I could see the fish going in all directions, and I walked home thoroughly wet."

Frank Read recalls that, in addition to the facilities provided by the builders, local tradesmen were keen to welcome the new residents: the local dairy, Job's, would "give you free milk for a start to get your custom." Jim Jolley, a baker's delivery boy with Turner's Bakery in Epsom from around 1935, and a barrow roundsman with the Devonshire Dairy in the same town later in the decade, expands on this practice: "As people moved in you were there with a loaf of bread, the milkman was there with a pint of milk, you got that free." The Devonshire Dairy roundsmen "used to leave a pint of milk, half of butter, anything in the dairy line – and a little carton of single cream, you'd wrap them all up in a bag, and you'd go round with the compliments of the Devonshire Dairy, and you left it." Competition bred a good-natured rivalry between the various companies: "If I got there and found United Dairy had been there before me, I used to up with the lid, pitch his and put mine in – 'I saw you do that' – it was really a laugh."

*At this junction, leave Edenfield Gardens and take the path to the right through the gates of…*

## Shadbolt Park

*Walk up the path, and continue in either a clockwise or anticlockwise direction around the Wood, the Tree Lawn and the Main Lawn until Shadbolt House comes into sight.*

The story of these gardens begins about 1921, when Ernest Ifill Shadbolt bought a piece of land known as Darkfield after a copse which stood near the top of The Avenue and "caused dark shadows to be thrown across the field by the setting sun."

Mr Shadbolt's career had been devoted to railway engineering in India. After training at the Royal Indian Engineering College at Coopers Hill he went out to India in 1874 at the age of 23, and was appointed to the Railway Branch of the Public Works Department. In the following decades he worked on railway construction projects in many of the Indian states, serving as executive engineer for the Sind-Pishin Railway, and engineer-in-chief on the railway surveys at Bezwada-Madras, Madura-Pamban, and Tinnevelly-Quilon. He was especially associated with the construction of large bridges, notably the Kotri-Rohri bridge carrying the line to Karachi over the Indus, in what is now Pakistan. From 1904 to 1906 he was Director of Railway Construction to the Government of India.

Mr Shadbolt was to enjoy almost thirty years of retirement, during which he was a keen supporter of the movement to promote open spaces, serving as treasurer and vice-chairman of the Metropolitan Public Gardens Association.[20] Having bought part of the "Dark Field" at the age of about 70, he began to lay out the gardens around his new home, and filled them with rare trees and shrubs from around the world. He was a man of determination: when an accident with a deck-chair crushed the left hand with which he played the violin, he taught himself to play with reversed hands, fingering with the right hand. In the design of his house, he showed an equal determination to achieve what he wanted: the pond was filled by collecting rain water from the roof and piping it under the lawn, and the house was built without chimneys, central heating being installed throughout.[21] He died on 16 June 1936, and the Epsom and Ewell Urban District Council was given the chance to buy the house and gardens for around half their market value.

In an article or leaflet written by Mr A E Owen, one of the founders of the Cuddington Residents' Association, and perhaps dating from soon after the purchase of the property, ambitious plans were outlined for the use of the park:

"The proposals for future development which had been put forward by the Association may be summarised in two parts, the House and the Gardens. In the House it is suggested a start be made with specimens of the 300 woods used for industrial purposes…. The nucleus of a Reference Library is already promised and the value of such a library dealing with trees, their diseases, pests, suitability for suburban gardens and so forth is obvious…. Another interesting section would be that of local finds in the soil, showing curious and unusual geological specimens.

"In the Gardens present arrangements to propagate more rare trees would continue, superfluous specimens being exchanged with other parks as at Kew…. The Association strongly recommends that a section of the gardens be devoted to the growth of specimens of every known species of English wildflowers… a nucleus of roots might be provided by school children from country rambles and would further encourage their interest in botany.

"Many interesting collections of botanical growths could be propagated in the grounds…. To the average suburban householders one of the most useful and interesting sections possible under this scheme is that of a model kitchen garden…Add to these suggestions a Rain Gauge, a Barometer, Thermometer and a Sundial and Cuddington would possess a miniature Botanical Gardens unequalled of its kind in Great Britain."[22]

Although most of Mr Owen's suggestions were not carried out, the Council has continued to maintain the gardens, initially by retaining a resident gardener and, since the late 1980s, by periodic visits. Occasional events have been held to draw attention to the flora in the park, such as a nature trail in 1973 and Tulip weekends in the mid-1980s. The house was used, not for a botanical library but for a small branch of the County Library, and after the closure of the branch the house was converted for use as a surgery in 1980 by Dr H H Bowen-Perkins.

*Follow the main drive past the left-hand side of the house, go out through the ornamental gates, cross over Salisbury Road and turn right.*

Salisbury Road branches off The Avenue and follows an elegant curving line to the Kingston Road. It was laid out some time before 1867, presumably by the Landed Estates Company to provide sites for villas which never materialised. No houses were built in the road until the 1920s. It was named after Edward de Sarisburie, a connection of the Codington family, the lords of the medieval Cuddington manor.[23]

As we walk up Salisbury Road, on the right we catch our best glimpse of the cream-painted walls and tiled gables of…

## The Croft

This attractive house, technically located in The Avenue rather than Salisbury Road, was built in about 1900 by the architect John Alick Thomas as his own residence.

Alick Thomas was born in Hertfordshire in about 1854. By 1881 he had come to Worcester Park, and was living in his widowed mother's house on the opposite side of The Avenue. On the census returns for that year he is described as an architect. With Richard Osborne Whitfield he formed the partnership Whitfield and Thomas: they had offices in Cockspur Street until 1900/01 when they moved across Pall Mall to Haymarket. The practice is listed at that address in London directories until 1915.

Whitfield and Thomas were not members of the RIBA, which makes it harder to trace their careers. However, it is known that they designed several churches, including All Saints' West Ewell (1893-94) and St. Mary's, Cuddington (1894-95), which will be described more fully shortly, and which Mr Thomas served as churchwarden from 1901 to 1920.

In March 1896 Mr Thomas showed the Vicar and committee of Emmanuel, West Hampstead, Middlesex, around St. Mary's, and was chosen to design a new church for that parish, to seat 750 at a maximum cost of £10,000 (including site). The chancel and four bays of the nave were built in 1897-98, and in 1902-03 Mr Thomas returned to complete the west end. He gave one of the stained glass windows in the church in memory of his partner Mr Whitfield. He also drew up plans for a new church in Merton in 1907 (St. James's). In the event the church was not begun until 1938, to the designs of another architect.

It is harder to find details of the practice's secular buildings, but they are known to have made additions to Northumberland House, Stoke Newington, and Peckham House, Peckham, in 1879. In our own area, they were responsible for the rebuilding of Ewell Court House, as well as The Croft.

Mr Thomas had two sons, both of whom were killed in the First World War. The elder, Capt. Alec Vaughan Thomas, was killed at Gallipoli in 1915: he was one of sixteen officers of the 2nd Hampshire Regiment who failed to return from an attack on the Turkish trenches on 6 August.

His younger brother, Lt Maurice Wotton Thomas, was sent to Osborne College in 1906 to train for the Navy, but was invalided out through illness in 1910. He recovered, however, and in 1914 joined the Royal Field Artillery. His obituary in *The Times* records that in July 1915 "it was decided that he was specially qualified by his training for the Royal Flying Corps [forerunner of the RAF], to which he was seconded as an observer. After many thrilling experiences he was wounded in an accident in December 1915 and came home. He made a speedy recovery and was sent to a reserve squadron and gained his wings. In May 1916 he was again sent out, doing much valuable work over the enemy positions." He was presumed killed on 5 August 1916.[24]

*Continue past The Croft to regain The Avenue, and turn left.* Before proceeding, we must devote a few moments to the section of The Avenue which we have missed. Opposite is Dene Close: the name may be a disguised compliment to the last owner of

Hazelhurst, which stood on this site: John Dean was the proprietor of Dean's Blinds and in 1903 became the first chairman of Fulham Football Club as a limited company. He died in 1944, having lived to see Fulham reach the semi-final of the F.A. Cup in 1936.[25] A few doors further down The Avenue, between Dene Close and Roland Way, stands no. 41, a modern dark red brick house. This marks the site of…

## Heatherlea

This house, demolished in about 1955, was for a brief period home to one of the most famous residents of The Avenue.

In 1896 H G Wells moved here from a small villa near Woking station, apparently because he wanted a study of his own rather than having to write his books on the dining-room table. He wrote to his friend Grant Richards, another novelist, in mock estate-agent's style, "On Wednesday next we move to Heatherlea, Worcester Park, a picturesque and insanitary house in the early Victorian style standing in its own grounds of half a quarter of an acre on the London clay. … The name of the house refers to the oak trees which grow luxuriantly in this district."[26]

Wells only stayed for about a year, before departing for the coast in order to benefit from the sea air, but Worcester Park made a sufficient impression on him to feature – under the name "Morningside Park" – as the setting for *Ann Veronica*, his 1909 novel of a young woman's attempts to escape from her middle-class ties.

In the opening chapter, he describes Ann Veronica arriving by train and walking "down the station approach, past the neat, unobtrusive offices of the coal merchant and the house agent, and so to the wicket-gate by the butcher's shop that led to the field path to her home." He sums up the locality in the following words:

"Morningside Park was a suburb that had not altogether, as people say, come off. It consisted, like pre-Roman Gaul, of three parts. There was first the Avenue, which ran in a consciously elegant curve from the railway station into an undeveloped wilderness of agriculture, with big yellow brick villas on either side, and then there was the Pavement, the little clump of shops about the post office [Park Terrace], and under the railway arch was a congestion of workmen's dwellings [Longfellow Road]. The road from Surbiton and Epsom ran under the arch, and, like a bright fungoid growth in the ditch, there was now appearing a sort of fourth estate of little red-and-white roughcast villas, with meretricious gables and very brassy window blinds."

Wells peopled his Avenue with "business men, solicitors, civil servants, and widow ladies", whose social leader was "the widow of a knight who had won his spurs in the wholesale coal trade"; she had a "trim garden, with its croquet lawn, its tennis net in the middle distance, and its remote rose alley", and "understood the art of bringing people together." It may be suggested, however, that Wells missed something of the cosmopolitan nature of his neighbours in The Avenue.

## The Avenue (continued)

*Continuing up The Avenue,* on our right we pass two tall "white brick" villas, nos. 49-51, formerly known as Homewood and Hillside. By c.1945 they had been bought by a Roman Catholic order of nuns, the Franciscan Missionaries of Mary (see below), who built a chapel between the two houses. The premises were sold to Servite Houses who opened a sheltered housing scheme in the houses and two large purpose-built wings behind in 1982. The chapel was turned into a common room for the residents. Servite Houses was founded in 1945 by Miss Joan Bartlett together with the Very Revd Francis McEnerney and the Revd G M Corr of the Servite Priory in Chelsea. This was in response to the situation faced by elderly people bombed out of their homes, many of whom Miss Bartlett had met as a Commandant in the Chelsea Red Cross. This scheme was a demonstration of the desire to care for others, which had been a feature of the Servite Order since its foundation in 13th-century Florence. In 1960 the first Servite sheltered housing scheme was opened, allowing elderly people to live independently in self-contained flats while having the reassurance of a resident warden.[27]

*St. Michael's, formerly Clevelands, in 1988*

Behind the fence that runs from these houses to the corner of Cleveland Road lies St. Michael's Close, developed in 1990. This marks the site of the house once known as Clevelands, which in the late 1930s was the home of Dr Christopher Petit. The house was bought by the Franciscan Missionaries of Mary who ran a nursing home for the elderly there, under the name of St. Michael's, thus echoing – perhaps unconsciously – the name of the family who had owned Cuddington manor for much of the Middle Ages. When they sold the adjacent convent premises they built new accommodation blocks for themselves in the grounds of St. Michael's.

*Continue up the left-hand side of The Avenue until you are standing opposite the junction with Cleveland Road,* which by the 1890s contained five houses. On the right, beyond Clevelands, were The Hermitage and York House. On the left, Mount Tavy was a prominent feature of the corner site. It boasted nine bedrooms including one in the tower, a first-floor billiard or music room, three reception rooms, stables with coach house, and "well-timbered grounds of about two acres... artistically and usefully laid out" including a tennis lawn and a vinery.[28]

The greater part of the left side, however, was occupied by the grounds of Malvern Lodge, home of Charles Smith. Although Orchard House, which was part of the property, still survives, the main house (later renamed The Grange), which stood just to the west of it, has been demolished. There was little change in the appearance of Cleveland Road until well into the 20th century, except for the construction of Dennington at the further end of the right-hand side. In the 1930s, Dennington was the home of W J Lavender of Cheam Common Lower Farm whose wife had, in her earlier years, been a maid there; the house was used as an old people's home from the mid-1940s until 1988. The site is now occupied by The Denningtons development.

Turning our attention back to The Avenue, on the left we see no. 66, which was the home of Sir Arthur Dean until his death in 1976. Sir Arthur was a civil engineer, who served in the Public Works department in India from 1919 to 1946, and was chairman of the Delhi Transport Trust from 1946 to 1948, Chief Civil Engineer to the Foreign Office Administration of African Territories from 1949 to 1952, and general manager of the Libyan Development Agency for the next ten years. Among the projects in which

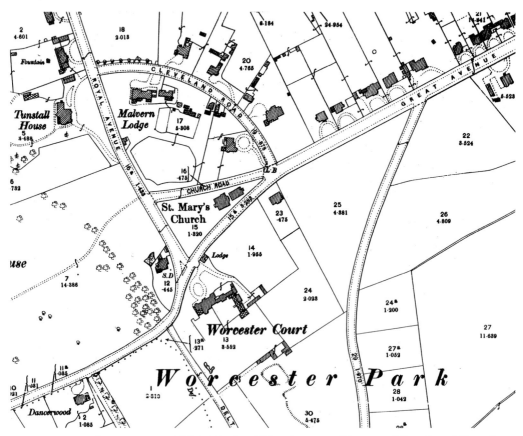

*Ordnance Survey map, 1894. Much of The Avenue, Cleveland Road and Royal Avenue is developed, but Salisbury Road and Delta Road are still empty. The new church is shown, but its iron predecessor has not yet been removed*

he was involved were the construction of a submersible road bridge over the Narbudda River near Jubbulpore in central India, and anti-malarial operations in Delhi.[29]

We are now reaching the end of the Victorian development of Worcester Park as a suburb. As the map opposite shows, the northern side of The Avenue was largely developed by 1895 and the southern side somewhat less so, while Cleveland Road, Church Road, Royal Avenue and Grafton Road boasted a total of fifteen large houses. What comment, then, can we make on H G Wells's description of "Morningside Park" as "a suburb which had not quite come off"? Sir Alexander Harris, who took up residence in The Hermitage, Cleveland Road, in 1883 and moved to Royal Avenue in 1897 (see page 42), described the situation rather more positively in his memoir of the period:

"Not unlikely it was the primary idea of the founders of Worcester Park to build a settlement of substantial houses adapted to the needs of business and professional men, who wished to have a home in the real country, and go to their daily work in London. The idea was well conceived, and had the effect of creating a rather choice and isolated district not specially well known and on that account attractive."[30]

However attractive this isolation may have been to the residents of the time, we can hardly suppose that it was entirely in accordance with the aspirations of the Landed Estates Company, whose proprietors saw several of the roads they had laid out standing almost empty. Why, then, did this development not "take off"?

There are perhaps several reasons, of which the first is hinted at in Sir Alexander's next sentence: "The touch of these varying houses with the outside world was obtained through a small business area at the bottom of the Grand Avenue": a post office and a small parade of shops were unlikely to supply all the wants of a Victorian family with the means to buy a house in The Avenue. The very isolation of Worcester Park (compared with, say, Surbiton, which was conveniently placed for Kingston) may well have made it unattractive to many potential purchasers. A noticeably high proportion of residents were former colonial officials or overseas traders, who may have placed a higher value on isolation, and had a lower expectation of convenient communications.

Another reason may have been the changing fashion in architecture in the late nineteenth century. The predominant styles until the 1870s were the Gothic and the Italianate, and thousands of villas were built in yellow brick, often with polychromatic decoration, pointed (Gothic) or rounded (Italianate) features, high gables, and fussy detail. We have seen surviving examples of these styles at nos. 13, 27, 35 and 49-51. From about 1880, this style became unfashionable for larger houses, although many of its features appeared on lower-middle-class terraces into the Edwardian period. The new style was vernacular, drawing on traditional English cottage building, using red brick, and featuring tile-hanging and half-timbering in a medley of styles from around the country. Immediately ahead of us is Copsemead, no. 68, built in a Queen Anne variant of this style, not unlike The Croft and the Old Vicarage (the right hand wing was added, in a style entirely harmonious with the original, in 1990); Hillcrest (see Royal Avenue, page 42) is a particularly fine example of vernacular style. The development of Worcester Park was, perhaps, begun at just the wrong time: by 1880 there were not enough old-style villas to make it a financial success, but there were sufficient to discourage architects from using the site for 'vernacular' schemes.

31

This point should not, however, be pressed too far: in 1925 James Sharwood, who lived at Homewood, bought Copsemead for his son-in-law and daughter Captain and Mrs Peacey.[31]

Finally, we have already seen the problems over the access from the estate to the Malden Road, which involved the company in much expense, and doubtless deterred potential tenants.

*Continuing past Copsemead, cross The Avenue and go through the wrought iron gates into the grounds of...*

## St. Mary's Church

As soon as development began in the 1860s in the 'parish without a church', as Cuddington had been since 1538, it was natural that the new residents wanted to see a church built, and it is not surprising that the preferred site was in The Avenue, the new centre of population, nearly two miles from the site of the medieval St. Mary's in Nonsuch Park (see St. Mary's Old Church, page 83). The goal of providing a permanent church was, however, to take almost thirty years to achieve.

When the Landed Estates Company bought the area of Worcester Park around The Avenue in 1865, the plot of land between The Avenue, St. Mary's Road and Royal Avenue was excluded from the sale, with the intention that it would be transferred to a public body and that a church would be built there. The Company paid for an iron church to be put up, and on 28 November 1866 the Bishop of Winchester licensed the Revd Thomas Smith, formerly curate of Chobham, to take services in this "temporary church situate in the liberty of Worcester Park in the parish of Cuddington."[32] The first services were held on 13 January 1867, with sermons by the Vicars of Malden and Ewell; a good attendance was reported despite a fall of snow on the previous day.[33]

The normal pattern of services on Sundays comprised an 8 am celebration of Holy Communion, 11 am morning prayer, and 3 pm or 3.30 pm evening prayer.

Thomas Smith remained in charge of the Iron Church until 1878, although he seems to have lived at Tulse Hill. The Revd Edmund Augustine Richardson, headmaster of Battersea Grammar School, took many of the services in the autumn of 1878, but later that year the inhabitants asked the vicar of Malden, Canon William Chetwynd Stapylton, to assume responsibility for the church, and he was licensed by the bishop on 12 February 1879. Canon Stapylton arranged with the Landed Estates Company that he would be responsible for the provision of two Sunday services each week, and the pastoral care of the local residents. He was to pay the expenses, including the organist's salary, and receive pew rents and fees in return.[34]

Stapylton already had responsibility for Malden, Chessington and Malden Rushett, and the Revd Henry John Wale was appointed curate in charge of the Iron Church. Mr Wale had enjoyed two careers: in 1845 he had entered the 15th Hussars in India as a cornet (he was subsequently promoted lieutenant). In 1854 he was ordered to the Crimea with the Scots Greys. By 1857 he had decided to return to England to seek a profession which would give him more freedom, and he was ordained deacon in 1861. His second career began with a curacy in Holy Trinity Church, at the unfashionable end of Weymouth; the parish included a large school, built under the superintendence of the vicar, where "most interesting services" were held. He later moved to Ringwood, but resigned that curacy because "a parish where the Church-people used to walk on

32

Sunday on the one side of the road, and the Nonconformists on the other, was full of difficulties, and I came to the conclusion a younger man would suit the vicar best"; from 1865 to 1878 he was Rector of Folkesworth in Huntingdonshire, and he served as secretary of the local branches of the Society for the Propagation of the Gospel, and the Church of England Temperance Society.[35]

In the 1880s it became clear that the situation was unsatisfactory. Sir Alexander Harris, despite his liking for Mr Wale, recalled that "the iron church was quite good as temporary buildings go…, but its status was far from acceptable to residents who were accustomed to an organised parish." Indeed, many residents had "found their way" to the more settled congregation at Malden. He discussed the matter with Canon Chetwynd Stapylton, who had continued to take an interest in the situation, and found that Stapylton did not see this migration to Malden as the solution; in fact, it was already causing concern in his parish.

By March 1884 a crisis had been reached. The churchwardens sent round a circular letter, in which they called "the serious attention of the Residents in Worcester Park to the present condition of affairs… 21 sittings have been given up during the past year and the income derived from Pew Rents is now only £135 per annum; the annual expenses of the Church being £200." They pointed out that non-parishioners had been unable to obtain seats in Malden Church prior to its extension in 1875, and that such problems would recur if the vacant properties in Malden were all to be occupied, or if the Iron Church closed and there were a further influx of a hundred applicants. The very state of uncertainty which was discouraging residents from attending the Iron Church was the root cause of the difficulty in obtaining a permanent clergyman. Mr Wale offered to resign, and a vestry meeting was called to decide "Whether the Iron Church shall be kept open or not, Whether Mr Wale's offer to retire shall be accepted or not, And if they decide to keep the Church open, How an annual income of not less than £200 is to be provided."

The meeting decided to accept Mr Wale's resignation, and the meeting was adjourned while investigations were pursued into an offer by Canon Brereton to pay half the stipend of a clergyman if he would assist in the management of his school. On 30 May 1881 John Hunter, as churchwarden, wrote to the chosen clergyman, the Revd William Atherstone Hales (who had been ordained in 1855, and had held curacies and parishes in Birmingham, London, Canterbury, Wandsworth, Bosley (Cheshire) and Plymouth). He explained that Canon Brereton had agreed to the arrangement "and I am therefore now in a position to ask you to undertake the duties of the Iron Church here after next Sunday up to Christmas next, for which period I can undertake to pay you £100 for your services. If by Christmas next you can arrange with the Bishop of Winchester and Canon Stapylton, who now holds the License, for the grant of the License from the Bishop to yourself, I hope that you will undertake the duties of the Church permanently, but, if you do this, I stipulate in the interest of the inhabitants that you should reside in the neighbourhood."

Mr Hales replied "I can only hope that our relative position will then [at Christmas] be such, that the rest of the programme may be happily and successfully carried out: and that the prospect of a permanent church and vicarage may make plain to me the duty and pleasure of coming to reside in or close to Worcester Park."[36]

By 1888 the financial situation had once again become serious. The insolvency of Canon Brereton's school had left Mr Hales without half his stipend, and the churchwardens without £70 pew rents which were due. They reported to the March vestry meeting that there was a deficit of over £64 in the year's accounts. It was resolved that the inhabitants and pewholders should indemnify the churchwardens, and Mr Hales offered to serve for a further year in return for the balance of income after the organist's salary and expenses had been deducted. In the event he received £99 0s 8¼d.

Throughout this time, the fact that the Church Plot remained in private ownership prevented any campaign for a permanent church being launched. As Mr Hunter had explained to Mr Hales in 1884, "The Church was built by the Landed Estates Company, then the owners of the Park... on ground not then conveyed to them but belonging to the person from whom they bought the rest of the Park. They subsequently [in 1871] gave this person £100 to convey the land to them and covenanted with him to use it only for a Church and Vicarage etc. The Company subsequently [in 1879] transferred the land to a subsidiary Company [the Worcester Park Building Company] who then transferred it to their late Managing Director Mr Chifferiel – on each occasion £100 was stated to be paid for it and the covenant to use it only for a Church and Vicarage was repeated. Mr Chifferiel is dead, his affairs are being wound up in the Court of Chancery and it is probable that his land will be offered for sale."[37] Mr Hunter judged that the current state of affairs was likely to continue until the land was conveyed to a proper set of trustees. He was over-optimistic: affairs were in fact to get worse, as Sir Alexander's memoir records:

"On a bright Sunday morning early in May, 1892, when the congregation assembled at the church, we found that there was a guard at the padlocked gates and no access to the church door was possible without dislodging the intruders." The churchwardens, although as surprised as anyone, did know the reason: the plot had been sold to Mr W J Bennett, and no covenant had been included to secure the position of the church. "Presently Mr Gilbert came up to me and suggested that we should make a charge and force the passage. 'We shall have an assault and battery' he said 'but no matter.' Mr Hunter, however, being a wise and sound lawyer, over-ruled any physical effort." Instead, Mr Hales conducted the full morning service in the double drawing-room at Sir Alexander's house, The Hermitage.[38]

A temporary compromise was reached, and services continued as normal until 2 October. The register of services records, under that date, "Church taken possession of by forcible entry and service conducted by Bennett's nominee." The financial situation added to the churchwardens' difficulties: Mr Hales received only £25 for six months' work, and left in September 1892. The Iron Church itself was in need of repair, and an estimate was obtained for a new temporary building.

In the following year, the tide turned. In August, the Church Plot was purchased from Mr Bennett for £500, and it was at last possible to think of planning a permanent church. A committee was set up the following month, and on 13 December John Alick Thomas of The Avenue (or, technically, his practice Whitfield and Thomas) was invited to draw up plans. Within seven weeks, the plans had been submitted and approved, and on 28 March 1894 a tender of £4392 from Goddard and Sons of Farnham was accepted. The foundation stone (which can be seen at the east end, on the outside wall facing the lych-gate) was laid by Bishop Thorold on 11 August.

In the meantime, services continued in the Iron Church, located on the lawn to the east of the foundation stone. From 1892, clergy were supplied by the Additional Curates

*Original designs for St. Mary's, including north and south porches*

Society (a charity which St. Mary's supported until 1991), until the Revd William Albert Cooke was appointed in March 1894. He served for six months, being paid £50, and was succeeded by the Bishop's chaplain, the Revd John Matthew Glubb.

The question of the choice of the first permanent vicar was raised later that year. The right to appoint vicars of the medieval church had belonged to Merton Priory, and it was unclear who had inherited this right. The tithes were paid to the Northey family, who had been lay improprietors as well as lords of the manor since 1755. The then head of the family, the Revd E W Northey, may have been embarrassed to find that, when his family had been receiving the tithes for so long, he was arguably entitled to appoint the vicar of a church built at the expense of the residents, although it appears that he had paid Mr Rice, the Rector of Cheam, £40 a year for pastoral work in the parish.[39] Whatever the reason, he had decided by November 1894 to transfer the advowson to the Bishop of Winchester. This was mentioned in a report of the Ecclesiastical Commissioners' Estates Committee dated 22 November; in a marginal note one of the officials had added, "Mr Northey tells me he has no idea how he became entitled – if he is entitled – to this Patronage." One can sympathise with the official, who wrote on the next page "Case altogether a very peculiar one."[40]

In July 1895 the new church was ready. The view we see as we walk up The Avenue today is very much as the original architect and builders intended. The funds available at the time, however, did not make it practical to build the whole of the nave. Only three of the intended five bays were built, and a temporary west wall with a small projecting porch was added. The plans provided for the eventual completion of the church with north and south porches, and a baptistery at the west end.

The last service was held in the Iron Church on 14 July and the new church was due to be consecrated on 17 July, but the illness and subsequent death of Bishop Thorold prevented this. The first services, nonetheless, were held on 21 July, with Mr Glubb officiating. The man chosen as vicar was the Revd William Edward Layton, who had served five curacies, mainly in East Anglia, since 1869, and was now being appointed a vicar for the first time. In August he was licensed to take services by the Archbishop of Canterbury (during the vacancy caused by Bishop Thorold's death).[41] The dedication of the church was performed by the new Bishop of Winchester, the Rt Revd Randall Davidson (later Archbishop of Canterbury) on 20 November. He preached on Psalm 68 v. 28: "Thy God hath commanded thy strength: strengthen, O God, that which Thou hast wrought in us." In December, Mr Layton was finally instituted as vicar.

The new church was dedicated to St. Mary, just as its predecessor had been. By an instrument of 5 March 1896 the Ecclesiastical Commissioners, the Bishop and the vicar brought to an end the period of over three centuries when Cuddington had been a parish without a church, and declared that the new St. Mary's was to be the parish church in substitution for the church demolished in 1538.

Since 1895, the church has had ten vicars. Mr Layton retired in 1907. His successor, the Revd Edwin Harding Eland, had served as curate in Dorking from 1896 to 1903, and since then had been a Diocesan Missioner, based in Winchester, and organising missions, quiet days, men's lectures and other activities around the diocese. He had a particular involvement in the ministry of lay readers, and served as secretary to the Diocesan Lay Readers Board almost from its establishment in 1904, a role which he retained on moving to Cuddington. Sir Alexander remembered him as being earnest in his views and having literary taste: he wrote three books, an introduction to the Book of Common Prayer, a guide for confirmation candidates, and an anthology of poetry and prose ranging across 'Life's Pilgrimage'. Horace Shrubb was a choirboy in the late 1920s, together with a number of his neighbours in Lindsay Road. They were paid monthly: "the basic was a half-a-crown a month, but you got an extra shilling if you went a full month, with choir practice, and on Sundays morning and evening services, and that was money to us in those days."

Until 1927 Cuddington lay within the diocese of Winchester, which covered almost the whole of Hampshire and much of Surrey (eastern Surrey had already been formed into the diocese of Southwark). In that year the diocese was divided, and Cuddington has since then been in the new Diocese of Guildford.

On Mr Eland's death in 1929, the Archdeacon was asked to point out to the Bishop that at two of the three churches in Worcester Park, St. John's Old Malden and St. Philip's, the services were high, and that St. Mary's was the only church in the area which met the needs of Low Churchmen. The new vicar was the Revd Eng. Capt. Francis Edwin Lamb RN (retd). He served until his death in 1941. His ministry coincided with a rapid rise in the population of Cuddington. When St. Mary's was named the replacement for the old parish church in 1896, it inherited the medieval parish boundary largely unchanged (except for the addition of 120 acres around The Avenue, including the site of the new church itself, which Henry VIII had added into his Great Park from Malden). The parish, therefore, stretched south-eastwards for three-and-a-half miles; except for the transfer of the area between Cheam Common Road and the railway line to the new parish of St. Philip's in 1906, this situation was unchanged in 1930. By 1931 the population – barely 500 when the Iron Church was opened – had reached 7000, and steps were taken to make provision for the newly developed areas. Initially, the southern part of the parish was transferred to the new parish of St. Paul's, Nork, and the northern part of Ewell (including the Ruxley Lane area as far as the Hogsmill, and Stoneleigh Hill) was transferred to Cuddington. This gave St. Mary's responsibility for the fast-growing communities of Stoneleigh and Ruxley, and led to the construction of two new churches, dedicated to St. John and St. Francis, in recognition of the names of Captain Lamb's sons Lt-Cdr John Lamb DSO and Surg-Lt Francis Lamb. For the history of St. John's, see page 74.

*Postcard of St. Mary's, showing the three-bay nave and temporary west porch*

Horace Shrubb when approaching 16 years of age was appointed the verger of St. Mary's having left the boys' choir. He was the verger at the time of Capt. Lamb's arrival. He recalls "During the autumn and winter months I had to go on Friday evenings to light the boiler fire to heat the church for the Sunday services. I started off by putting into the boiler a lot of newspaper, followed by a number of bundles of firewood, and then shovelling in coke to get the boiler going. Gradually I built up the fire until it was ready to be shut down with the damper to keep the fire going through the night. I had to go on Saturday morning and again in the evening, to rake out the ashes and then bank up the fire with fresh fuel to maintain the heat. This would be repeated on Sunday morning to complete that side of my duties.

"One Saturday evening when I was about to go to bed I had a sudden thought whether I had shut down the boiler damper: in a panic I got out my bike and cycled as fast as I could. When I reached the church my fears were justified as there were loud hissing noises coming from various parts of the church where steam was gushing from valves connected to the heating system. Capt. Lamb and his wife were already outside having been disturbed by the hissing. Instead of being angry, he greeted me by saying 'It's all right Shrubb, it's under control' and did not rebuke me, much as I may have deserved it. After everything had subsided and I had attended to the boiler, I went home more than a little thankful."

On Sundays the verger's responsibilities continued throughout the day: "I arrived at about 7.30 am to open the church and make the necessary preparations for the 8 o'clock Communion service. After cycling home and having some refreshment, I then returned to the church about half past ten, to be ready for the 11 o'clock service, and I would sit just inside the main entrance door and see that everybody had whatever they wanted, and I would have to tidy up, and then I would go back home. Then in the evening I had to ring the bell, so I'd be there by about six o'clock. I would see the evening service through, and after closing up at the end, switching off all the lights as necessary, that was it. And at various festival times I had to change the altar frontal."

The worship at St. Mary's was still low church in character. Real bread was used at Communion services, cut into tiny squares. The clergy, like the choir, wore cassocks and surplices. Candles were used – and it was another of Horace Shrubb's jobs to light them – but they were perhaps only lit on Easter Day and other festivals. Such occasions were also marked by a procession of the choir from the original vestry behind the organ "down the aisle, and around to the door, and then up the centre, singing whatever was appropriate: that happened on these festival days, Whitsun and so on."

Captain Lamb's successor, the Revd Arthur Robert Winnett, was inducted in 1942. He found himself in a parish where low-church practices remained strong, and he had difficulties in making changes such as introducing servers or altering the parish magazine. His obituary in *The Daily Telegraph* records that he "belonged to the now endangered species of scholar parish priest... Winnett chose to combine his research and writing with the pastoral responsibilities of four different Surrey parishes; he was equally highly regarded in both spheres, and each contributed to the other." After leaving Cuddington, he served in Rowledge, Grayshott and Ockham; he produced books on the Church's attitude to divorce and remarriage (on which he was prepared to make plain he had changed his mind) and on the 18th-century Irish bishop and philosopher Peter Browne, as well as a history of the young diocese in which most of his ministry had been spent. He "was a gifted preacher and teacher as well as a sensitive pastor."[42]

The Revd Idwal Jones, who had served two curacies in his native Wales and had been an army chaplain since 1944 (when he had landed on the Normandy beaches with the 79th Armoured Division), became vicar in 1950.

There was soon to be a change in the pattern of services. The practice of having a service of Holy Communion as the main morning sung service, which would have been regarded as a high-church practice earlier in the century, was now becoming much more accepted across the country. Idwal Jones introduced a 9.15 am Communion service on red-letter Sundays in 1951, and it became a weekly service from Advent 1953, initially referred to as Sung Eucharist and, from 1955, Parish Communion. Although the 11 am Sung Mattins continued until 1973, Parish Communion became the most popular service; as Canon Jones recalls, it brought "new and vigorous life in our Sunday worship."

Three important changes were made to the church's facilities during Canon Jones's ministry. The first was the laying-out of the garden of remembrance to the east of the church, as a memorial to the fallen of the Second World War, and to be used for the interment of cremated ashes. The lych gate was added by Mr and Mrs C B A Greenfield; over the gateway is inscribed the message of the Christian hope of resurrection, "Resurgam – I shall rise again".

The next project was the construction of a larger church hall. A site was chosen on a portion of the vicarage garden, on the corner of The Avenue and Royal Avenue, and plans were drawn up for a large hall, with a foyer giving access to a kitchen, committee room and cloakroom, and a stage at the further end. The foundation stone was laid by Bishop Montgomery Campbell on 5 March 1955. The day was cold and blusterous and, when the Bishop returned to Farnham and found a proposal on his desk to transfer Cuddington to the Diocese of Southwark, he was tempted to assent.[43] The Large Hall was opened on 3 June in the same year, and quickly became a centre of activities both for the congregation (by 1955 there were five Sunday Schools catering for 330 children) and for the wider community. Users of the hall included an old-time dancing group and a badminton club.

The hall, with its fine stage, also provided a home for the Cuddington Players. The Players had been founded in 1953, as a drama group, and the earliest productions had been given in a marquee during the evening of the Summer Fair. The company was soon using the new hall to stage a variety of shows, including dramas, comedies and murder mysteries.

In 1958 an Operatic Section of the Cuddington Players was formed, mainly by members of St. Mary's with a nucleus from the church choir. The inaugural production was Gilbert and Sullivan's *The Gondoliers*. Other G & S operas followed as the main autumn productions, whilst lighter musicals such as *Free as Air* or revues were often staged in the spring. Two of the most notable productions were the world premières of two musicals by Nigel Brooks and Robert Bowman: *Turpin* (based on the career of the

*Fight scene from the Cuddington Players' production of 'Turpin', 1964*

highwayman Dick Turpin, who was said to have associations with the Plough at Malden) and *Morgan* (based on Captain Morgan, buccaneer and lieutenant-governor of Jamaica), in 1964 and 1967. Later performances ranged from grand opera (*Carmen*) to American musicals (such as *Oklahoma*).

In the 1960s the Players assisted with the construction of a suite of dressing-rooms, having previously used tents pitched behind the hall for the purpose. These rooms were also used as classrooms by the Sunday School. The Players continued to use the hall until it was demolished, when they moved to Ewell.

By the 1940s the church, which had seats for 220, had become crowded. Once the new hall was open, it was time to revive plans for completing the nave. The Parochial Church Council decided to maximise the seating area by dispensing with the north and south entrances proposed in 1894, and invited David Nye, the diocesan architect, to draw up some alternative plans. The chosen design incorporated a single entrance at the west end with a cloakroom, and a gallery. The work was carried out during 1959, and the extension was dedicated on 20 November.

The Revd John Hamilton Atkins succeeded Idwal Jones, and served from 1963 to 1972. He led a stewardship campaign, encouraging members of the congregation to give their time and talents, and to give financially in a more planned way. Several youth groups were formed, providing social activities and scope for charitable work. The Revd Harvey Pentreath (1973-80) brought two links with his native Cornwall: he invited the Mousehole Mole Valley Choir to sing, and in 1973 introduced the old custom of 'clypping' the church on Mothering Sunday, in which the congregation formed a circle around the outside of the building. In 1973 the modern-language Series 3 liturgy was introduced for Communion services, and the 9.15 am service was moved to 10 am, the sung mattins being discontinued. A new musical setting was composed for this service by Bill Wright, a member of the choir. As well as continuing to be used at St. Mary's, it has been exported by clergy and organists to other churches from Cornwall to Kuwait, where John Avery, organist at St. Mary's for many years, served as organist while working in the country. Music of another kind was provided by the Bethany band, made up of young members of the congregation; they won the Guildford Diocesan Song Contest in 1976.

The Revd Barry Preece (1981-88), under the motto 'fun and fellowship', combined a humorous exterior with a devotional commitment that became apparent at quieter services, and was recognised in his appointment as diocesan adviser on spirituality in 1992. His preaching was notable for his openness about the obstacles he had overcome in the development of his faith. The Revd Colin Cheeseman (1989-96) developed the parish's ministry to families with young children, as well as sharing with the congregation his interests in academic study and social affairs (he served as a part-time prison chaplain during his time at Cuddington, and left to take up a post in that field). The present vicar, the Revd Bryan Owen, was inducted in 1996, and has sought to deepen the congregation's spirituality, drawing on the Celtic tradition of the Iona community and icons of the Eastern Orthodox churches.

As we look at St. Mary's today, we can see three phases of development: firstly the major part of the church, built in 1894-95 and, to our left, the Old Vicarage facing St. Mary's Road, which was designed by the same architect, Alick Thomas, and built in 1895 for £1556. Secondly, we see the two western bays of the nave, added in 1959. Finally, adjoining the western end of the church, are the new meeting rooms, built with the same materials of flint and brick. The construction of these rooms in 1994-95, and the planning process which preceded it, had occupied much of the ministry of Colin Cheeseman, and much of the energy of his churchwarden Peter Leverton. The existing Large and Small Halls were demolished, and the site of the former was sold for housing development.

The interior of the church is also rewarding to the visitor. If the church is locked, access can be gained on weekday mornings (except Mondays) by contacting the Parish Administrator in the meeting-rooms complex. Copies of Robert Leach's detailed history of the church – the building and people – may be obtained from the parish office.

On entering, one is drawn to the carved reredos over the High Altar, depicting Christ welcoming children to his presence in the face of his disciples' disapproval. In the chancel, notice the fine late-Victorian woodwork of the stalls and the screen with its two angels, and the organ pipes on the north side. The organ was built by the renowned Henry ('Father') Willis and installed in 1896. The original console was located below the pipes; it was powered by hand-pumped bellows until an electric blower was substituted in 1925. In 1974, a full overhaul was carried out. A choir manual was added, the existing great and swell manuals were restored, and the console was moved to its present position in the nave. This was made possible by the replacement of the manual tracker action with a solid-state electronic action, which only required a much lighter touch. Barry Rose, organist of Guildford Cathedral, was so impressed with the system that it was introduced into the Cathedral organ.[44]

Most of the windows in the older part of the church were filled with stained glass soon after the building was opened; the nave windows depict New Testament saints (south side) and saints and bishops from the Diocese of Winchester (north side). In the 1959 extension, there are two windows at the end of the nave, in a more modern style, one depicting the nativity, and one combining the institution of the Lord's Supper and the agony in the Garden of Gethsemane. Most striking of all is the great west window above the gallery. It was given by Charles Greenfield in memory of his son, Flying Officer A C A Greenfield, who was shot down over France on D-Day. Appropriately it depicts Christ triumphing through the suffering of the Cross.

In this part of the church are a number of pieces of woodwork made in light oak by Glyn Smith, a cabinet maker and former churchwarden, including the book-cases for hymn-books by the main door; he also made the portable font stand and bishop's chair, which are only seen in church on occasions when they are in use.

As we return to the church door, we pass the font, paid for with pennies collected by 220 children, and still used at many baptism services. In the porch, notice the stones from the medieval church displayed on the wall. These were secured by the vicar at the time of the excavations, Idwal Jones. He recalls visiting the dig, looking into the trench, and announcing "I'm the vicar of Cuddington." The diggers thought they had seen a ghost.[45]

*Turn left out of the church and walk round the outside. Leave the gardens by the small iron gate presented in memory of Cinderella Child of The Lodge, and turn left onto St. Mary's Road* (previously known as Church Road, but renamed in 1956 to avoid confusion with Church Road in Old Malden). Pass the Old Vicarage and its 1985 successor. *At the end of the road we reach…*

# Royal Avenue

*Stand here and look to the right.* The word 'avenue' was popular in the 1930s as a name for suburban roads, in Worcester Park as elsewhere. In this instance, however, there really was an avenue of trees (as shown on the map on page 131), said to have formed part of the royal route from Hampton Court to Nonsuch. We shall shortly turn left, thus joining the route, but we should first stop to examine the later history of the road.

By 1866 there were three houses on the western (opposite) side of Royal Avenue. A fourth, Drumaline, was added around 1926, nearest to the point where we are now standing.

Drumaline was built for Sir Frederick George Dumayne, who lived there until his death in 1930. He was another former colonial official, serving as secretary to the trustees of the Port of Bombay for many years, as vice-chairman of the Commissioners for the Port of Calcutta, 1901-13, and as a member of the Bengal Legislative Council in 1910. It is possible that he chose this Scottish-sounding name for the house in commemoration of his wife, Mary MacAdam, who lived near Drymen above Loch Lomond, and who died less than a year after their marriage in 1896. There is a Drumline Farm about ten miles from there, and one may speculate that this name had some significance for Sir Frederick.[46] During the Second World War, Drumaline was used to accommodate men serving in the Dutch Navy who had been shipwrecked and were unable to return to Holland on account of the German occupation. The house was demolished in about 1973, and the top of the Drumaline Ridge development roughly indicates its location.

The next house on the left-hand side was Tunstall House. By 1930 this formed the premises of the Worcester Park Nursing Home. Daphne Court stands on the site of the house, and Drumaline Ridge extends across its grounds.

The third house was Manor Lodge. This was the home of the Wearne family. Mr and Mrs Wearne had four sons of whom two died in the First World War, within six weeks of each other. The eldest, Keith Morris Wearne, joined the Essex Regiment in India in 1911, and also served in South Africa before the outbreak of war. Captain Wearne was

*2nd Lt F B Wearne*

*Manor Lodge, shortly before its demolition in 1971*

severely wounded at Gallipoli, but was sent to another front where he was killed on 21 May 1917.[47]

His brother, Frank Bernard Wearne, went up to Corpus Christi College, Oxford, from Bromsgrove School in 1913. The following summer, when war broke out, he immediately volunteered, and soon obtained a commission in his brother's regiment. He was sent to the Western Front and was badly wounded at the Battle of the Somme in July 1916; it was only in the following May that he was fit to return to the Front.

Lt Wearne was attached to the 11th Battalion of the Essex Regiment, based near Lens in Northern France; his battalion was alternately manning trenches near Loos, and recuperating at the small village of Les Brebis. On the 12th June he wrote to his young cousin Margie, "Though we are not actually in the fighting for Messines there is a tremendous lot of shelling. We don't mind that much when we are in deep dug-outs, but when we are walking about in the trenches it makes us awfully funky. You should see me bob down like a rabbit when I hear anything coming."[48]

Eight days later the 11th Battalion returned to the line, under orders to carry out a trench raid on the 28th June. A force of around one hundred men was to capture a section of the German front line, take prisoners, and destroy dug-outs and mine-shafts. The force was divided into four parties; Lt Wearne commanded Party B, comprising twenty men, and had the task of attacking to the left of the other parties and preventing German reinforcements reaching the other parties as they destroyed the dug-outs and mine-shafts. Soon after 7.10 pm Party B advanced and took part of the enemy's line. *The Times* records the result:

"During this period Sec Lt Wearne and his small party were repeatedly counter-attacked. Grasping the fact that if the left flank was lost his men would have to give way, Sec Lt Wearne, at a moment when the enemy's attack was being heavily pressed and when matters were most critical, leapt on the parapet, and, followed by his left section, ran along the top of the trench, firing and throwing bombs. This unexpected and daring manœuvre threw the enemy off his guard and back in disorder."[49]

Lt Wearne must have been fully aware of the sacrificial nature of his actions. The conclusion is provided in a letter written by his companion Pte J Voller to Wearne's father:

"I do not think the enemy realized we had left the trench until we had started in with our bombs and rifle grenades. It was as complete a surprise as ever German soldiers had. When the enemy in the trench started to retire we followed him up. One of the Lewis gunners was wounded and Mr Wearne went towards him. But hardly had we reached him when a bomb, landing between us, Mr Wearne received his first wound (in the leg). I do not of course go into details but it was a wound that would have fully justified going back to our lines, but he refused to go. I bound him up as best I might but, as I had been hit in the chest by the same bomb that wounded him, I could not do it very well. However the enemy having retired I got him into the trench where he sat directing things as coolly as ever."

Shortly afterwards Wearne was hit again, on the forehead. Pte Voller continues, "... I was doing my best of course to help him when he was hit yet again at the back of his neck and rolled over. When I saw his face, sir, I knew beyond doubt that my officer was dying. I sat beside him holding his shrapnel helmet over his face to keep off the flying stones and fragments. He turned his head towards [me] and said, 'You have done well,

Voller. Tell…' And then he died with the same smile on his face it always wore when it was pleased."[50]

The following month, Lt Wearne was awarded the Victoria Cross posthumously, the citation recording that, "By his tenacity in remaining at his post though severely wounded and his magnificent fighting spirit, he was enabled to hold on to the flank."

The family's third son, G W Wearne, served with the Canadian forces; he survived the war, albeit suffering from severe shell shock. A fourth brother survived unharmed and went into the wine trade.

Manor Lodge was demolished in 1971, and the Royal Close development was constructed on the site. This development shows the Georgian features which were popular at this time, but are rarely found elsewhere in Worcester Park.

The final house on that side of Royal Avenue was Barrow Hill, the home of Auriol Barker, whom we shall meet again in the park that bears his name (see Auriol Park, page 64). This house too has gone, but the steep hill descending about 45 feet in 150 yards to Old Malden Lane is still called Barrow Hill. It seems likely that the name originates, not from the presence of any barrow (burial mound) in the area, but from the name of the (Derbyshire) family home of Mr Auriol-Barker's grandmother.[51]

At the top of Barrow Hill, Royal Avenue continues as a footpath to St. John's Church, Old Malden. Although this marks the end of Cuddington parish, we should remember that the Worcester Park postal district continues as far as the Malden Manor railway bridge. This trail, however, does not attempt to do justice to Old Malden's history as a separate village. If we were to continue along the footpath, we would emerge onto Church Road opposite the Manor House, the front portion of which probably dates back to the early 17th century. The manor of Malden was acquired in about 1240 by Walter de Merton, later Chancellor of England and Bishop of Rochester. In 1264 he established Merton College, the first college at Oxford to be set up as a corporate self-governing community; he granted the manor to the newly-formed college, and established at Malden an administrative house, under the rule of a Warden, to run the Surrey estates for the benefit of the Oxford students. Ten years later the Warden and his colleagues were moved to Oxford, and since then the manor house and estates have generally been leased out by the college.

Beside the Manor House is the church of St. John the Baptist, which is of Saxon origin (the name Malden means 'the Cross on the Hill'). By 1609 it was badly decayed, and was largely rebuilt, with the active support of Thomas Ravis, Bishop of London, biblical translator, and a native of Malden. In 1850 William Chetwynd Stapylton began his forty-four year ministry as vicar. He found a church filled with box pews appropriated to the use of a local landowner's tenants. During his incumbency there were three major phases of alteration to the church: open pews were installed in 1863; a lean-to north aisle was added in 1867; and in 1875 the north aisle was replaced by a new nave and chancel. The 17th-century church survives as the present south aisle and Lady Chapel.[52]

Beyond the church and the footpath to the Hogsmill river is the Percy Gardens development. Here, almost at the edge of the Worcester Park postal district, is perhaps the earliest site of habitation in the area: excavations in 1991-92 revealed an Iron Age settlement dating back to the 4th-5th centuries BC.

*We now, at last, turn left into Royal Avenue.* To the right is Parker's Field, part of a larger field used by the Parker family of Malden Green Farm from 1940 for growing hay and exercising horses. In the 1950s St. Mary's summer fair was held in Parker's Field. This included, in a large marquee, a flower and vegetable show with classes for handicrafts and cakes as well. The person who gained most points was rewarded with the Baskerville Cup, given by the Baskerville family of Mount Tavy, and awarded annually from 1953 to 1965. This field also saw the start of the Pets and Ponies service.

On the right beyond Parker's field is Hillcrest, designed by John Giles and previously known as The Homestead and Koryfi. From 1897 it was the home of Sir C Alexander Harris, who had previously lived in Cleveland Road. He was an official in the Colonial Office during his time at Worcester Park, serving as private secretary to the Under-Secretary of State for the Colonies from 1894, and as Principal Clerk from 1898. Later, from 1917-22, he served as Governor of Newfoundland.

As we continue along Royal Avenue, we must imagine it as perhaps the "race or way... sett forth betwixt two rowes of well growing trees set in a direct line answering the body of the sayd Worcester House which extends it selfe a measured halfe mile in lenght from the same... a speciall ornament both to the house and parke", as the Parliamentary Commissioners described it in 1650. Sir John Millais, two centuries later, described it as "one of the finest avenues of elm trees I ever saw."[53]

*As we reach the junction with The Avenue*, we have come to a spot which was not only on the probable royal route to Nonsuch, but also one of the highest points in the Great Park. Little wonder, then, that this was the site selected for the Keeper of the Great Park to have his residence. We must therefore imagine travellers from the Nonsuch period continuing, not into the modern Worcester Gardens development, but into the courtyard in front of the Keeper's Lodge, known for much of its history as...

## Worcester House

We have very little idea of what buildings stood on this site in the early years of Nonsuch, although we find references to a keeper living in the Great Park in the 1540s-50s. Our information becomes more specific in the reign of James I, who took the park back into royal hands in 1605, and gave orders the following year for the re-paling of the park, and the enlargement of the two lodges. It was around this time that a semi-circular piece of land on the opposite side of the Hogsmill was taken into the park, comprising the Riverhill area (where Tolworth Hall built in the 19th century) and Wighill (a name possibly connected with Wiggelonde, named in a deed of c.1240, perhaps meaning 'Wicga's Land'). In May 1607 a payment of £600 towards the building or rebuilding of a lodge was made to the Earl of Worcester, who had been appointed Keeper. It was in his honour that the lodge became known as Worcester House, and that the Great Park became known as Worcester Park. Since he is, therefore, the man from whom the present district of Worcester Park derives its name, it may be worth looking more closely at his career.

Edward Somerset was born about 1550, and succeeded to the title as fourth Earl of Worcester in 1589. Thereafter he seems to have made rapid progress in the final years of Elizabeth I's reign, becoming a Knight of the Garter in 1593, Master of the Horse in 1601 and a Privy Councillor in the same year. When James I succeeded Elizabeth in 1603, the Earl – who had been an Ambassador to Scotland to deliver an official message of congratulations on James's marriage in 1590 – continued to rise: he served as Earl Marshal at James's coronation, was made Judge of the Court of Requests in 1621, and served as Lord Great Chamberlain at Charles I's coronation in 1626.

Why was the Earl of Worcester chosen by James as the keeper of his Great Park? It appears that he was, in fact, well-qualified for the position. He was said to have been "In his youth a very fine gentleman and the best horseman and tilter of the times." The same source also suggests another possible reason: "...and when years had abated these exercises of honour he grew then to be a faithful and profound Counsellor": the Earl's own residences were Raglan Castle in Monmouthshire, and his London home – confusingly, also known as Worcester House – in the Strand (close to the site

*Edward Somerset, 4<sup>th</sup> Earl of Worcester.*
[Reproduced by kind permission of the Duke of Beaufort
Photograph: Photographic Survey, Courtauld Institute of Art]

of the Savoy Hotel), so his appointment to the keepership gave him the use of a country estate from which he could easily be summoned if his advice was required.

The Earl died in 1628; in 1639 one Charles Kirke was appointed Keeper. The Civil War caused Worcester House to be put to another use for a short period in Kirke's keepership: in November 1642 a labourer working on the hedges saw about two hundred Cavaliers arrive on horseback. He observed them dispersing to the various lodges in the parks, and lights in all the rooms of the houses. He hurried to Kingston to warn the commander of the Parliamentary forces, but in fact the Cavaliers entered Kingston, to the accompaniment of "ringing of bells for joy" on 13<sup>th</sup> November.

The eventual Parliamentary victory in the Civil War meant that the royal estates were seized, and valuations were made with a view to their sale. We are fortunate that, as a result, we have a detailed description of Worcester House as it stood in 1650.

The house was described as "consisting of one intire pile of very good brick building fower stories high covered with tile well built and ordered." The lowest storey contained the kitchen, with associated wine and beer cellars, dry and wet larders and other ancillary rooms. Above these were a hall (wainscoted and tiled), a parlour and a withdrawing room (wainscoted and boarded), a great chamber (wainscoted), two other chambers, two closets and two rooms for servants. The third level contained a wainscoted dining-room ("large and fayer"), a withdrawing room, four bedchambers and two closets, while six garrets ("all boarded and well lighted") occupied the top floor.

To the north-east was a garden enclosed by a ten-foot high brick wall, and in front of the house was a "handsome greene Court", behind another ten-foot high wall, with a flight of ten steps leading to the hall door. A walled kitchen garden, a railed back court, and a yard containing a coach house, pigeonhouse and poultry sheds were described by the Commissioners as "all very useful and necessary."

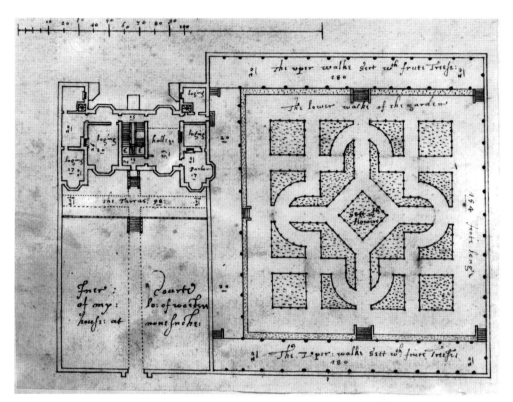

*Plan of Worcester House and its garden, probably by Robert Smythson, 1610*
[British Architectural Library, RIBA, London]

They valued the building materials of Worcester House, together with the adjacent timber lodge, two old lodges elsewhere in the park, and two barns, at a total of £1820, although they pointed out that, with the exception of the two old lodges, they were "not fit to be taken downe or demolished."

The Commissioners submitted their report on 6 April 1650. In a foretaste of things to come in later property booms, a contract for the sale of the estate was agreed six days later. The purchaser was Colonel Thomas Pride, who had been a drayman or brewer, and had quickly risen to senior rank in the Parliamentarian army. He is best known for his 'Purge' of the House of Commons in 1648, when he expelled the more moderate members who refused to sit in judgement on Charles I.

Pride's purchase included not only Worcester House, but also the park, described in 1650 as containing over three hundred deer, timber worth £280, and several coppices worth over £1084. It seems, however, that Pride and, later, his widow effectively disparked the estate, cutting down trees and converting it to agricultural use. On his death in 1658 he bequeathed an annuity of £400 out of the rents of the Great Park to his wife, the remainder being divided between his sons William and Samuel, while his son Joseph succeeded to his interest in brewhouses at Kingston worth £4000.[54]

At the Restoration in 1660 the Crown regained control of the Nonsuch estate, and in 1663 the Great Park and Worcester House were leased to Sir Robert Long. (The lease was granted, as was common at this period, not for a fixed term of years, but for the lifetime of two named individuals; a third name was added in 1670, after Sir Robert submitted a petition pointing out that he had spent £2500 on restoring the buildings.)

Sir Robert may not be one of the best known participants in the Civil War, but his career is worth describing in some detail. He was born into a landed family in Wiltshire around 1600 and, as the fourth son, had to forge a career for himself. By 1626 he was sitting in the House of Commons as MP for Devizes. In the 1630s he held a number of positions, including (in 1636) the role of Commissioner for Preventing the Export of Butter. He was also granted the reversion of the post of Auditor of the Receipt, in the Exchequer, although the then holder of that office retained it until his death in about 1662. In 1641 he became Surveyor General to Charles I's Queen, Henrietta Maria, on whom Nonsuch had been settled at her marriage in 1624: this appointment was doubtless one of the factors leading to his obtaining the Great Park for himself.

In 1645 Long became Secretary to the Prince of Wales; four years later when Charles I was executed and the Prince became, in the eyes of royalists, Charles II, Long followed him into exile in Paris and continued to serve him as private secretary. The British Library holds a small collection of his official papers, showing that he handled matters ranging from the appointment of ambassadors to grants of settlement rights in the American colonies. It is a little poignant to see the exiled king granting, for instance, a swathe of Northern Virginia between the Potomac and Rappahanocke rivers, without knowing at the time whether a grant in his name would ever have any value.[55]

Also in the British Library is a key to the cipher used by Long in 1649, presumably adopted in case his correspondence fell into Parliamentary hands. As may be seen from the reproduction, it was a fairly sophisticated numerical cipher, in which each letter was represented by one of two alternative numbers, and the most common letters were represented by any of three numbers, thus making it harder to identify them. Frequently-used words or phrases could be conveyed using three-figure codes such as 295 for 'Secretary Long'.[56]

Long fell out of favour in 1652 as a result of a quarrel with Sir Edward Hyde, later Earl of Clarendon. At the Restoration, Clarendon's appointment as Lord Chancellor might have impeded Long's progress, but he resumed his office as Surveyor-General to Henrietta Maria in 1661, and the following year was made a baronet when he finally 'inherited' the post of Auditor of the Receipt. He had also returned to the House of Commons, representing Boroughbridge in Yorkshire in 1661, and continued to represent the town until his death.[57]

When Sir Robert was negotiating his lease of Worcester House in 1663, the Great Park was not in fact a hunting park in anything but name, and he arranged for a declaration to be issued officially recognising the fact that it had already been disparked; the remaining deer were given to Sir Robert to dispose of.[58]

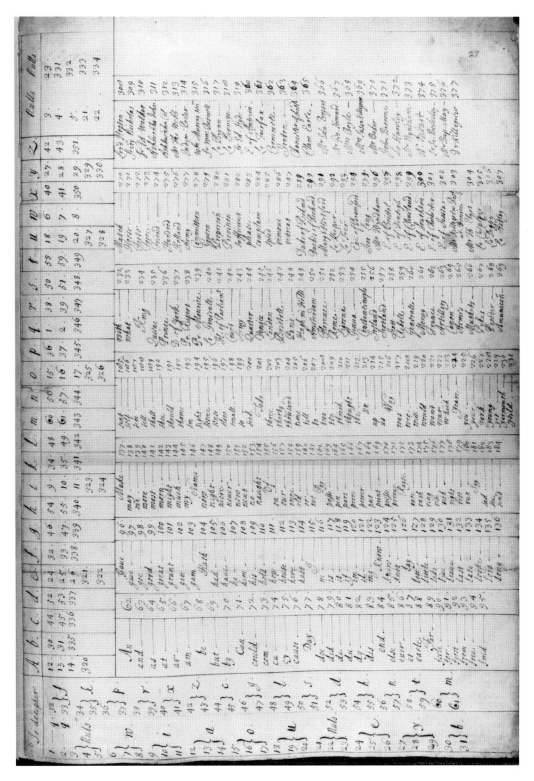

*Cipher used by Sir Robert Long to communicate with other Royalists, 1649*
*[By permission of The British Library, Add MSS 33596 f21]*

49

The Restoration of the House of Stuart to the English throne did not restore Nonsuch Palace to its place in courtly life. Queen Henrietta Maria is not known to have returned to the Palace, and there is just one record of a visit by Charles II in 1664. The following year, as the Plague drove the court away from London, the Palace took on a more mundane role as a temporary home for the Exchequer. The choice of Nonsuch may have been linked to Sir Robert's position as Auditor of the Receipt.

While the Exchequer was at Nonsuch, it was visited on a number of occasions by Samuel Pepys, in his capacity as an official in the Navy Office. The entry in his diary for 28 November 1665 records that, after completing his business at Nonsuch, he continued "to Sir Robert Long's house; a fine place, and dinner-time ere we got thither… where had a good dinner, and curiously dressed, and here a couple of ladies, kinswomen of his, not handsome though, but rich… and mighty merry we were."[59]

Sir Robert retained his position in the Exchequer until his death, and was the key official in the Lower Exchequer. It was said that if any one man could work out the current Exchequer balance between income and expenditure it was the Auditor of the Receipt. He died in July 1673: most of his estates passed with his baronetcy to his nephew Sir James Long, but his will reveals that he had already settled his lease of Worcester Park on Sir Richard Mason, the husband of Sir James's daughter Margaret.

The Mason family had been prominent in Bishop's Castle, Shropshire, for over a century. Richard was secretary in the 1640s to Lord Percy who, like Sir Robert Long, was a member of Henrietta Maria's circle of Royalist exiles at the Louvre. At the Restoration in 1660 he became avenor (chief officer of the royal stables) and in 1671 he received both a knighthood and the post of Clerk-comptroller of the green cloth (responsible for the financial affairs of the royal household). In 1673 he was also appointed agent for taxes, and was reported as fulfilling his duties "much to the King's benefit with much less expense." Sir Robert Long gave him the manors of Sutton and Coulsdon, as well as the reversion of Worcester Park; he died in 1685 and was buried at Sutton.[60]

It is not clear when the lease on Worcester House and its Park expired. By 1731, however, it had once more become part of the Nonsuch estate, which was then in the hands of the Duke of Grafton. In that year his estates were sold piecemeal, the purchaser of the Great Park being the Duke's former steward, John Walter.[61]

In 1750 the Park was sold to William Taylor, whose family retained it for about a century. Taylor's connection with Worcester Park had begun thirty years earlier when he opened the Malden or Worcester Park Powder Mills on the Hogsmill River beside Old Malden Lane. The site he chose was probably close to the location of the early powder mills built by the Evelyn family, perhaps in the 1580s, which had presumably closed when the area was incorporated into the Great Park in 1606-07.

Gunpowder was originally made on the battlefield by combining saltpetre, charcoal and sulphur with a pestle and mortar. The resulting mixture, however, tended to separate again rapidly. The solution was to incorporate the mixture by pounding it with stamps to form a mass which could then be broken up into particles. The original gunpowder mills consisted of stamps operated by water or animal power.

In the eighteenth century a new method was introduced using vertical circular stones rolled on their edges over the mixture, which was then compacted in presses. John

Smeaton, better known as the designer of the Eddystone lighthouse, developed a new bottom-driven incorporating mill for the Malden site in 1771.[62] By 1762 William Taylor was operating the business on a capital of £4000.[63]

The Taylors continued to run the mills until at least 1849, after which they leased them out. There were at least two explosions in the 1840s, and another in 1854. By 1872 Jabez Hover, a miller and baker, had a corn mill here; he also leased a shop in Park Terrace.[64] It is said that this mill was burnt down in 1891: eight years later Webb & Thompson Ltd (who took over the corn chandlery in Cheamside soon afterwards) appear to have been running a mill there. By the 1890s some of the mill streams had been converted to watercress beds. Maurice Upperton recalls that, on summer afternoons around 1920, "My mother would send me with a strawberry basket, with tuppence in my hand, and for tuppence they would fill my little pannier with watercress." In about 1919 the mill was converted to a silk printing works, which was run by W Wilks & Sons for two decades.

Roger Wilks recalls the three different printing methods used by his father Charles in the early to mid 1930s. Traditional hand block printing involved carving a pattern onto a wooden block, dipping it into dye, and pressing it onto the silk. A separate block was required for each colour, and patterns involving up to eight colours were produced at the Old Mill: "At that time the silk works were producing paisley patterned scarves for ladies, bedspreads and other items for buyers like Liberty's of London and John Wannamakers of Philadelphia." A cheaper method was silk screening, in which one colour of the pattern was drawn on a silk sheet fixed to a wooden box frame, and the colour was applied using a squeegee. Finally, there was batik printing, in which part of the fabric was tied with raffia twine to keep the dye off, and the fabric was dipped into dye, producing unique sunburst patterns.

The mill pond was used to rinse the raw silk before printing, and in particular to remove the rice flour in which silk imported from China was covered. "The flowing mill stream going slowly through the mill pond provided the needed washing action. I can still remember the long strips of silk gently floating on the water. The stream was also used to rinse off the unused dye." The watercress beds nearby assisted in keeping the water clean. The Wilks family also dealt in coal, and operated a haulage business after closing the mill. The remains are now incorporated into the premises of Adams Bristow, beside the old mill house.

The fate of Worcester House has not been precisely recorded. By 1797 the Taylors had built a new mansion, Worcester Park House, further down the hill and the old site was occupied by...

## Worcester Park Farm

The farmhouse may have been the smaller keeper's lodge which was described in 1650 as being on the northern side of Worcester House, or may have been a replacement building on the same alignment as Worcester House.

In 1851 Worcester Park, which for the last half-century of its royal ownership had increasingly lost its connection with the nation's cultural life, suddenly found a new artistic connection when two leading members of the Pre-Raphaelite Brotherhood took up lodgings in the farmhouse.

The Pre-Raphaelite Brotherhood originated in the discovery by three young artists, William Holman Hunt, John Everett Millais and Dante Gabriel Rossetti, that they shared a distaste for the sentimental and sombre stylisation of contemporary art. They aimed to paint directly from nature, with a heightened attention to detail, choosing subjects with an underlying meaning, and in particular presenting religious subjects and contemporary social problems with a fresh realism that could be shocking to observers.

Rossetti's brother, William Michael Rossetti, summarised the aims as being to have genuine ideas to express, to study nature attentively, so as to know how to express them, to sympathise with what is direct and serious and heartfelt in previous art, and to produce thoroughly good pictures. One of their inspirations was the work of Italian painters prior to Raphael, and in imitation of the brilliant clarity of their work they adopted the painstaking practice of painting a tiny section at a time on a wet white ground. In 1848, with four like-minded friends, they formed the Brotherhood to provide mutual encouragement in their pursuit of these aims.[65]

Holman Hunt had become familiar with the Ewell area during boyhood holidays spent at Rectory Farm, the home of his uncle William Hobman (his middle name was intended as a compliment to his uncle, but Hunt chose to adopt the mis-spelling recorded on his baptism certificate). Millais, too, had spent holidays at Ewell, visiting the Lemprière family.

At the end of June 1851 Hunt and Millais decided to use the River Hogsmill as the background for their next compositions. They set out from Ewell, and Hunt found, probably near Ewell Court Farm (site of the Meadow Walk Estate), a location for *The Hireling Shepherd*, depicting a herdsman leaving his sheep to wander into a cornfield while he concentrated his attention on his girlfriend. Millais's chosen subject was *Ophelia in the Stream*, the death of Hamlet's tragic lover.

The two friends walked for some distance downstream without finding a suitable site, until finally "round a turn in the meadows at Cuddington" they found "the exact composition... he had dreamed of... and we sat down to enjoy its loveliness." The exact position has long been a matter for debate, but Barbara Webb has now produced a very convincing argument in support of the section of the river at Old Malden below the Manor House garden. The evidence includes the distance from their lodgings to the site, the steep banks shown in the picture, the position of the shadows and a memorandum made by the then vicar of Malden, Canon Chetwynd Stapylton. If, as seems likely, this identification is correct, Millais would have worked from the Six Acre Meadow, across the river from St. John's Church and the Manor House[66].

Initially the two artists took lodgings in Surbiton. These were, however, four miles from Hunt's site and two from Millais's, and when they were joined by Charles Collins (a member of their circle, although not officially a member of the Pre-Raphaelite Brotherhood) they decided to move to larger and nearer accommodation. The place they chose was Worcester Park Farm.

In September, Hunt and Millais began to make sketches for other pictures. Hunt's design showed the figure of Christ before a weed-entangled door, illustrating the saying "Behold, I stand at the door, and knock: if any man hear my voice, and open the door, I will come in to him." The choice of a long-abandoned door to symbolise the unawakened soul was inspired by the sight of an old powder-mill hut down on the

Hogsmill (not, as is often said, by the door of Malden Church). This picture, *The Light of the World*, was perhaps the most widely-reproduced painting of the 19th century.

Millais, meanwhile, had decided to paint two lovers whispering by a wall. The dramatic context was provided by the theme of the massacre of French Protestants in 1572: *A Huguenot on St. Bartholomew's Eve* shows a young Protestant refusing a girl's attempt to make him wear an armband to indicate he was a Catholic.

Both men were able to paint the background to these pictures close at hand. Hunt used the orchard beside the farmhouse, and Millais's wall was the old garden wall that dated back to Worcester House's heyday. Even so, the coming of autumn was to test their commitment to drawing from life. Millais describes Hunt as "deeply immersed in his new work, *The Light of the World*, and still painting out of doors, though the weather was bitterly cold. By day he was still working on his sheep for *The Hireling Shepherd*, but every night from 9 pm until 5 am he went out to paint his moonlight, sitting in his little sentry-box made of hurdles, with his feet in a sack of straw to protect them from the elements."

Millais's diary records some of the obstacles they encountered:

4 November: "Frightfully cold morning; snowing. Determined to build up some kind of protection wherein to paint. After breakfast superintended in person the construction of my hut – made of four hurdles… covered with straw… Hunt painting obstinate sheep within call…"

5 November: "Painted in my shed from Ivy… My man Young… was employed by Hunt to hold down a wretched sheep, whose head was very unsatisfactorily painted, after the most tantalising exhibition of obstinacy…"

6 November: "…Hunt employed small impudent boy to hold down sheep. Boy not being strong enough, required my assistance to make the animal lie down …"

7 November: "…During the day Hunt had a straw hut similar to mine built… Twelve o'clock. Have this moment left him in it, cheerfully working by a lantern from some contorted apple tree trunks, washed with the phosphor light of a perfect moon…"

Over the course of the following month, it became too cold for outdoor work, and on 6 December the artists left Worcester Park. Work on the figures for their paintings could be continued in London, and one final Worcester Park connection was made: Emma Watkins, a servant at the farm, went to London to sit for the young woman in *The Hireling Shepherd*.[67] The long-suffering sheep, we hope, were left undisturbed until the 1860s brought farming on this site to an end.

The 1867 Ordnance Survey map shows the farm buildings still surviving. However, the name Worcester Park Farm had by this point migrated to a farmhouse adjoining what is now Central Road, near Windsor Road (see Central Road, page 129), and the old farmhouse may have seemed increasingly anomalous as the Landed Estates Company's development grew up around it. In 1873 it was replaced by a new and substantial house, known initially (and confusingly) as Worcester House, but for most of its existence as…

## Worcester Court

This became the home of Alexander Hector, who had spent much of his career developing both commercial and diplomatic links in Baghdad. In 1835, with service in an expedition on the Niger already to his credit, he joined the Government's Euphrates Expedition, which had been sent out to survey the Euphrates and Tigris rivers with a view to finding a more rapid overland route from the Mediterranean to India, under the leadership of General Francis Rawdon Chesney.[68] His official role was to act as store-keeper and purser, but he was also active in arranging the transport of vessels, and on one occasion had to rescue the expedition's diving-bell from muddy water using bamboo feelers.

Towards the end of the expedition, Mr Hector took charge of the postal line through Arabia. He settled in Baghdad, and came into contact with Sir Austen Layard, who was soon to become well known for his excavation of the ancient city of Nineveh at Nimrud, and was later an under-secretary for foreign affairs. Layard attempted to assist Hector in his struggle to establish trading ventures. In December 1842 he wrote to Sir Stratford Canning, the British Ambassador at Constantinople, in support of Hector's resistance to various duties imposed on his commerce, pointing out that Hector had established a cotton and wool press, and was considering building a steamer for use on the Tigris and Euphrates "which would... contribute greatly to the extension of British interests." Hector was continually frustrated, however, by the somnolence of the British Residency: in March 1843 he complained to Layard that, whilst the consul, Colonel Taylor was away, "I have had occasion to apply several times to the Consulate... and was told that my letters would be forwarded to the Colonel as soon as any *pressing business occurred*."[69]

Alexander Hector's wife Annie French was a notable Victorian novelist. She was born in Ireland in 1825, but her family came to England in 1844, living first in Liverpool and then in London. She was befriended by W H Wills, co-editor of Charles Dickens's periodical *Household Words*, in which her first published work appeared. She also published two novels in the 1850s, prior to her marriage. Mr Hector's health broke down soon after this, and she resumed writing, publishing *Look Before You Leap*, *Which Shall It Be* and *The Wooing O't*, between 1865 and 1873. She published these under her maiden name; after Mr Hector's death in 1875 she wrote over forty more novels, borrowing his forename and calling herself "Mrs Alexander". Her books mainly concerned young girls presented with choices between money, family and love.[70]

In 1939 Worcester Court became home to Blakesley School, a preparatory school for boys and girls which had been established by E G (Jack) and Alice Dudley in 1913. Mr and Mrs Dudley, who had met as members of staff at Merton Boys' School, began the school in Blakesley House, near the Nelson Hospital in Merton, and moved it to Worcester Court when the original building was taken over as a wartime first-aid post.[71] The School was to spend over 15 years in the premises. Canon Idwal Jones, who knew the school both as a parent and as Vicar of St. Mary's, recalls that the staff – Mr and Mrs Dudley, Miss Ivy Rowe and Mrs Haydn Davies – "gave themselves unreservedly to a good basic children's education, with a good foundation of the three Rs... The school maintained a good standard of discipline while maintaining a very happy atmosphere for a good variety of pupils... The numbers in our Sunday Schools multiplied exceedingly and at one time reached nearly 400 pupils. We had some accommodation in the Stoneleigh and Cuddington Schools, but with cheerful kindness Mr Dudley allowed us to use Blakesley School."

Mr Dudley was also responsible for the formation of the 2nd Cuddington (Blakesley) Scout Group in October 1943, with a view to equipping children returning from evacuation for their part in the post-war world. Under the leadership of Mr D H F Luftman, scoutmaster, and Miss Rowe, cubmaster, the scouts and cubs quickly began to take a role in district competitions. Meetings were initially held in a small building behind the gardener's cottage – or, during the flying-bomb period of 1944, in the school shelters. Mr Dudley offered a building on the school premises as a headquarters, and this was ready by 1948.[72]

*Postcard of Royal Avenue looking from St. Mary's Road to Worcester Court in The Avenue, postmarked 1906*

The school closed in 1959, and in the following year 2nd Cuddington moved to a purpose-built hall in Salisbury Road, later named Rowe Hall in honour of Miss Rowe, and rebuilt in 1987 after a fire. The Worcester Gardens development was built on the site of the school but the lodge to Worcester Court survives facing The Avenue.

*Continue to the right in The Avenue, around the bend, and past the junction of Delta Road into…*

## Grafton Road

This was one of the roads laid out before 1867 for building development which, in the event, hardly touched it until the 1930s. At this point we should note one of the former residents of Delta Road, Haydn Davies MP who lived at no. 4 (not visible from this end). Mr Davies had been a schoolmaster in London and a journalist, serving as education correspondent of the *News Chronicle* and industrial correspondent of *The Star*. He stood unsuccessfully as Liberal candidate for St. Pancras SW in 1929, but later joined the Labour party and won the same constituency in 1945. At the 1950 election, boundary changes forced him to seek a new constituency, and he stood for York. Here, however, he was defeated by the Conservative candidate, Mr Harry

Braustyn Hylton-Foster, by 77 votes, a margin of 0.1%. Sir Harry, as he became, went on to serve as Speaker of the House of Commons from 1959 to 1965. It is a curious coincidence that he also had Worcester Park connections, as his family had lived at Tolworth Hall.[73]

*Postcard of Hanbury's Hill, c.1900: the junction of Delta Road and Grafton Road*
*[Copyright of Surrey History Service, 6348]*

From the corner there is a fine view to the North Downs (according to Sir Alexander Harris's memoir, it was possible to see Leith Hill from one corner of the adjacent garden of Hillcrest). To the right, Tolworth Tower is just visible.

*Cross over Grafton Road and stop on the corner of...*

## Grafton Close

The map opposite shows that a drive already existed by 1894 on the present line of Grafton Close, providing access to Harbybrowe and Copthorne. Its present name, however, only dates from 1973 when the process of building houses on the left-hand side began, a process which continued gradually until 1997. Much of the belt of trees between the main driveway and the new houses has been retained, giving the road an unusual charm.

On the corner of the drive was Dancerwood (a modern bungalow of the same name in Grafton Road occupies part of the site). Until 1923 this was the home of Walter George Hanbury, who in 1867 married Isabella Lemprière of Ewell. Her brother Arthur had been used by Millais as the model for the Huguenot 16 years earlier. An early 20th-century postcard which seems to depict the hill leading down Grafton Road towards

Dancerwood is captioned "Hanbury's Hill". I was unable to find any confirmation of this until Lucy Bell-Chambers told me that, as a child, she knew it as "Ambridge Hill".

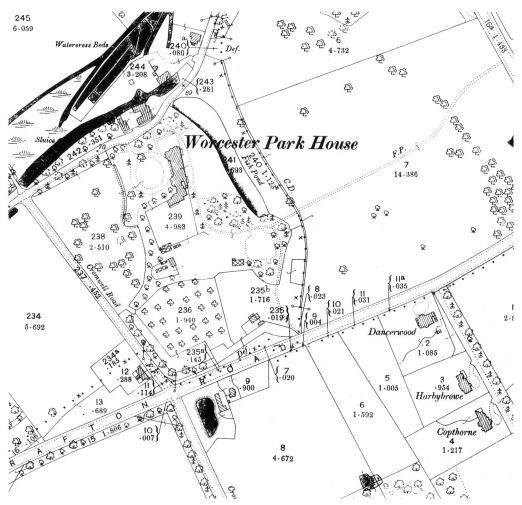

*Ordnance Survey map, 1894*

Harbybrowe is the only one of this group of houses shown that survives. This attractive house, which displays the timber and tile motifs of the late-19th-century vernacular style, was the home, until his death in 1924, of Sir Nathaniel Highmore, who spent most of his career in the Inland Revenue. Having joined this department around 1864, he rose to be solicitor to His Majesty's Customs from 1903 and solicitor to His Majesty's Excise from 1909. He retired from both posts in 1913 and was made KCB, but "When the war broke out he resumed duty at the Custom House as representative of the Board of Customs & Excise on the Committee on Trade with the Enemy. From 1915 till its close in March, 1919, he was secretary to the War Trade Department, and in 1920 his services were recognised by the honour of the GBE."[74] His wife Annie Louisa, Lady Highmore, was awarded the Order of Mercy in 1918: this decoration was given by the League of Mercy (founded in 1899 under the presidency of the Prince of Wales) to those who participated in the League's work of collecting subscriptions for the maintenance of voluntary hospitals before the establishment of the NHS.[75]

Beyond Harbybrowe stood Copthorne, which was made into the clubhouse of the Northcliffe Sports Ground, used by the staff of Associated Newspapers Ltd (publishers of the Daily Mail) and named after its founder Alfred Harmsworth, Viscount Northcliffe. In 1982-83 Ideal Homes developed Northcliffe Close, Auriol Park Road and Auriol Close on the land.

Looking across the field on the opposite side of Grafton Road, we see the woods which extend to Old Malden Lane past the site of…

## Worcester Park House

We now return to the Taylor family, whom we have already encountered at Worcester House. The younger William Taylor is said to have built Worcester Park House in 1797. John Nash, the architect better known for developing Regent Street and Trafalgar Square, and rebuilding Buckingham Palace for George IV, made improvements to the house.

In the middle years of the nineteenth century, Worcester Park House had a number of occupants, some of whom may have been tenants of the Taylors. In 1841 the printer and publisher William Clowes was living there with his family. His firm, founded in 1803, was noted for such feats as printing half-a-million sheets in a week, typesetting and printing a 1000-page Parliamentary report in the same time, and producing the Nautical Almanack, consisting of 500 or 600 pages of figures without a single error and in sixteen or seventeen days.[76] The company later went into partnership with a firm in Beccles, where William Clowes & Sons Ltd continues to trade; its most famous product is perhaps *Hymns Ancient and Modern*.

*Worcester Park House, c.1910*

By 1861 Worcester Park House was the home of Harvey Drummond, a partner in Drummonds Bank at Charing Cross, patronised by Sir Humphry Davy and Sir John Herschel.[77] Later in the same decade, the house passed into the hands of James Pennethorne.

In the mid-1870s Mrs Portia Wheeler moved to the house with some of her 16 children. She was the widow of Henry Wheeler, who appears to have made his fortune as a general merchant and had died in 1873 at Bolingbroke House, Wandsworth Common, where the family had lived for over 40 years. Mrs Wheeler is said to have come from the aristocratic Guadiano family in Palermo.

The 1881 census shows Mrs Portia Wheeler as the head of the household, living with seven of her children and six servants. Mrs Wheeler died in 1889, and some of the children set up home elsewhere (her son Frederick, for instance, became Commissioner of Police in Brisbane), but several of the unmarried daughters remained at Worcester Park House into the 1930s.[78]

Lord Ironside, a great-nephew of the Misses Wheeler, remembers visiting the house with parents – "I think in 1933, for lunch, when I was aged nine. I remember clearly that my mother and father were, after lunch, taken for a horse-drawn carriage drive, whilst I and my sister, together with our cousin… were told to take the boat and go and amuse ourselves on the lake."

*Photograph of members of the Wheeler family outside Worcester Park House, c.1905. They probably include the Misses Laura, Nina, Alice, Portia and Ellen*

Gerald Woods recalls seeing the surviving daughters in the 1920s: "I remember being with my father on the old rake behind the horse, raking all the hay up from that meadow… They were little old maiden ladies, they had tea under one of those trees."

The final years of the house are somewhat mysterious. The house and grounds appear to have been sold by 1938, initially to the catering firm Goodhews, which retained only the corner site on which they opened the Hogsmill Tavern in the 1950s, the rest of the estate being transferred to an investment company. However, according to at least one account the Misses Wheeler remained there until a bomb fell on the stables and they moved to the countryside; the late Mrs Elsie Rodd believed that the bomb had been jettisoned by a bomber shortly before it crashed in the Riverhill area. The house was left unprotected, some of the fittings were removed, and eventually an accidental fire reduced it to ruins.[79] It is not clear how this relates to the fact that in 1940 the house and the nearest part of its grounds were sold to John Dean of Dean's Blinds, who lived in The Avenue; he bought it on the understanding that he could use the house as a residence or build a replacement house, and that he could use it as offices for the duration of the war.[80]

Various attempts were made to develop the grounds in the 1950s, either for housing or to provide a new site for Stoneleigh West County Secondary Boys' School. In the event, only a small part of the land has been developed, with the opening of Linden Bridge School for autistic children in about 1974, to which the Spring Centre for maladjusted children was added in 1987.

*Continue down Grafton Road*. On the left, the view opens out across the Wandgas Sports Ground towards the surviving fragment of…

# Dancer Dick Wood

The intriguing name of this ancient piece of woodland is supposed to derive from a highwayman. Local legends suggest that he made his victims dance, and either that he evaded capture by disguising himself under voluminous skirts, or was caught by officers adopting the same stratagem.

In 1938 a distinctive house was built on the front part of the wood facing Salisbury Road by the French architect Hippolyte Kamenka for Fernand L Boulanger, owner of a knitwear factory in Motspur Park. Many will remember this house, with its creamy-pink walls and matching gateway, shown opposite. The house was originally named Bois Jean, but, as the local people developed the habit of pronouncing this "Boys Jean", M Boulanger gave it the name of the wood instead. At the beginning of the war, the house was transferred to his partner, a Belgian named Mr Lombert or Lombard, and M Boulanger left for France. During the war years it was painted with a camouflage pattern, which could still be seen years later in wet weather, through many coats of paint. The dark blue pantiles also presented an air-raid hazard, as they glittered in the moonlight, but nothing could be done about that. Although M Boulanger returned to Worcester Park after the war, he moved to Manor Lodge in Royal Avenue, and Dancer Dick Wood was sold to a Mr Collar. In 1950 it was bought by James Ratcliff, who lived there until 1985.[81] A sheltered housing scheme was built on the site in 1986 by McCarthy & Stone, and was named Worcester Court (not to be confused with the earlier Worcester Court: see page 53).

*Dancer Dick Wood in 1985, shortly before its demolition*

*Continue down Grafton Road* alongside the Wandgas Sports Ground which has been used by the staff of local gas companies since it was bought by the Wandsworth & District Gas Company in about 1939. The company was founded in 1834, and took over the Epsom and Sutton gas companies in 1912 and 1931 respectively. *After passing the pavilion and Gadsden Villa, turn left at the crossroads into Cromwell Road.* The half-timbered gable of Harbybrowe is visible across the field. *Continue to the end of Cromwell Road.*

*The main route lies straight ahead, but an alternative, avoiding a short stretch of enclosed footpath and unpaved ground, may be taken by turning left into Salisbury Road and, after 300 yards, turning right through the gates into Auriol Park, rejoining the main route at the Thorndon Gardens exit from the park.*

*Otherwise, go straight ahead into…*

## Timbercroft

The Davis Estate, made up of Timbercroft and Sterry Drive, was developed by Davis Estates Ltd in 1935-39 on the site of the house and grounds known as Parkside.

The house was turned into a boys' preparatory school by Mr Thomas Hill in 1879. His widow, writing in 1929, recalled "It is now 50 years since my husband started the school with, I believe, four boys… We sent boys to Eton (a good many), Winchester, Clifton, Malvern (a good many), one or two to Wellington and Haileybury. Those who came to see us as Old Boys constantly told Mr Hill that the work they did at Parkside carried them on so well at Eton that they hardly required to do any work there for years, for which they seemed unduly grateful."

The pupils in Mr Hill's time included the Thakor Sahib (later Maharajah) of Morvi. Mrs Hill remembered that "He brought a native valet, two native cooks (which we declined to have) and an English groom and carriage."[82]

In 1902 Mr Hill retired and was succeeded by Alfred Vaughan Pott, who remained Headmaster until 1916 when, as he later wrote, "a little pulling of string could overcome objections of health and age, and allow me to go to the war in an active or quasi-active capacity" as a private in the Italian Red Cross. Four of his former pupils were awarded the VC: Lt Tom O L Wilkinson (killed 1916) received the decoration for "great courage in driving back the enemy and attempting the rescue of wounded comrades"; Lt Alec B Turner single-handedly halted an enemy thrust down a communication trench near Vermelles in 1915, and died of the wounds he received on that occasion; his brother Lt-Col Victor Buller Turner twenty-seven years later won the only VC awarded at El Alamein, for leading his battalion in repulsing an attack by some 90 German tanks; finally, Brigade-Major Billy Congreve, who won the VC in the Rifle Brigade in 1916 was a private pupil of Mr Pott (but his brother Sir Geoffrey Congreve DSO was a pupil at Parkside). [83]

A prospectus for the school, dating from the 1920s, announced "The school... stands on sandy soil in its own grounds of 12½ acres, which includes a cricket ground of 3¾ acres, two football fields, asphalt playground, swimming bath, 40ft by 20ft, tennis courts and a large kitchen garden & orchards...

"The buildings provide accommodation for 45 boarders. There is a very fine dining room, a private chapel, large schoolroom, classrooms, dormitories, sick room, library of 500 books, playground and gymnasium (60ft by 30ft), changing room, Matron's room and carpenter's shop."

The centenary history, from which the above quotations are taken, includes recollections from Old Boys of the school's time on this site. Mr Christopher Bull (a pupil from 1920) recalled "The building had two fine features, its chapel and its dining hall. The Chapel was like a miniature college chapel, with pews facing inwards... On two Saturday afternoons in that Christmas term we went beagling with the Worcester Park beagles over the fields of the neighbourhood." Mr C E R Levi, who arrived as a pupil in 1929 and became joint headmaster in 1969, wrote "We had one large, flat and well-drained field for Soccer, Cricket and Hockey, and another for Rugger... the dining room was splendid, with a raised dais at one end, and the scholarship panels around the walls... ET Davis had taken over the school the year before, and he must surely have been one of the great Headmasters.... His teaching of Latin, French and Maths in the top form was such that learning was never a chore.... Other memories come back to me: The honour of being asked to play tennis with the Davis family on an excellent grass court far beyond the gooseberry bushes – hours of rolling the cricket field – the toast given by Mrs Davis to the prefects at tea-time – dorm. feasts – grass-snakes and adders – the very senior privilege of shooting rats, prevalent in a copse behind the pavilion."[84]

The development of the surrounding area caused E T Davis to move the school in 1933; after sharing premises with another school in Epsom for a year it moved to East Horsley, and is now at Stoke D'Abernon.

*Walk down Timbercroft and stop at the entrance to Sterry Drive (first left).*

The company which bought the Parkside site, Davis Estates Ltd, had been founded by A F Davis who began building at Kingsbury in 1929. By 1935 the company was advertising twenty suburban developments around London.

The style adopted on this development was very different from the cottagey vernacular style we have seen on most of the 1930s roads in Worcester Park. The painted, rendered walls, the streamlined windows with metal frames and a horizontal emphasis, and features such as corner windows and (on a few detached houses) balconies, are all features of this 'moderne' or 'suntrap' style. The origins of this style can be found in the International Modern movement in Europe, which presented the house as "a machine for living in", in which the function dictated the form, and exploited modern manufacturing methods whilst avoiding unnecessary decoration. A number of detached houses appeared in England which followed these principles whole-heartedly, with flat roofs and sun balconies.[85] There are a couple of examples in Worcester Park, in Salisbury Road (no. 95, designed by Connall, Ward and Lucas) and in Church Road, Old Malden (Woodthorpe, opposite Brockenhurst Avenue).

Advertisement for Davis Estates suntrap houses from the Homefinder Small Property Guide, 24 August 1935

Several developers, including Davis Estates, exhibited examples of modernist houses at the Ideal Home Exhibition in 1934. They were, however, cautious in their use of the style for complete estates and, as in the Parkside Estate, used conventional layouts and pitched roofs in combination with modernist-style windows and façades. If we look carefully at the houses in Timbercroft, this caution becomes increasingly apparent: nos.

61-63, for example, display the suntrap and corner windows with an equally modernist flat-roofed porch; if we look at nos. 57-59, however, we find suntrap windows combined with brick porches that seem to draw more on a Norman baronial style than on 1930s continental themes. The fact that, in recent years, Georgian-style doors and windows have appeared on several of the nearby houses suggests that the developers' ambivalence was not misplaced. In a promotional film made in 1935, Davis Estates stressed the healthy climate of their developments: "For the benefit of the men and women of the future, money should buy health and comfort... Sunlight and air bring new life and new ideals and give the kiddies their chance." The film also strikes a balance between the modernity of the stainless steel sink and chromium-plated cupboard handles in the kitchen, and the patriotic solidity of British-made bricks.[86]

Occasional examples of this style can be found elsewhere in Worcester Park: in Seaforth Gardens, for instance, there are two pairs of moderne semis (nos. 49-55) presenting something of a contrast to the adjacent Ideal-Homesteads-style chalets.

*Turn left into Sterry Drive.* This road rejoins Timbercroft at the corner of the green which adds so much to the character of this development. *Our route, however, lies up the footpath in the angle of the road, between nos. 24 and 26. At the group of pine trees, fork right and continue with the green railings on your left to reach the top of Chestnut Avenue*, developed on the site of "Astbury" around 1931.

*Turn left into...*

# Auriol Park

The boundary we have just crossed probably marks the edge of the Great Park which we left near Sterry Drive and are now re-entering.

The land which makes up Auriol Park was sold in four plots by the trustees of the Landed Estates Company to various purchasers in the 1870s. The plots were clearly intended as the sites for substantial residences similar to those being constructed in The Avenue: they were priced at around £1,000 each, and covenants were inserted in the conveyances stipulating that no buildings should be constructed other than detached houses valued at £1,000 or more. The failure of the Company's development to reach this area caused the value of the land to fall dramatically, and the plots changed hands for around £300 each in the 1880s. In 1900 James Brand Pinker of The Oaks in The Avenue acquired all four plots for a total price of under £2000: it is likely that he kept horses in them, as Sir Alexander Harris recalled Mr Pinker's four-in-hand carriage.[87]

The site of the Park was acquired (possibly in the late 1920s) by Auriol Barker or, to give him his full name, Auriol Allan Henry Auriol-Barker (he added the Auriol to his surname by deed poll). He was a solicitor who had chambers in Gray's Inn for many years, and lived at the house called Barrow Hill (see Royal Avenue, page 42). He is best remembered, however, for his sporting interests.

These interests began when he was growing up at Bolton Hall, near Gosforth on the Cumberland coast, where he kept a pack of foxhounds and, with his brothers, hunted them on foot. He was also a keen steeplechase rider, and was later to enjoy numerous victories on his horse Best Man. In about 1902 he was instrumental in the foundation of the Worcester Park Polo Club, and he continued to play until he was over 80; he also coached the Prince of Wales and Duke of York (later Edward VIII and George VI). At the age of 82 he remained an active follower of the Mid-Surrey Draghounds, and an incident in which he had to be extricated from under his horse did not deter him from entering, and winning, gymkhana events at Ranelagh in the same year. He died on 11 April 1938, aged 89.[88]

Mr Auriol-Barker probably kept polo horses on the land that bears his name. Dick Levi, a pupil at Parkside School from 1929, recalled that there was a polo ground at the back of the school's property[89], although the land was probably not flat enough to be used for matches. The matches were probably played at the Club's ground in Motspur Park, where Purbeck Avenue is now situated. Its main tournament was the Cicero Cup, presented by Lord Rosebery, whose horse Cicero won the Derby in 1905.[90]

The Bystander, June 23, 1926

MR. AURIOL BARKER

By "The Tout"

A famous figure in the Polo World. Though he is the oldest player still in the active list he plays as vigorous a game as many a "young 'un"

*Caricature of Auriol Barker by The Tout in The Bystander, 23 Jun 1926*

In 1924 a syndicate was formed to buy the Motspur Park ground and the adjoining land (almost the whole of the Portland Avenue and Chilmark Gardens estate) in order to avoid the possibility of the land being developed, and to provide additional polo facilities for the London area. Two full-size grounds and a practice ground were laid out, and in 1926 over 600 chukkers were played there. Although the Hurlingham Polo Association leased the ground for three seasons, there were never enough subscriptions to make the new Club a financial success; in 1928 it was decided to let the pitches to football and cricket clubs, and by 1931 twelve sports clubs were playing matches on Saturdays. In 1933 the land was sold for development, its value having risen to £800 per acre, as against £480 per acre at the time of its purchase.[91]

In Salisbury Road, meanwhile, Mr Auriol-Barker's field was soon to be secured as an open space. In June 1934 Epsom Urban District Council entered into a contract to buy the land.[92] The council showed foresight in acquiring the land while it was available. It did not, however, have the resources to lay it out at the time. Mr Harry Butcher (Parks Superintendent to the Council from 1936 to 1964) recalls:

"When I first came the coal merchants, Parkers, used to park their coal carts and horses in the fields there. Then during the war I pegged out about the whole of Auriol Park for allotments, and the top part I made permanent." After the war the rest of the allotments "were done away with, and then we had to get a firm to level it off enough to have a football pitch on there, and a cricket pitch as well." In 1965, a pavilion, bowling green, putting green and tennis courts were added in the upper part.[93] Two years later, the Auriol Bowling Club, with ladies' and men's sections, was authorised to take over the bowling green.[94]

*Follow the path around the right-hand side of the Park.* In the next corner is Cuddington Copse, planted by the pupils of Cuddington County First School in National Tree Week 1993 to mark the 60th anniversary of the inclusion of Cuddington in Epsom Urban District (now Epsom and Ewell Borough).

*At the junction with the main drive (rejoining the alternative route), turn right.* As we walk up the path we leave the Landed Estates Company's Worcester Park Estate, and enter the Stoneleigh Hill Estate.

At the top of the path, notice the ornamental gateway which records the alternative name for the Park, King George's Field. Like the recreation grounds of the same name in Poole Road, West Ewell, and Jubilee Way, Tolworth, it is one of the open spaces purchased with the help of a fund established in 1936 to provide a national memorial to George V, in the form of a nationwide network of playing fields. By 1946 schemes totalling over four million acres had been approved for grants from the fund, in commemoration of a king who "had deeply at heart the welfare of the rising generation."[95]

*Leaving by the Park gateway, we turn left into…*

## Thorndon Gardens

The area between Thorndon Gardens and Stoneleigh Station was developed under the name Stoneleigh Hill Estate. Like the lower-lying Stoneleigh Park Estate on the further side of the railway, it was part of the farmland bought by John Jefferies Stone in 1860.

Although this land, like the area around The Avenue and Salisbury Road which we have just visited, was part of the Great Park of Nonsuch, it developed in a very different way. The division in ownership seems to have occurred by 1746; by this time the area which was to become the Stoneleigh Estate, stretching from Thorndon Gardens to the London Road and from Walsingham Gardens to Central Road, was owned by Thomas Lewis. By 1780 it had passed to Mary Lewis, and soon after 1800 it was acquired by Robert Ladbroke. It was his kinsman Felix Ladbroke who sold the property to Mr Stone in 1860, possibly as a result of the financial difficulties sustained by the family in the development of the area around Ladbroke Grove in North Kensington.[96]

When the Great Park was divided into farms, what is now the Stoneleigh Hill area became Coldharbour Farm, and was run from a farmhouse situated between Seaforth Gardens and Amberley Gardens. For much of the 19th century it was amalgamated with Bowling Green Farm on the other side of the railway and the farmhouse was used as accommodation for farm employees. According to Thomas Pocock, Coldharbour was held by Clara Curtis of Fitznells Farm, Ewell, in the early 20th century. She kept a dairy herd of Guernsey cattle on her main farm, supplying dairy shops in Ewell and Balham. Coldharbour was used to accommodate young stock who would be taken into the main herd later.[97]

Although the land continued to be used for farming during his lifetime, John Jefferies Stone could foresee its suitability for development. On his death in 1879 he left the estate to his trustees Edward and Frederick Stone, for the benefit of his children, but with the "earnest request and recommendation" that it should never be sold at agricultural values: they were to retain the property until it could be sold at building land prices.

Apart from some negotiations with the London County Council in 1902 for the purchase of the Stoneleigh Estate as a site for 'cottage homes' for Londoners, the trustees (Walter, Ralph and Kenneth Stone by this point) waited until the 1930s before seizing their moment. In 1931 Walter Hobbs, a contractor from Carshalton, offered £250 per acre for Coldharbour Farm; he completed his purchase of much of the farm in 1933.

Most of this estate was developed by small building firms. Part of Walsingham Gardens, however, was developed by Wimpey's, who advertised detached (£725 or 17s 5d weekly) and semi-detached (£615, 14s 11d weekly) houses, announcing "If you were given a free hand to plan an estate exactly to your wishes – this would be the answer!"[98]

Many of the builders sought to attract buyers by means of innovative features or stylish decorative schemes. Frank Petley recalls that the King & Stone chalets built in Seaforth Gardens in 1937 included a china cabinet fitted in the dining room, dark oak skirting boards, and kitchen units such as a fold-down flap with an enamel working surface, and an ironing board fitted into a tall cupboard.

*Walk up Thorndon Gardens as far as the school playing field. At this point our route continues to the right. Straight ahead is…*

## Cuda's Close

The name of this road presents us with an opportunity, albeit a slightly incongruous one, to consider the origin of the name Cuddington. The English Place Names Society's volume for Surrey interprets the name as "Cuda's farm". Cuda was presumably an Anglo-Saxon who founded a settlement in the area, perhaps in what is now Nonsuch Park where Cuddington village stood in medieval times. Nothing more is known of him.

There are three other Cuddingtons in England, a parish in Buckinghamshire about five miles south-west of Aylesbury, a hamlet about twelve miles east of Chester and a village called Cuddington Heath about the same distance

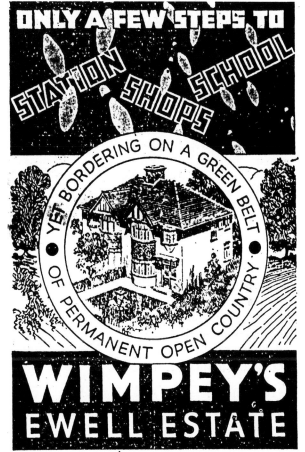

*Advertisement in the Epsom Advertiser, 26 Sep 1935, for Wimpey's houses in Walsingham Gardens*

southwards from Chester. In each case the derivation is the same, although we must assume that there were at least three men named Cuda who founded these settlements.

*Turn right into Newbury Gardens beside the school field, and take the first left into…*

## Vale Road

Centred on the junction of Vale Road, Cunliffe Road and Cuddington Avenue we find two schools, two parades of shops, a public house and a scout hall. It would seem fair to describe this spot as one of the focal points of Cuddington and Worcester Park, and it therefore comes as something of a surprise that the junction marks the boundary between the Worcester Park and Epsom postal districts, and that the modern parish boundary between Cuddington and Stoneleigh runs behind part of Cunliffe Road.

The schools complex to our left was originally known as Stoneleigh West, and consisted of a Central, later Secondary School in the building facing Vale Road, and a Junior Mixed & Infants' School in the two-storey building facing Cuda's Close, both opened in 1937.

Mr G D Echlin was appointed as first Headmaster of the Central Mixed School. Miss B V Wheeler was appointed Chief Woman Assistant, and eight assistants were selected in May 1937 (Messrs Frost, Weston, Jolly and Bradford, and Misses Gercke, Viney, Kendrick and Hobart). Miss B Hayter was chosen as Headmistress of the Junior Mixed and Infants' School, assisted by Misses Fordham, Wylie, Low, Clee and Berry, and augmented at the end of the year by Misses Bissell and Mason and Mr Evans.

By 16 September 1937 Miss Hayter had 40 children, mainly infants. No provision had been made for lunches, and Mrs Metcalfe, the caretaker's wife, suggested that she could provide a choice of a two-course hot meal, or a cheaper one-course meal such as barley broth.[99] Ruth Bissell recalls that Mrs Metcalfe provided a meal for the staff. Miss Bissell also remembers the disruption that was soon to be caused by the war: "There were air raid shelters all round the edge of the property." Once the children were in the shelters "we used to tell them stories and have sing-songs, but that was about all." In the summer of 1944 "I was evacuated to Leicester for about four or five months, with pupils from our school and from Sparrow Farm Road as well; we mixed in with the local classes."

In 1949 the Infants' section was made into a separate school in single-storey buildings facing Cuddington Avenue. 199 children were transferred from the existing classes, and 132 more admitted, making a total roll of 331 divided between seven classes. The opening of the school on 19 September was not without problems: no head teacher had been appointed, so the school was run by Miss V E Lovett, the principal infants' teacher, under the supervision of Miss Hayter of the Junior School. Three of the classes were taught by supply teachers. The central block of the new building had not been finished, so the children had to use the Junior School washing facilities. School dinners were served on four days at each end of the building, the children eating in their classrooms, and each class had to bring sandwiches or go home to lunch one day per week.

These problems were resolved over the following weeks. Miss Florence Clarke arrived as Head Teacher on 31 October, and two more appointments were made the following month. The official opening of the school took place on 9 November, a walnut tree

68

being planted to mark the occasion, and the dining hall was taken into use on 28 November. In January 1950 numbers reached 392, and an eighth class was formed. However, 99 children were transferred to the new Cuddington school in 1952, and the numbers were reduced: by September 1955 the roll had fallen to 187, divided between five classes.

The school was inspected in October 1952, and was commended for its "delightful atmosphere of goodwill and friendly efficiency", its use of teaching aids such as pictures and an aquarium, the successful remedial work, and the practical number exercises such as weighing and shopping. The Head Teacher had set herself a programme of teaching small groups engaged in woodwork, clay modelling and gardening, with the result that "she not only stimulates throughout an interested and purposeful industry but encourages initiative and experiment."

The reorganisation of secondary education in Epsom and Ewell in 1973 meant that the Secondary school left the Stoneleigh West site. The Junior school, which became Auriol Middle School, moved into the Secondary premises, while the Infants' School took over the Junior building in addition to its other premises. It was renamed The Mead First School, and accommodated pupils aged 7-8 who would previously have been transferred to the Junior School. The Mead opened on 4 September 1973, with five classes in the main building and three in the annexe. The roll, once the admission process had been completed, exceeded 250. Each of the two buildings housed one class of the Partially Hearing Unit, which had previously been housed at Riverview School but was now integrated into The Mead. The school is still called The Mead, but is now once again an Infant School.[100]

*The Gamecock under construction, October 1955*
*[Copyright of Surrey History Service, 3995]*

Across Cuddington Avenue from the schools stands the Gamecock. Plans for a public house on this site were submitted by the brewers Courage and Co. as early as 1935[101], but local opposition meant that their applications were refused until after the war. Frank Read recalls that, in the years before the war, the site "was a gypsy encampment where they used to make pegs; they used to come round selling lavender and that sort of thing." In 1940 the Borough Council took over the land for use as wartime allotments.[102] Not until 1955 did Courage's get the chance to make use of their land.

Across Vale Road from the Gamecock is The Parade, the first set of shops to be built in Vale Road. By 1938 they included a stationer (The Avenue Bookshop), a fruiterer (F N Rudkin & Co.) and a grocer with Post Office (Astill Bros.) at nos. 2, 3 and 4 respectively.

The nearer parade, Cunliffe Parade, is much newer. Although Atkinson and Marler proposed to extend the shopping facilities in 1935, and plans were revived for a row of seven shops in 1948, they were not built until the 1950s.

*Cunliffe Parade, June 1968*
*[Copyright of Surrey History Service, 3995]*

*Continuing past Cunliffe Parade, turn right into…*

# Cunliffe Road

This road, together with Alsom Avenue, Wolsey Close and Cardinal Close, lies above the site of the Worcester Park Brick Company's works, established by 1905, and is named after a former owner of the property. The brick works had its own goods siding from the adjacent railway line. Frank Read recalls that there were plans in the late

1930s to turn the flooded clay-pit into a lido. When war broke out, however, a concrete platform was constructed half-way up, and fire-fighting equipment installed for use in air raids.

On the left is the scout hut of 1st Cuddington Sea Scouts, formed in 1931 by the Revd Captain Lamb, vicar of St. Mary's and a former naval officer. Originally the troop met in the coach-house of 47 The Avenue, and had one old whaler (they now have 50 boats). After using other premises, they bought the present site in 1954, and the present hall was opened six years later. It is now known as Fancourt Hall, after Les Fancourt who became cub master in 1937 and group scout leader in 1952. He retired in 1976 and died 19 years later.[103]

*Walk to the end of Cunliffe Road, enjoying the cherry-blossom if it is springtime, and turn right into Stoneleigh Park Road.* This road, as laid out in the 1930s, stopped just above Stoneleigh Crescent, as the Brickworks property blocked its route to connect with Ardrossan Gardens. After 100 yards however, we re-enter the Stoneleigh Hill Estate (see Thorndon Gardens, page 66). *Take the first right into...*

# Stoneleigh Crescent

This road, shown as Newbury Crescent on the map in Pile's 1938 Directory of Sutton and Cheam, and known as part of Stoneleigh Park Road prior to the adoption of its present name in 1939, contains some good examples of the 1930s vernacular style, beginning with the 'Jacobethan' exuberance of the first house on the right. Following the road round to the left, we find some pairs of semi-detached houses built on a 'halls-adjoining' plan by Carters (Modern Builders) Ltd. This arrangement, which had the obvious advantage of providing a sound buffer between the living-rooms, was fairly common in the Edwardian period. In the 1930s, however, the emphasis placed on making each house an individual entity made this plan unfashionable.

The grassy traffic island half-way along the crescent is a feature of many roads in Stoneleigh. Probably designed to enhance the rural appearance of the estate, these roundabouts also provided a 'traffic calming' measure, long before the term was invented. They also had other uses: Thelma Jones, who grew up within sight of one in Stoneleigh Avenue, recalls that the United Dairies milkman "used to come with a horse in the wartime... and the horse used to stand by that island and eat the grass." Frank Petley recalls that a similar island in Amberley Gardens was used as a wartime ARP post. At the end of the war, the island near no. 49 Woodlands Avenue was the scene of a VE-Day party. Margaret Trickett recalls being given a fairy cake at the party "baked in a paper cup, and it wasn't a white cup, it was a coloured one, and I remember picking it off so carefully because I'd never seen a coloured one before."

*On the right-hand side of the Crescent is...*

# Stoneleigh Methodist Church

The first Methodist services in Stoneleigh took place in the homes of individual members. "During the winter of 1936", as Florrie MacDonald, a founder member of the congregation, recalled at the time of the church's 50th anniversary, "a group of twelve Methodists met one evening in the home of Mr and Mrs Frank Curnow in Stoneleigh Park Road, to discuss the ways and means of establishing a Methodist Society in Stoneleigh... Before the meeting adjourned, a site had been suggested and agreed upon whereon to build, in the first instance, a hall for worship with enough land on which to build a church... In order to lay the foundation and in preparation for this, we 'Founder Members' met together on Sunday evenings in a schoolroom in Stoneleigh West Infants School." On Whit Sunday, 23 May 1937, the first full service of the newly-formed Society was held "in the hall of Stoneleigh West School... The Rev Wilfred Hannam [Superintendent Minister of the Wimbledon Circuit] conducted the service and a small choir had been formed who sang an anthem." A few months later the foundation stone was laid for the dual-purpose church / hall, which was opened on 26 February 1938.

The opening of the church made it possible to extend the range of the society's activities. 1938 saw the foundation of the Women's Fellowship, the 3rd Stoneleigh Scout Group, and the 2nd Stoneleigh Guide Company (under Miss Olive Civil). By the late 1940s over 600 young people were attending weekday meetings in Stoneleigh Crescent, and a youth hut was added behind the church to ease pressure on the accommodation.

Despite the difficulties in obtaining Government consent for building work in the post-war period, plans were drawn up for a new church alongside the 1938 building, which was to become the church hall. Building commenced in 1954, and the church was opened on 10 September 1955. A further development was the building of the Link Room in 1972-73, which not only formed a physical link between the church and hall, but also provided space for organisations which would strengthen the congregation and its connections with the local community at large.

In subsequent years the church's life and witness have developed in varied ways, ranging from the youth choir "Thanks" which was invited to sing at the Methodist Conference in 1979 to the ecumenical Stoneleigh Care Scheme established in the mid 1980s to serve the community.[104]

As we walk along Stoneleigh Crescent, we pass through the fields once known as Nearer and Further Thistley Hills. *We now rejoin Newbury Gardens and turn left.* As the pair of 6-inch maps opposite shows, this road lies along the line of part of the footpath running from Royal Avenue via Delta Road towards Nonsuch. It also marks the ancient parish boundary between Cuddington (on the left as we walk down the hill, but on the right on the map) and Ewell. The houses on the right stand on the site of a field called Neds Oaks (Who was Ned? We had better move quickly on, before we begin inventing a legend about the Tudor Prince Edward sheltering under an oak tree).

At this point we are at 173 feet above sea level, and there is a fine view of the North Downs, with Epsom Grandstand clearly visible. Closer at hand, on the further side of Stoneleigh Park Road, no. 68 was the home of the playwright John Osborne as a boy between 1936 and 1938. It is perhaps unsurprising that the writer of *Look Back in Anger* was unimpressed with Stoneleigh, which he described in his memoirs as "not Stockbroker's Tudor but Bank clerk's Tudor." His grandparents lived in Clandon Close; his grandfather once pointed out a man as a Socialist, which he defined as 'a man who never raises his cap to anyone'. Osborne later commented "It didn't occur to me then that no-one in Clandon Close ever wore a cap except to play golf at weekends."[105]

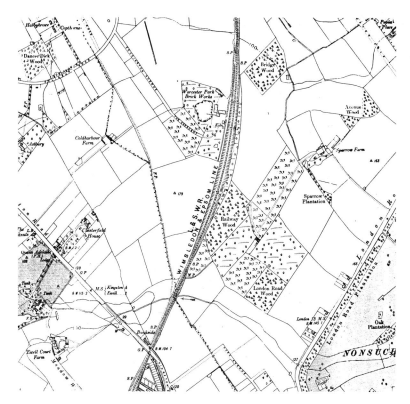

Ordnance Survey 6-inch maps of 1911 and 1938, showing the rapid development across the fields of Coldharbour and Sparrow Farms. The later map was compiled as an emergency measure before the outbreak of war, so the newest groups of houses are shown in outline, and some of the street names are slightly misspelled

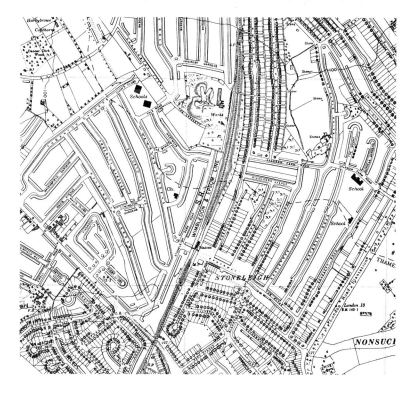

*Continue down Newbury Gardens, and cross Stoneleigh Park Road. As we enter Station Approach, we pass (on the right)...*

## St. John's Church

Stoneleigh lies across the boundary of the ancient parishes of Cuddington and Ewell, but in 1931 the Ewell part of Stoneleigh, together with the Ruxley Lane area, was transferred to Cuddington. It soon became apparent that St. Mary's could not provide sufficient accommodation for the rapidly developing communities, and the Vicar, Captain Lamb, set them on the path to separate parochial status.

The first step was the opening of a dual-purpose church / hall in Dell Road in July 1936, dedicated to St. John the Baptist. A curate, the Revd A Warnock Smith, arrived to take specific responsibility for Stoneleigh in the following January. By April 1938 Professor A B Knapp-Fisher had been chosen to design a permanent church, and the foundation stone of the present building was laid on 15 October. The church was designed to seat 450, but it was decided initially to build sufficient accommodation for 300, omitting the western end and porches.

The church was consecrated on 13 May 1939. It had already been assigned a 'conventional district', making it semi-independent from Cuddington, serving an area roughly covering the south-eastern half of Stoneleigh Hill, Stoneleigh Park between Briarwood Road and Sparrow Farm Road, and Nonsuch Park as far as the avenue. In 1948 it became a separate parish, with slightly altered boundaries, the Calverley Road area being added. The Revd John Mascall Evans was appointed as the first vicar.

The west end of the church was completed with the construction of a tower and gallery in 1956. More recently, a new complex of meeting rooms has been added on the north side, replacing both the parish room (which had stood on that site since 1960) and the original hall in Dell Road, which was sold in 1994 to the Para Sakthi Society for use as a Hindu meeting place.

Since Mr Evans's departure, the church has been served by Michael Buckley, who arrived in 1952, Martyn Farrant (1968), E John Richardson (1975), Christopher Morgan (1979), Alan Le Grys (1984), David Renshaw (1992) and Pauline Moyse (1997).

## Stoneleigh Station

The development of Stoneleigh, as of most of the inter-war suburbs around London, was dependent on its transport facilities. As most of the advertising of homes in the area was aimed at those living in London or the inner suburbs, it was essential to provide the new residents with a speedy means of reaching their London workplaces. It is not, therefore, surprising that as early as 1930 negotiations began for a new station in the heart of the estate.[106]

In July 1931 an agreement was reached between the Southern Railway and the Stone Trustees, under which the trustees were to contribute nearly half the cost (£3,000 out of £7,750) and provide land and access roads free of charge. The station was opened on 17 July 1932, and consisted of a simple island platform and open footbridge.

The original name selected for the station was Stoneleigh Park. Even before it was opened, however, it was decided that a concentration of four consecutive 'Park' names would be excessive, and, with the consent of the Stone Trustees, the second word was omitted.

Very little progress had been made with the development of the immediate vicinity by the time the station was opened, although the Ewell Court Estate (Bradford Drive and Meadow Walk area) was well advanced, and the newly-installed residents there benefited from the new facility. E W Sams, writing in 1956, recalled:

"In 1932 I… had a house built on the Ewell Court Estate in Courtlands Drive… Stoneleigh station stood on its own, with hardly a house in sight, no street lamps to guide you from the station down to the Kingston Road, a very hazardous walk on a foggy evening when you stumbled into a gypsy's horse hobbled by its front legs to prevent straying."[107]

The rapid development of Stoneleigh placed heavy demands on the railway service, and the Stoneleigh Residents' Association, formed in 1933, soon began to channel demands for improvements. Weekday trains to London between 8 am and 9 am were gradually increased from four in 1932 to seven in 1936, and in that year a number of trains began running non-stop from Motspur Park to Waterloo, thus reducing the journey from Stoneleigh to twenty-three minutes.

The station, with its narrow footbridge, was soon found to be inadequate for the rush-hour passengers: in 1935 the Residents' Association counted 1,500 passengers leaving for London between 7.20 am and 8.40 am. A new covered bridge was added, incorporating a booking office and a wider staircase to the platform. It was completed in 1939, by which time over 3,000 people were using the station daily.[108] Arthur Saitch, who was a booking clerk in the station at the time, recalls that the booking office had previously been situated on the platform.

*Cross the railway using the covered bridge.* (An alternative route avoiding the steps is available by continuing for 200 yards down Stoneleigh Park Road and turning left into a footpath leading under the railway; then turn left along Kenilworth Road to rejoin the Broadway.) *We emerge from the station into…*

# The Broadway

The Broadway is the focus of Stoneleigh, and it is perhaps symptomatic of Stoneleigh's reliance on the railway that, while it is easily reached from the station, the approaches by road – from both the Kingston and London Roads – are distinctly tortuous. Indeed the road pattern of the whole neighbourhood is unusual, almost haphazard. This has had the happy result of reducing through traffic in Stoneleigh, and nowhere is this more apparent than in the comparison between the Broadway, with its distinctive stone-edged flowerbeds, and the contemporary parades at Ewell Court and Ruxley Corner, both situated on the main Epsom-Kingston road.

On the right-hand side of The Broadway, the first building is the Stoneleigh Hotel, opened in 1935. Like many public houses in neighbouring suburbs, it is a Tudor-style super-pub, designed to evoke the respectable coaching inn rather than the gaudy corner pubs of the inner suburbs. Its facilities included a restaurant, a billiard room and a hall where dancing lessons were soon being held. The site opposite was still vacant when war broke out, despite a scheme to build a cinema there, and the modern parade

SL 9        THE BROADWAY, STONELEIGH        A TUCK CARD

*Postcard of The Broadway, with the Stoneleigh Inn on the right, postmarked 1952*
*[Courtesy The Francis Frith collection ]*

of shops was not built until the 1950s. In April 1966 Stoneleigh Library was opened in the first shop, previously occupied by Granville's supermarket.

After the Hotel, across Kenilworth Road, is the first block of shops built in the Broadway, which were mainly let by November 1933. The next block of shops, running as far as Dell Road, was built in the following year. There was immediate concern over the choice of an urban classical style: the Stoneleigh Residents' Association magazine *The Resident* for December 1935 described it as "adding an unwanted touch of suburbia." It must have come as something of a surprise to the housebuyers enticed by the estate agents Atkinson and Marler's promises of surroundings "where in the spring the trill of the lark may accompany the worker as he walks to the station." The shopping facilities were increased, and the architectural character of The Broadway balanced, by the addition of the vernacular and classical blocks on the north (left) side, in 1937 and 1939 respectively.[109]

By 1938 The Broadway could boast a comprehensive range of shops, including six grocers, five other food shops, two chemists, two newsagents or tobacconists, four hardware or domestic dealers, four drapers or outfitters and two cleaners. There was also one hairdresser, shoe repairer, wireless dealer, bookseller, dancing school and estate agent, a branch of the Midland Bank and a showroom for the local Electricity Authority. Most of the businesses were run by independent shopkeepers, but a few had more than one shop in the area, such as the greengrocer A A Smith and the chemist Sydney Best, who also traded in Stoneleigh Park Road and Ewell village respectively. There was also a branch of the South Suburban Co-operative Society, which is still operating, whilst the oldest family business is probably the electrical retailer Bradbury's, opened by George Bradbury in 1942.

76

Greta Mallin recalls the choice of food shops in the 1930s: no. 60 "for many years was Frost's, where they had double counters and you shopped over the counter in the original way; you went to the provisions or the grocery counter." Latterly "you could help yourself to certain things off the shelves, but you had to carry them in your hands to the counter and they would go on serving you. As well as Frost's we had Walton, Hassell and Port, which is a very old-established grocer's, and we had Payantake's: you didn't get provisions – ham or bacon or anything like that – there, it was all dry goods, but they were very good shops." Further choice was provided by shops in Ewell which would deliver to Stoneleigh: "Sainsbury's at The Organ delivered, but not for long… and a grocer in Ewell Village would come once a week and take your order down for next week. Sutton Creameries on The Broadway delivered in one of those little push-carts."

*Payantake Stores at 38 The Broadway in January 1967*
*[Copyright of Surrey History Service, 3995]*

No. 22 was, by 1940, occupied by Peggy Brown's cake shop. Mrs Mallin (who later assisted in the shop herself) recalls "Peggy Brown came to this country and had the idea of opening up a shop and doing all the baking herself: she was one of these people who insisted on everything being home-made." Cakes and bread were sent over daily from her main shop in Surbiton, and the shop also sold speciality honey and biscuits that were not available elsewhere.

*Continue to the end of The Broadway.* We are now near the centre of the Stoneleigh Park estate, developed in 1932-35 between Park Avenue and Sparrow Farm Road. As on the Stoneleigh Hill estate, the houses were constructed by many independent builders. The layout and marketing, however, were managed by Atkinson and Marler, a firm of estate agents. They took care to produce a harmonious estate by enforcing building lines and minimum house values.

# E. F. MILBOURNE
## *BUILDER*
### BRIARWOOD ROAD
# STONELEIGH PARK ESTATE
#### EWELL
Telephone EWELL 1771

DECORATIONS THROUGHOUT ARE TO PURCHASER'S OWN CHOICE

——

STONELEIGH STATION ONLY TWO MINUTES' WALK AWAY

EACH BUNGALETTE HAS TWO ELECTRIC POWER POINTS NINE LIGHTING POINTS and SIX GAS POINTS

"A" TYPE BUNGALETTES

| | | |
|---|---|---|
| DRAWING ROOM | 16' into bay × 13' | |
| DINING ROOM | 15' × 11' 9" | |
| KITCHENETTE | 9' × 10' | |
| BATHROOM | 9' 6" × 7' | |
| SPARE ROOM | | |

**FIRST FLOOR**

| | |
|---|---|
| FRONT BEDROOM | 15' into bay × 12' 6" |
| BACK BEDROOM | 13' 3" × 12' 6" |

**PRICES AND TERMS**

| | | |
|---|---|---|
| FREEHOLD | .. .. .. | £760 |
| DEPOSIT | .. .. .. | £35 |
| WEEKLY OUTGOINGS | | 22/9 |
| RATES | .. .. .. | 3/10 per week. |
| GAS | .. .. .. | 4/1 per 1000 cubic feet |

ELECTRICITY LIGHTING 5d. per unit

HEATING & COOKING 1½d. & 1d. per unit

These Prices and Deposits include all Road Charges, Legal Charges, Mortgage Costs and Survey Fees.

### EACH HOUSE HAS ROOM FOR GARAGE

# BUNGALETTES   £760   FREEHOLD

*Advertisement from Atkinson and Marler's promotional brochure for the Stoneleigh Park Estate, c.1933*

Atkinson and Marler's promotional brochure announced: "Ewell is, undoubtedly, one of the prettiest of the Surrey villages near to the Metropolis, and it is being made still prettier now that the Stoneleigh Park Estate is being developed... There are few places around London with the same residential qualification as Stoneleigh Park. Certainly none have better travelling facilities to and from Town... Get into your train at Waterloo..., ride in ease and comfort, alight at Stoneleigh Park, and, hey presto, there's your front door!... Here you get a quiet journey, refreshed in body and mind when you reach the other end...

"What is the urge which induces people no longer to live in stuffy, unhygienic towns, but to... seek a region where the sun may throw its brightest beams unrepelled by smoke and fog...? It is not only, we think, the desire to seek out healthy conditions for one's self and one's family, but also because people are more and more striving for individuality in their daily life... It is at such spots as Stoneleigh Park that this ideal of individuality is so intensely realised. A street in town is like any other street, and a house is like any other house. But at Stoneleigh every street and house is distinctive... a resident at Stoneleigh... has a very real and very distinct place in the sun... [and yet] at Stoneleigh are so many people who are really strongly knit together by this common aim and object – that of getting away from the vast herd... – [that] this common fundamental background will provide a communal meeting-place in which every man will find his own joyful little niche."[110]

*Continue past the roundabout straight ahead into...*

## The Glade

This road of attractive chalet-style houses was developed on the site of the London Road Wood around 1933. Like most of southern Stoneleigh, this area had been part of Bowling Green Farm. The farmhouse, which stood between Ewell Park Way and Elmwood Drive, was transformed by J J Stone into a country residence, "Stoneleigh", as a nucleus for his Surrey estate. Many of the fields to the north of the London Road Wood are named "Lampreys" on the tithe map of 1840, but this may be a corruption of the name "Lumleys" given in a terrier of 1746.[111]

Greta Mallin recalls visiting the estate after it had been advertised by Atkinson and Marler at the Ideal Home Exhibition in 1933 or 1934: "When we got here to see the place, Briarwood Road was built, and all the other roads were laid out in concrete. The Broadway was there, but the Stoneleigh Book Shop, a paper shop, was the only shop that was open. Mr Cox had a show house in Briarwood Road"; Mr Cox built the two styles of chalets in The Glade, of which the larger type cost £850 including a garage. "You could have a choice of fireplaces, bathroom fittings and wallpaper, and that was an attraction to young couples starting off, that they could have everything how they liked it."

At the far end of The Glade is Stoneleigh Baptist Church. The congregation began by holding services and a Sunday School in 1934, in a sports pavilion in Richlands Avenue, but the first Baptist meeting-place on this site was a hall, intended to be used as a dual-purpose church and hall until the construction of a permanent church, and opened on 21 September 1935. The door was unlocked by Mrs J J Goldsmith, with the words "Within its walls may the weary find rest and peace, may sinners find their Saviour, and may children be led to the Children's Friend." The hall, which included the main Church Hall, Primary Hall and kitchen, was built for £2700 on a site donated by Arthur Itter.[112] Mr Itter was Mayor of Peterborough in 1934, and was a tireless worker for Baptist churches in Peterborough and at regional and national levels. He was involved in several development companies, including Stoneleigh Estates Ltd, and it is possible that nearby Waverley Road was named after his mother's house in Totteridge near Barnet.[113]

The congregation was initially under the care of the Revd J Aubrey Moore, but in September 1936 the Revd Horace Warde moved from Surbiton to become the first permanent Pastor. A range of organisations was set up to meet the needs of different age groups: by November 1939 these included Boys' and Girls' Brigades, a Women's Fellowship and a Girls' Covenanters Class.

Mr Warde had intended to retire from the pastorate at the end of the three years for which he was originally appointed. He was asked to stay on for a few more months until the next year's students from Spurgeon's College were ready to take up posts, after which he was again asked to remain in post because of the outbreak of war. The war brought many other changes: the secretary, Mr Wood, had to leave after his firm was evacuated to Bath; the Sunday School was moved to the Sparrow Farm Road schools where shelters were available, and was later split between private houses; and although attempts were made to keep the youth organisations operating, the Men's Fellowship had to suspend its activities.

*The opening of Stoneleigh Baptist Church, pictured in the Epsom Advertiser,*
*26 Sep 1935*
*[Reproduced by kind permission of the Croydon Advertiser Group]*

Mr Warde (who was described as "a wise councillor and a faithful minister in every sense of the word") retired in the summer of 1942, and the Revd David W F Jelleyman became Pastor, although Mr Warde continued to assist, especially when Mr Jelleyman joined the YMCA for six months' service on the Western Front in 1945. Despite the strains of the war, it was possible in 1946 to clear the debt on the construction of the hall and a new fund was immediately opened in preparation for the building of a new church.[114]

The foundation stone of a new church on the southern side of the hall was laid on 10 June 1961, and it was opened the next year. The present complex was opened in 1998. The design, by Brian Drury, incorporated the 1962 sanctuary facing The Glade, which was heightened to allow additional natural light to enter. A new hall and complex of rooms was built on the site of the old hall and the courtyard between the two buildings. As an act of faith, the congregation committed itself to a project costing £850 000, of which all but £50 000 had been raised by the time it was opened.

*Turn right at the end of The Glade into Chadacre Road, and left into Briarwood Road, leaving the Stoneleigh Park Estate through the brick gateway. Turn right onto the London Road*, which runs roughly on the line of the Roman London-Chichester road, Stane Street. *Continue a short distance along the London Road as far as the right-hand bend. Cross the London Road with great care.* (The nearest light-controlled crossing is at the Ewell By-Pass junction, though even there the crossing on that side of the London Road has no pedestrian phase.)

*Turn left into Nonsuch Park. As we walk through the gateway and along the avenue through the park,* we are not only entering the estate surrounding the Mansion House and the former Little Park of Nonsuch Palace, but also approaching the site of the medieval...

# Cuddington Village

We have already seen that Cuddington was probably founded by an Anglo-Saxon named Cuda. We have little knowledge, however, of later Saxon owners, except for the last, Leofwin, who was a younger brother of Harold Godwinson, the last Saxon King of England. Leofwin was Earl of the South Eastern Shires, and Cuddington would for him have been one manor among many.

The Earl was killed at the Battle of Hastings, and William the Conqueror gave the manor to his half brother Odo, the Bishop of Bayeux.

In 1086 the commissioners compiling the Domesday Book recorded that, in Leofwin's time, the manor had answered for an area of 30 hides, of which he held 20 himself, and that the Bishop now controlled 26 of the 30, but that they were held under him by Ilbert [de Laci]; there were seven villagers, nine smallholders with six ploughs, and four slaves; there was also a mill. On the remainder of the manor, the commissioners found four villagers and four smallholders with one plough. The whole manor had been worth £11 before 1066; the value had dropped to 100s after the devastation following the Conquest, but had now climbed back to £9 12s.[115]

Ilbert de Laci, although sub-tenant of this manor, was a considerable landowner, having nearly 150 manors in Yorkshire, and others in Nottinghamshire and Lincolnshire. His son Robert, however, forfeited these estates after the death of William II, when he supported Robert, Duke of Normandy (William II's elder brother) in his struggle against his younger brother Henry I for the English crown.

In 1101 Henry gave the de Laci estates to his adherent Hugh de Laval, and Cuddington remained in his family's hands for just over a century. In 1203 the de Lavals also suffered from the tensions between England and Normandy: King John's growing unpopularity in Normandy, and the determination of the French king Philip Augustus to incorporate the dukedom into his kingdom, forced those barons with lands in both England and Normandy to choose between the claims of England and France. Guy de Laval took Philip's side, and forfeited his English estates.

In 1203 the manor was granted to William de St Michael, and it remained in his family (which by the 1350s had adopted the surname de Codington) until once again a king stepped in to alter the course of Cuddington's history. The de St Michaels were a branch of the Wateville family, but little is known of the early years of their time in the manor, except that William was succeeded by his son, grandson and great-grandson who were all called Lawrence. The third of these left no sons, and the manor eventually passed, in 1354, to his nephew Sir Simon de Codington.

Sir Simon is the first member of the family of whom more is known. He served as Sheriff of Surrey in 1353 and 1362, and represented Surrey in at least eleven parliaments. On his death in 1374 an inventory of his goods was compiled, which enables us to walk around his manor house, room by room.

The valuers began in the chamber. The most valuable piece of furniture in the house, the bed, was found here and with its tester and ridells was valued at 26s 8d. The chamber also contained some cloaks, three tunics and a gown, two pairs of shoes (much worn), five chests (four without locks), two pairs of spoons, and a number of weapons including a sword, two bows and two cross-bows.

Moving to the hall, they found a set of blue and white hangings, with three bench covers and six cushions, a dining table with a trestle and two forms, and some bowls and ewers and fire irons. In the pantry and buttery was a range of cooking utensils and cloths, as well as a silver cup with its silver cover and three pieces of silver (40s). The kitchen contained a number of cooking-pots, tin saucers and brass dishes, but the valuers were unimpressed, describing many of them as worn, broken, or both. Continuing on to the bakehouse and brewhouse, they recorded 50s of malt along with the necessary equipment.

In the grange they noted £4 worth of wheat; they also found a fan [in the sense of a winnowing instrument] and set it down at 6d before moving on to the livestock – three steers (26s 8d), 26 oxen (£13), a bull, 16 cows and 3 heifers (£6 13s 4d), 9 steers and heifers (45s), 572 sheep and lambs (£33 3s 4d), 26 pigs and piglets (34s) and 12 geese and ganders (4s). They added £38 16s 6d for 194 acres of corn sold after Simon's death.[116]

The estate passed to Sir Simon's son Ralph Codington (who seems to have dropped the "de" from the surname). Like his father, Ralph represented Surrey in the House of Commons (in 1391, 1399, 1402 and 1407), and undertook the duties of Sheriff (1400). The fall of Richard II, and assumption of the throne by Henry IV, first of the Lancastrian kings, in 1399, seems to have been beneficial to Ralph Codington: as well as his appointment as Sheriff, he was made a member of the commission of enquiry set up to list Richard II's possessions at Portchester Castle beside Portsmouth Harbour, and he received some of the forfeited estates of the Duke of Norfolk. By 1412 his Surrey estates (which included property in nearby parishes) were said to produce an income of £40 a year.[117]

Less information is available on Ralph Codington's activities within the manor. We do know, however, that a dispute had begun by 1402, which was to continue intermittently for over a century, over the status of Sparwefeld or Sparrowfield. This was a large common, partly lying in the northern part of Cuddington but stretching to, or across, the boundaries of Cheam, Malden and Morden. Its name was later applied to one of the farms in the Great Park (see Sparrow Farm Road, page 100). The grazing rights of the tenants of the various manors were ill-defined, and in a lawsuit of 1402-03 Ralph Codington prosecuted William Curson of Malden for trespassing on Sparwefeld.

The 1420s-30s saw disputes between the Warden of Merton College, on behalf of Malden manor, the Prior of Christ Church, Canterbury, on behalf of Cheam manor, and the Codingtons – Ralph, his son Simon and Simon's brother and successor Thomas. In January 1427 an agreement was reached, by which the parties were to be "gode frendes", and to share the pasturage rights, and the Warden of Merton College was to give Thomas "a robe of gentilmannes liverey with a liverey furre, or elles a mark of silver... atte Cristemase." This was not the end of the matter, however: in 1508 Merton College decided to seek the Bishop of London's help in fending off the bailiff of Christ Church Priory, who had seized some Malden cattle, and a year later John Codington was recorded as preventing the Malden tenants from exercising their common rights.[118]

John Codington, son of Thomas, had succeeded his mother Margaret as lord of the manor in 1470. After John's death it passed to his son Richard, who proved to be the last member of the family to hold the manor, when Henry VIII, seeking to enlarge his hunting estate around Hampton Court, selected Cuddington as the site for a rather unusual hunting lodge.

As we shall soon see, Henry's plans were to cause a complete transformation of this piece of spring-line countryside. Before this happened, however, the king's surveyors drew up a description of his proposed acquisition, which suggests a distinct rise in comfort and status since the days of Sir Simon.

The manor house was built around a courtyard, 140 feet by 100 feet. On the northern side was a gatehouse set into a stone wall; the western and eastern sides contained timber barns with tiled roofs, that on the east measuring 155 feet by 36 feet. On the southern side lay the house itself, centred on a hall (fairly small, at 24 feet by 18 feet), with three parlours and chambers at the ends "with oute Castes of bey wyndowys above and belowe, very pleasaunte in the vewe and Shewe at the entre into the same and in the saide parler and Chamber be Chymneys very goode"; there were also seven servants' chambers, two small cellars used as a pantry and buttery, a kitchen, pastry-house, two larders and four ovens. The hall and parlour looked out over a garden and orchard which, with the cook's garden, extended to an acre.[119]

Within about two hundred yards were four farmhouses with barns and stables "wherein dwellyth and inhabiteth foure honest mene and tall persones mete and able to do the Kynges service." The southern part of the parish contained arable fields, and stretching to Banstead Downs, "commodious country" full of pheasants, partridges, foxes, hares and badgers. This suggests that the surveyors realised the attraction of the manor for its hunting, but they may have supposed Henry intended to take over the house, "a fayre place well buyldede and withoute decay" and convert it into a modest hunting lodge. The King's own idea was very different.

Unfortunately for us, and perhaps because they were unaware of the magnitude of the royal plans, the surveyors did not describe the other principal building in the village, which adjoined the manor house, namely...

## St. Mary's Old Church

The architectural history of the old Cuddington church was established during the 1959 excavations of Nonsuch Palace. The discovery of a number of post holes suggests that there may have been an early wooden church. The first stone church was built around

1100, and was a simple rectangular structure of nave and chancel. In about 1250 this was replaced with a larger building, including a western tower, north and south aisles, and longer chancel. A century later, further alterations were made, involving the demolition of the south aisle and the enlargement of the north aisle; the final touch, some time later, was the addition of a north porch. The majority of graves found within the church were situated in the north aisle, which suggests that this may have been a chapel for the Codington family, perhaps the "chapel of St. Katherine" where Anne, widow of John Codington, wished to be buried, according to her will made in 1500/1.[120]

In 1491-92 the church was in need of repair: Richard King bequeathed a red cow with a white patch on her back towards the repair of the steeple, and Alice Rogers bequeathed her lands for the same purpose. William Rogers left two wethers and two ewes for repairing the church "of our lady of Codyngton."[121]

*Nonsuch Palace excavations, 1959,*
*including Cuddington church (centre rear of this picture)*

So much for the architectural outline: but what would the medieval worshipper have seen as he entered the church? We must forget the present-day interiors of churches that have survived from the period, with white-washed walls and plain interiors. The medieval churchgoer, hearing a Latin liturgy chanted by a priest who was frequently not trained to preach, relied on ritual and symbol for his religious education. The church would have been colourful, with painted columns, hangings, and perhaps statues and stained glass. There would have been candles: in 1274 it was recorded that, as part of the rent for his house in the village, Philip Hereward had to provide a wax candle in the chancel, to burn before the altar each day during services, and in 1492 the church received a bequest from Alice Rogers of a quart of barley for the maintenance of the Paschal light, a candle which was carried in procession during the Easter vigil service to symbolise the dawning of the light of Christ after the darkness of Good Friday.

At funerals, torches might be used, and the service could be followed by a feast. The will of Robert Rogers of Ewell, proved in 1533, directed his executors to buy five torches for use at the burial, at which fifteen priests were to be present. The ceremony was to be followed by a feast of three fat sheep, ten pigs, ten geese, a quart and a half of wheat and two and a half quarts of malt brewed in drink. Although the arrangements relate primarily to Ewell, where a priest was to say masses for Rogers and his parents, Cuddington church was to be given one of the five torches.[122]

Feasting may perhaps also have taken place on the dedication festival of the church each year: in 1404 the Bishop of Winchester gave the parish permission to alter the festival from the third day after the feast (15 August) of the Assumption of the Virgin Mary, to a Sunday shortly after that feast, so that harvesting work did not prevent it being celebrated "with festivity and solemnity."[123]

Some ceremonies would have taken place outside the church building: we know that in the 1420s a wooden cross of the same height as the Holy Cross, was set up on Sparwefeld, and that the people of Cheam used to process there on Rogation days for the service of the litany (rogation days, in late spring and early summer, were marked by processions through the fields and prayers for the crops). We only know this, however, because of the legal repercussions of an incident in May 1426 when the cross was pulled down and dragged away, presumably in connection with the Sparwefeld boundary disputes.[124]

We know the names of over thirty of the clergy who served in St. Mary's. In the thirteenth century the church had rectors, Master Robert (1218), Walter de Merton (1238) and Ralph de Mare (1284). The second of these was the parish's most famous clergyman: he went on to be the Keeper of the Great Seal from 1258, Chancellor of England from 1260, and Bishop of Rochester from 1274. In 1240 he acquired Malden manor; with the support of its revenues he founded Merton College at Oxford, which in 1264 became the first university college in England to receive a foundation charter.

Soon after the construction of the first permanent church, it was granted, with its land and tithes, to Bernard the Scriptor by Hugh de Laval in trust for Merton Priory, which was founded around 1114 by Gilbert the Knight. In 1284 the revenues of the church were appropriated to the Priory, by an order of Pope Martin IV. This was confirmed by the Bishop of Winchester in 1310, recording that, through no fault of their own, the monks had become unable to support themselves and make provision for guests and the poor unless their income was augmented.

As a result, Cuddington church ceased to be served by Rectors who received tithes from the parishioners, and instead was entrusted to vicars appointed by Merton Priory. The first vicar, Low Thomas of Kingston, was instituted in 1311.

When Henry VIII acquired Cuddington manor in 1538, it soon became apparent that the church had no place in his plans. Merton Priory, which had remained patron of the living, was closed in the same year as part of the Dissolution of the Monasteries, and its property had been confiscated by the Crown. The worship which had been offered on this spot for over four centuries was halted, and for the next 328 years Cuddington was to be a parish without a church. The site of the church now lay within the inner courtyard of…

## Nonsuch Palace

Monarchs of the medieval and early modern period had an itinerant way of life, travelling around the country from one palace or castle to another. This served a number of purposes: the large retinue of the court was able to move on to a new well-provisioned and well-aired residence as necessary, and the king was able to be seen by, and dispense justice among, his subjects throughout the kingdom. Those kings, such as Henry VIII, for whom hunting was an abiding passion, were keen to take advantage of the deer parks attached to many royal residences. For instance, in his youth Henry frequently led his court to Woodstock, and would sometimes retreat with a few associates to the surrounding satellite hunting lodges such as Langley and Ewelme.

As travelling became more irksome to Henry, he decided to establish a new hunting forest nearer to London. He already had a suitable residence on which the forest would be centred, at Hampton Court. This had been built by Henry's powerful minister Cardinal Wolsey, and in contrast to the traditional fortified castle it was designed to be both magnificent and luxurious, where visiting ambassadors would be impressed with the quality of the Biblical and classical tapestries and paintings, and the comfort of the bed-hangings and the piped water supply. When Wolsey failed to secure Henry's divorce from Katharine of Aragon in 1529, he fell from favour, and Hampton Court became, what it already appeared to be, a royal residence. Henry moved in during 1530, and soon began to enlarge the palace, adding a Great Hall 106 feet long.

Hampton Court was sufficiently large to accommodate the whole court, and Oatlands, which Henry began constructing at Weybridge, provided an outpost in the western part of his new forest. Henry wanted something more, however: a building which at the practical level would be an intimate hunting lodge, a "privy palace", but which would also serve the symbolic purpose of portraying the House of Tudor, newly-secured in 1537 by the long-awaited birth of a prince, as one of the great royal houses of Europe and an inheritor of the Classical ideals of virtue. And Cuddington was the place in which he chose to build it.

The king's new hunting estate was formally established in 1539 by act of Parliament, as the Honour of Hampton Court, and extended in 1540. Parts of the estate, such as the land around Nonsuch, became Parks, owned by the king himself and reserved almost exclusively for deer. The remainder of the Honour, although remaining in other hands, became subject to forest laws which, as in the New Forest, protected the deer which roamed it. From 1540 the Honour stretched from the Epsom and Walton Downs to Wandsworth and Battersea in the east, and Walton-on-Thames in the west. As the Privy Council recorded in 1548, a year after Henry's death, it was set up because "hys Hignes… might not travayle so readyly abrode, but was constreyned to seke to have hys game and pleasure ready at hand."[125]

What became of Richard Codington and his wife Elizabeth as a result of this scheme? When they surrendered Cuddington to the king, they were given in return the priory of Ixworth in Suffolk (which, like Merton Priory, had recently been dissolved). This may not have been an unwelcome move: the Priory's property included Ixworth manor and tithes from many parishes, bringing in an income of nearly £170 in 1535. As Charles

Abdy has pointed out, Elizabeth had been a widow when she married Richard, and her first husband had been Thomas Bokenham of Great Livermere, the parish adjacent to Ixworth. Richard died childless in 1567, and so on Elizabeth's death four years later the Ixworth estate passed to a grandson by the Bokenham marriage, thus enabling that family to consolidate its Suffolk landholding.[126] Richard and Elizabeth are depicted on a memorial brass in the chancel of Ixworth church, which also records their acquisition of the Priory in exchange for Cuddington.

Back in Surrey, events moved rapidly. Although the formal surrender was not completed until July 1538, work began in April. On the 22nd, two clerks began work. By 29 April, six freemasons, two bricklayers and six labourers had joined the payroll. During the summer, the workforce increased rapidly: the list of men present on 15 July comprised 44 masons, 95 bricklayers, nine chalk-diggers, 88 carpenters, 27 sawyers, seven carters, a scaffolder, a hodmaker, four clerks and a labourer.

These workmen came from a wide area: masons were paid to travel as far afield as Herefordshire and Northamptonshire to press men into service. The building materials, too, came from many sources: during the summer of 1538 over 3500 one-ton loads were brought from a rather convenient quarry in Merton (formerly renowned as a centre of devotion and education); at least in the early days, many of the loads from the Priory included carved stone, which was useless for the masonry above ground, and was incorporated into the foundations. More stone was brought from Richard Aynscombe's quarry at Reigate, or carried by boat from London to Ditton.

Tiles were brought from Kingston and Streatham; timber was selected in woods as far away as Bookham and Newdigate, and as near as Rutherwick copse (in the Riverhill area of Worcester Park); scaffolding was brought from Dorking, and fencing from many of the parishes around Dorking and Reigate. Even the residents of Cuddington could extract some benefit from the situation: Thomas Fenner of Cuddington sold three hand-barrows at 4d each, and Thomas Carpenter was paid nearly £15 for elm board, firewood and straw. Kilns were built at Nonsuch for burning bricks and lime; they were located near the banqueting house and the present Mansion House. The costs incurred included payments to three men from Stoke D'Abernon, who produced 600,000 bricks at a rate of 2s per thousand, and compensation to four farmers (Robert Hall of Ewell, Richard Bray and George Codyngton, and Raynald Wilkyns of Ewell) for the damage caused to neighbouring crops. (This snippet of information makes one more sanguine about the fate of those Cuddingtonians who were dispossessed of their lands altogether.)

These details are drawn from the building accounts, which survive for the period April to September 1538. Regrettably, only summary accounts survive for the subsequent period of construction down to 1545. Even by September 1538, however, it seems likely that the foundations of the Inner Court had been largely constructed, and the building of the walls begun; metal and timber for the window frames had already been purchased, and the hall of the manor house had been re-tiled so that it could be used for accommodation (whether for the builders or for a possible royal site inspection is uncertain).

By June 1541, work appears to have begun on the decoration of the Inner Court; payments are recorded to Nicholas Modena and his slate workers and 24 mould makers, in connection with the exterior stucco-work, while the 70 carpenters on site at the time were probably making and installing wainscoting inside. Stone was still being packed up at Merton Priory, and bricks were being burnt by thirty brickmakers, presumably in readiness for the construction of the Outward Court. Between November 1543 and May 1544 the carvers and gilders worked for 204 days, presumably on the slate decorations, and in July 1544, six French clockmakers were on the payroll. By November 1545, expenditure on the palace had reached £24,536 7s 7d (in comparison with less than £1650 incurred in the construction of Loseley House, which was built around 1570 near Guildford, and still stands).

Let us now follow in the footsteps of visitors to Nonsuch in its heyday. We are fortunate that several detailed descriptions have survived, notably those of Anthony Watson, Rector of Cheam (probably written between 1581 and 1592), Paul Hentzner, a German visitor in 1598, and Thomas Platter of Switzerland, who visited the palace in 1599. These may be compared with the Parliamentary Surveyors' report of 1650, the findings of the 1959 excavation, and the surviving drawings by Joris Hoefnagel (1568), John Speed (1610), a Flemish artist whose painting is held by the Fitzwilliam Museum (c.1620) and Hendrik Danckerts (c.1660). What follows is based largely on John Dent's synthesis of these sources,[127] and I have adopted his convention of referring to the palace as facing north, whereas the true orientation is north-north-west.

The visitor from London will have proceeded down the London Road, with the palings of the Little and Great Parks to his left and right. As he reaches the turn in the road, he is confronted by the ornamental gateway a couple of hundred yards ahead, and, through the gateway, his first sight of the palace. His initial impression is of a fairly traditional stone battlemented gatehouse, not dissimilar in style to the brick gatehouse at Hampton Court albeit on a smaller scale. "Very strong and graceful" it may have been, as the surveyors thought, but "none such"? Surely not, he thinks.

Entering the gateway, he passes along "a long grassy avenue enclosed by wooden palings" (Platter) between lines of alternating elms and walnuts (Pepys). If the court was in residence, as in the summer of 1599, the meadow on the right might have been full of tents, accommodating those – servants and nobles alike – who had not been able to find rooms in the diminutive palace. As we follow him along the modern roadway, we are walking a few feet to the right of the original avenue.

In front of the palace, the post-and-rail fence opens out to enclose a bowling green ("neate and handsome", the surveyors thought). Crossing the green, the visitor reaches the gatehouse of the outer court, and *we reach the first of the three obelisks beside the modern roadway*. Passing through the archway, beneath a ceiling constructed to form an echo that returned "the voice and sound of trumpets, not merely one time, but four or five, very distinctly",[128] he reached the courtyard of the Outward Court, 135 feet by 115 feet, and cobbled except for flagstone paths connecting the gatehouses and various entrances. The walls were faced with ashlar (square-cut stone), although this seems to have been a facing added to a brick core.

Very few of the rooms in the outward court can be identified with certainty. The 1650 survey lists the occupiers of the rooms during Queen Henrietta Maria's ownership of the palace: the housekeeper had six rooms on the ground floor and two on the first; there were rooms for the gentleman ushers and quarter waiter, for the groom porter and for Henry Jermyn, captain of the bodyguard. The Groom of the Stool (Lady Denbigh), Lady Carlisle, the Lord Chamberlain (Lord Dorset) and the Queen's Almoner all had apartments around this court.

To the left (east) there was a passage to the Kitchen Court, which could also be reached from the front of the palace through a yard. This arrangement matches the plan at Hampton Court, where the kitchens have been restored and convey a vivid impression of the cooking arrangements of a Tudor palace, albeit on a much larger scale. The Nonsuch kitchens included, as well as the main kitchen, a pastry room, a boiling house, a bottle house and a coalhouse. The 1959 excavations revealed four ovens, and a well which fed a pump in the kitchens. Among the objects found in the well-shaft were several pewter plates, pierced with square holes "as though", Dent suggests, "the kitchen lads had used them as targets and then taken fright and slipped them into the well."

On the opposite side of the courtyard, was a corresponding archway leading to stabling and a wood-yard. Near here the excavations revealed the foundations of a massive wall, probably part of the 155-foot barn that had stood on the eastern side of Cuddington's manor house.

On the southern side of the Outward Court was the central block dividing the two courtyards. The upper rooms were apparently approached from the Inner Court, but the lower storey contained two cellars reached by steps from the outer court. The wine cellar was one of the most impressive features of the excavation, and contained many fragments of bottles and flasks. The eye of the sixteenth-century visitor, however, will have been drawn to the Inner Gatehouse in the centre of this range. So far, all he has seen is an assertion of the military strength of the House of Tudor, and its reinvigoration of the medieval monarchy after the disorder of the late fifteenth century. As he ascends the eight steps and walks through the gatehouse – *and as we, in our turn, reach the second obelisk* – what will he, and we, find?

On entering the Inner Court, the visitor is once again surrounded by four ranges of buildings. This time, however, above the stone ground floor, is an upper storey covered in a dazzling display of stucco ornamentation, which at times was white-washed to preserve its impact. Around the top were busts of thirty-one Roman emperors; below them were panels depicting classical deities, while the lowest row contained the labours of Hercules on the left, and personifications of the liberal arts and virtues to the right. Facing the visitor across the courtyard, surrounded by the precedents of imperial power and legendary daring, was Henry himself, depicted either in relief or as a statue. There was to be no doubt that the Tudor dynasty was taking its place among the great heroes of the past, and the Renaissance monarchies of the present, and that this was to be the inheritance of the infant Edward VI.

Although some visitors were deceived into thinking that all this decoration had been produced in stone, the upper storey of the Inner Court was actually a timber construction. Between the timbers were plaster panels, around two inches thick. It is likely that the plaster was put up wet, with planks backing it, and that the plaster was moulded in situ, with further layers added as required. The carvings were in high relief, up to nine inches thick in the case of a Roman soldier discovered in the excavations. The timbers between the panels were concealed (and protected from the weather) with panels of slate, decorated with trophies, birds, fruit and flowers, crowns, grotesques, flaming torches and scrolls, and in many cases gilded. Whilst the stuccoes were inspired by the decorations at Fontainebleau, one of the palaces of Henry's rival Francis I of France (indeed, Nicholas Modena alias Bellin was probably responsible for overseeing both projects), the slate decoration was a unique touch. None such, indeed. Looking behind him, the visitor would have seen that in "the middle gatehouse (which outdoes the first gatehouse by a tower, a clock, chimes and six golden horoscopes), the projecting windows might be thought to have been hewn from the heart of the rock." (Watson)

*Painting of Nonsuch Palace in c.1620 by an unknown Flemish artist (detail),*
*showing the bowling green in front of the outward court;*
*the "none such" inner court is visible on the right hand side*
[Reproduction by permission of the Syndics of the Fitzwilliam Museum, Cambridge]

The ground floor rooms around this courtyard were mostly occupied by royal servants and officials: the 1650 survey mentions rooms for the Queen's dresser, priests, equerries, master-cook and waiters. On the first floor, behind the plasterwork heroes, were the apartments for their successors, the queen's suite of rooms to the left (east) and the king's to the right. Watson records the arrangement of the king's apartments. A staircase led from the guard chamber to a waiting room. Beyond this was a sequence of rooms of increasing privacy and status: the presence chamber (with tapestried walls, but a straw-covered floor, except for a carpeted path to the queen's canopied chair, according to Platter), the privy closet (for private interviews) and, approached by a wide corridor parallel to the closet, the privy chamber, where the king took his meals, and where Watson noted a fountain in which water trickled from the mouth of a serpent. These rooms occupied the west range; the plan of the south range is less certain but, based on Watson's description, Dent suggests that it contained the privy gallery, running along the courtyard side, and the king's bedchamber, with other rooms, overlooking the garden.

The queen's apartments could be reached either from an entrance, guarded by a sculpture of Penthesilea (in Greek mythology, the valiant queen of the Amazons: was this really the much-married Henry's concept of an ideal queen?), opposite the

90

entrance to the king's side, or by continuing along the gallery. Watson recorded that the queen's quarters "are accorded the unrestricted benefit and use of the gallery and are marked by the same spaciousness and ornamentation as the king's." Elsewhere, a feature recorded by Watson was the library, assembled by Arundel and Lumley and later made the nucleus of the British Library.

Now that we have reached the royal apartments, it is time to turn to their various occupants. More information on them, as on the palace itself, is available in John Dent's *The Quest for Nonsuch*. The first name is, of course, that of Henry VIII. Nonsuch, however, was a project of his latter years, and he spent much less time there than is often assumed. We know for certain of only three visits, of which the best-recorded lasted from 4 to 7 July 1545, and included both meetings of the Council and a hunting trip, which the king watched from a cushioned "standing" in the park.

In 1547 Henry was succeeded by his son Edward VI, who is known to have visited Nonsuch in 1550. Edward's sister Mary I, who succeeded in 1553, apparently found the palace an unnecessary burden, and three years later granted it, in exchange for some Norfolk manors and a cash payment, to Henry Fitzalan, Earl of Arundel, who had helped to secure her accession. Arundel's relationship with her successor Elizabeth I was more unstable: in 1559, probably after completing numerous embellishments at Nonsuch, he entertained the Queen with lavish feasts and a masque, and it was rumoured that he was seeking her hand. In the 1560s-70s, however, he was involved in various plots centred on Mary, Queen of Scots, and was at times imprisoned or confined to his house. This does not seem to have discouraged Elizabeth from visiting Nonsuch. Indeed, she unashamedly wrote to him in March 1567 reporting that she had paid a visit while he was abroad, and "had dyvers wayes very good contentation. And did so well ayre every parte of your house, as at your comming we thinke you shall fynde it seasonable for you."

Arundel died in 1579; his son-in-law John, Lord Lumley, who had long made his home there, succeeded not only to the palace but also to Arundel's debts. By 1591 his situation was becoming unmanageable, and Elizabeth's continued visits to Nonsuch during the 1580s inspired a solution: in January 1592, Lumley conveyed the Nonsuch estate to the Queen, in return for which the debts were expunged, Lumley was granted a lease of the parks, and he was allowed to continue living in the palace as Keeper.

Elizabeth thus acquired a property which she had long admired, and Lumley remained in residence freed both from his debt and the cost of maintaining the palace. The most famous incident connected with her tenure of Nonsuch is her interview in her bedroom with the hasty Earl of Essex, at which he sought to explain his failure to obey her orders as Lieutenant of Ireland. She would, perhaps, have preferred to remember her hunting trips onto the downs.

Elizabeth's successor James I settled Nonsuch on his queen, Anne of Denmark, in 1603, although Lumley remained as Keeper until his death in 1609. The palace was frequently visited by the new queen's sons, Henry Prince of Wales and Charles Duke of York. Prince Henry, who is said to have derived great pleasure from riding, died of typhoid fever in 1612, and so it was James's younger son who succeeded as Charles I. Nonsuch was settled on his bride, Henrietta Maria of France; the royal accounts refer to expenditure on the palace, ranging from the installation of a great altar to the replacement of stolen gutters.

The Civil War caused the Queen to flee to France in 1644. Parliamentary forces had certainly taken possession of the palace by July 1648, and in 1650 the palace buildings were valued at £7020, in terms of demolition value. It was assigned to one of the Parliamentary regiments, as security for arrears of pay, and in 1654 was sold to Major-General John Lambert, who paid £14,800 for the palace and Little Park. Lambert had been a successful general in the Civil War, and was influential in securing the offer of the title of Protector to Cromwell, although he later vehemently opposed the suggestion that Cromwell should be given the title of King. Lambert had a love of gardening, and had a fine collection of plants at Wimbledon House. It is not known whether he spent much time enjoying the gardens at Nonsuch. He came to prominence again after Cromwell's death as a key republican, but his plans were unsuccessful. He was imprisoned on Drake's Island until his death in 1684.

Charles II was restored in 1660, and Henrietta Maria, the Queen Mother, resumed ownership of Nonsuch. There is no record of her visiting the palace again before her death in 1669, and it was used as temporary offices for the Exchequer in 1665 and 1666, when plague and fire in quick succession made London uncongenial.

By this time Nonsuch was in decline. In 1670 it was granted to trustees for Charles II's mistress, Barbara Villiers (Countess of Castlemaine, Baroness Nonsuch and Duchess of Cleveland). It is unclear whether she found any use for it before 1682; in that year, probably in debt for gambling, and perhaps faced with heavy repair bills, she obtained permission to demolish the Palace and sell its materials. Some of the fabric was re-used in the construction of Durdans at Epsom by George, Lord Berkeley, who had been Keeper of the Palace and Little Park since 1660. Much of the basic structure survived in ruins for decades: even in 1757 there were foundations visible above ground. In the nineteenth century, however, the exact position of the palace passed out of memory, and it was only established again for certain during the excavation conducted under the direction of Martin Biddle (now Professor Biddle) in 1959.[129]

Let us now move from the Palace building to its gardens. Staircases in the towers led from the royal apartments to the walled Privy Garden, laid out around three sides of the Inner Court. Our knowledge of the Nonsuch gardens largely relies on descriptions from Elizabethan times, and we cannot be certain how many of their features dated back to Henry VIII's time. It is likely, however, that the original style mirrored that of Henry's innovative garden at Hampton Court. There, the Privy Garden below the royal apartments had been transformed into a vehicle for displaying the heraldic ancestry of the House of Tudor, with gilded carvings of the King's Beasts – dragons, greyhounds, lions, antelopes and so on – mounted on poles. We know that, later in the century, Hampton Court also boasted a collection of animal and human figures in topiary, made of evergreen shrubs or rosemary trained over dry branches, which may have been another of his innovations.[130]

Our only pictorial information on the Nonsuch Privy Garden comes from Speed's 1610 engraving. Even this only shows a small part of the garden, which extended just over 200 feet from the Palace. It does, however, give an indication of the knot gardens, small beds edged with dwarf hedges. Watson described them as "plants and shrubs mingled in intricate circles", and referred to deer, hares, rabbits and dogs, either of topiary or statuary, mingled with them. Also visible in Speed's depiction are two popinjays, perched on columns. This bird was an emblem of the Lumley family (later included in the Sutton borough arms), so these must have been added during Lord

Lumley's tenure of the Palace in Elizabethan times, following the heraldic style of garden ornamentation developed by Henry VIII and possibly replacing a set of royal emblems. In the centre a fountain is shown, around which by 1650 there were "six trees called Lelack trees which trees beare no fruit but onely a very pleasant flower." By this date there were also 140 fruit trees, two yews and a juniper. The flowers grown here in Elizabethan times included hyacinths, thyme, rosemary and roses.

Outside the Privy Gardens, a less formal garden extended westwards towards...

## The Banqueting House

You may now like to make a detour to see the banqueting house platform, the only part of the palace visible above ground (apart from the section of walling around the Mansion House garden).

- *If you prefer not to take the detour, continue walking along the avenue to the left.*

- *The following paragraphs describe the detour route.*

*Take the tarmac path to the right at the point where the avenue turns to the left, and immediately turn right into a narrow unsurfaced path, following the 'London Loop' waymark.* This footpath probably runs just outside the garden enclosure, perhaps following the line of the medieval route called the Portway. All the paths to the banqueting house tend to become very muddy in wet weather; the path suggested below for the return route is the least likely to become impassable.

For the first 100 yards or so, we must imagine ourselves walking with the Privy Garden wall to our right. Thereafter, we are walking along the edge of the area known as the Wilderness. As Watson pointed out, it was "in fact, neither wild nor deserted": the term was used to indicate a landscaped garden in which a natural look had been carefully contrived. As Sir Roy Strong has suggested, the Wilderness as ornamented by Lumley in the 1580s-90s was a pioneering style of gardening, in which heraldic decoration was replaced by a more subtle symbolism. The fountain in the Privy Garden, in the shape of Diana, the Romans' chaste moon-goddess, prepares us for the theme of the Wilderness, a celebration of the Virgin Queen Elizabeth I.[131]

The basic layout of the Wilderness, perhaps dating back to Henry's time, consisted of three paths, the middle one sandy and the others turfed, running through the evergreens, fruit trees and other trees and shrubs. Parts of the paths were partitioned off with high boards to make alleys for ball games (Platter), and to the north was a wide-spreading plane tree, its branches supported on posts (Watson). There were also animals and birds, although our sources are too fanciful to make it clear whether these were real creatures, statues or a mixture of the two.

*Three hundred yards after leaving the avenue, we reach a fork in the path, marked with Bollard no. 4 in Professor Biddle's Nonsuch trail. Fork right into the Wilderness, and then keep on the higher path to the left.* At the point where the path swings left again, we are close to the area known as the Grove of Diana, probably located in the dell below us, near a natural source of water. Platter describes the grotto as follows: "here we came to a rock out of which natural water springs into a basin, and on this was portrayed with great art and lifelike execution the story of how the three goddesses took their bath naked and sprayed Actaeon with water, causing antlers to grow upon his head, and of how his own hounds afterwards tore him to pieces." The ensemble consisted of Diana and two nymphs among the rocks with, fifteen paces away, the over-daring Actaeon, symbolising unbridled sensuality, and his dogs.

Nearby was a summerhouse in the form of a temple or bower, embellished with verses drawing the lesson of the sculptures: "From an impure fountain impure springs, from an unpleasant mind a sight defiled." Also close by was an arch, and two pinnacles decorated with a phoenix and a pelican. These were Elizabeth I's personal emblems, and they lead the visitor to see the tableau in the grotto as a compliment to the chaste and victorious Queen. Lumley's horticulture was not altogether serious, however: not far from the arch was a trick pyramid with heads which "while counterfeiting dryness in the mouth, discharge small streams of water" on the unwary visitor.[132]

The garden enclosure tapers at this point, so as we continue along the footpath we pass out of it. *After another hundred yards we turn left in front of a dell and up a few steps on the left back into the enclosure*; ahead of us is the brick platform of the Banqueting House, almost certainly built in Henry VIII's time. The surviving wall encloses a mound with cellars at its core, as revealed by excavations in 1960. In the middle of the platform, reached by steps on at least three sides (including one set at the point where the ramp is now situated), stood a two-storey timber building, 44 feet by 38 feet. The lower storey, probably 4 or 5 feet above the level of the platform, contained a wainscoted hall and three other rooms; on the upper floor there were five rooms, and at each corner of the building was a balcony.

The function of the building was not banqueting in the modern sense. Rather, it was a setting for entertainment, accompanied by light refreshments such as marzipan, cakes and "counterfeit fruits". Hunting would presumably have been one of the entertainments provided, as the balconies would have commanded a view of much of the Nonsuch estate.[133]

The Banqueting House was demolished in 1667 by Lord Berkeley, then serving as Keeper of the Little Park to Henrietta Maria. The platform survived, and by 1780 had passed into the hands of Thomas Calverley, the owner of the predecessor to Ewell Castle. He planted the mound with trees, as a focal point for his garden.

*Continue across the grass to the left of the Banqueting House platform, past bollard 6, and onto a narrow path ahead. Go straight across the footpath at bollard 5, and turn left onto a parallel footpath running behind the gardens of the houses in Castle Avenue. This path has a concrete kerb and lies somewhat higher, so it is less likely to be waterlogged in wet weather. After 400 yards, we reach the tarmac path connecting the Palace site and Castle Avenue. Continue straight across it and over a concrete platform on to a path partly formed by an abandoned concrete road, running along the north-western boundary of…*

## Warren Farm

The name 'The Warren' was certainly applied to this area by 1731, when it was used to denote three fields on a map of the Little Park, although it did not become a separate farm until some time later. In 1839 the site later occupied by the farm buildings contained a sheephouse, barn and yard, and the land was part of a farm run by James Martin and occupying much of the former Little Park. It had one farmhouse adjoining the Mansion House, and another, known as Lower Farm and later as

Nonsuch Court Farm, in the centre of the land developed as Gleesons' Nonsuch estate from 1935.[134] The Sutton-to-Epsom railway was built across the farm in 1847, and a tunnel was constructed connecting the two portions.[135] The tunnel still survives, leading from the site of the Warren Farm buildings to Holmwood Road. In 1938 Nonsuch High School for Girls was opened on the eastern part of the farm fields. Part of the remainder continued to be cultivated into the 1980s. Recently the western part has been developed, while the central section has been transferred to the Woodland Trust as an open space.

This farm extended to the Cheam Road, which curves around the perimeter of the Little Park and was doubtless diverted away from the direct line through Cuddington village when the park was enclosed. The ancient parish of Cuddington extended for over a mile south-eastwards beyond the park boundary, taking in the area between Banstead Road and Harefield Avenue, including the land now occupied by Cuddington Golf Course and the Howell Hill nature reserve (the latter name is believed to date back at least to 1201, when it appears in the form Hawelle, and probably means 'spring on the spur of land'[136]). By 1839 almost the whole of this area was included in Cuddington Manor Farm, run by Robert Lewin. The farmhouse, later known as Cuddington Court Farm, has since been made into a clubhouse for Sutton and Epsom Rugby Club.[137]

- *If you have been following the detour, continue for 600 yards along the concrete road until a prominent footpath from Warren Farm (marked with a footpath sign) crosses it; turn left onto the footpath, and cross over the avenue onto the path nearly opposite.*

- *If you have been keeping to the avenue, turn left at the path leading off diagonally.*

*Follow the path as far as the hedge and through the gateway into the gardens. Keep straight on to the forecourt in front of the main entrance to the…*

## Mansion House

It is now time to continue the story of the Little Park after the demolition in the 1680s of the Palace which had been its raison d'être. In 1731 the trustees of the Duke of Grafton's estates sold it to Joseph Thompson. Later that year, he had a plan of the estate made, entitled "A Survey of Nonsuch Park, the seat of Joseph Thompson." The focus of the Park had now moved from the Palace site to the land where the present Mansion House stands.

This land had certainly been occupied during the lifetime of the Palace, as shown by the Tudor wall which we shall see shortly. It is even possible that the site incorporated some earlier farm buildings. Its function during the Palace period has not been conclusively proved. Although it has been suggested that the Palace stables stood here, the most likely explanation is that it was the location of the Lodge for the Keeper of the Little Park, described in the 1650 Parliamentary Survey as standing "a pretty distance" from the Palace. It contained a hall, parlour, kitchen, buttery, larder, scullery, dairy, bolting house, deer house, coal house and ten chambers, as well as a stable, two barns, and a garden or orchard.[138]

Joseph Thompson appears to have enlarged the house, as the laundries in the present Mansion House service wing are eighteenth-century in style. It is likely, however, that he retained most of the existing structure: William Gilpin, who was headmaster of Cheam School and thus a near neighbour, described it in 1798 as "a house, now modernised, which is said to have been formerly the habitation of Queen Elizabeth's Maids of Honour." It is hardly likely that Gilpin, a noted writer on "picturesque beauty", should have believed the house to be two centuries old if it had been built within the previous 70 years.

Joseph Thompson died in 1743, leaving the property to his nephew Joseph Whately. It is said that Thompson made the bequest on the condition that his nephew should take Holy Orders. No such condition appears in his will, however, under which Joseph was to inherit Nonsuch on reaching the age of 25. Such a condition would seem contrary to the general tone of the will, in which he "with much indifference" expresses the wish that Joseph should take steps to adopt the name Thompson, but only "if it be not unsuitable to his own Inclination and his parents" and asks to be buried at Cheam, Ewell or Epsom "without any building or covering over my grave than the earth" except for a simple headstone.[139]

Joseph owned Nonsuch until his death in 1797. It was occupied for much of this time by his elder brother, Thomas Whately. Thomas, as well as serving as MP for Ludgershall and Castle Rising, as Secretary to the Treasury in the mid-1760s and as Under-Secretary of State and Keeper of His Majesty's Private Roads in the early 1770s, was notable for his interest in gardening. His *Observations on Modern Gardening*, published in 1770, was described as "the grand fundamental, and standard work on English gardening", and he began the landscaping of the Mansion House gardens.

In 1799, the trustees of Joseph Whately's will sold the house and Little Park to Samuel Farmer, MP for Huntingdon. He already had an estate in Cheshire, and this purchase increased his Surrey landholding to 2000 acres. He commissioned two architects to draw up plans for a more substantial house. One design was submitted by John Nash, but we know nothing of its style, nor whether his work at Worcester Park House (see page 58) was carried out around this time. The chosen plan was that of Jeffrey Wyatt.

The house as we see it today is very much as Wyatt planned it. The style is Gothic, perhaps deliberately chosen in order to portray the new house as the successor to the Palace: the entrance tower is certainly reminiscent of the Tudor outward court. Wyatt was to use the same style in the 1820s for the restoration of Windsor Castle, which transformed that building from dereliction to magnificence, and transformed the architect from Mr Wyatt to Sir Jeffrey Wyatville.

To the right of the entrance lay the library, later made into a morning room. Most of the principal rooms are situated on the further side of the house, facing the garden. To the left is the service wing, which is now regularly opened by the Friends of Nonsuch, and provides an opportunity to see a set of early-nineteenth-century kitchens restored to their original style of furnishing. The servants' hall, on the nearer side of the service wing, is now used as the public tea room. Conveniences, including facilities for disabled people, are located in the former stable block to the left (replacing those in the old dairy in the gardens).

*Continue along the drive around the service wing. After a sharp right turn*, notice (over the wall to the right) the turret of the game larder, designed for cool and ventilated storage of meat, poultry and fish. *At the end of the service wing, turn right through the gate into the gardens,* noticing the chequer-board pattern in the wall, formed by alternating flint panels and chalk blocks: this is the Tudor wall that probably surrounded the Keeper's house and garden.

*Turn left into the formal flower garden.* On this side of the wall is a fine wisteria, perhaps a descendant of the 120-foot specimen described in 1860. Much of this area was planted by Samuel Farmer's grandson, W F G Farmer, in the 1840s, including the trellis walk and the pool (originally surrounded by alpine plants). The most striking feature of the garden, however, is perhaps the central Dell. This former chalk pit, perhaps associated with the construction of the Palace, was landscaped by Thomas Whately in the 18th century, in accordance with his preference for a natural style. The London plane, now 23 feet round, was perhaps one of the trees planted by him.[140]

*Walk alongside the wall, and take the first path on the right into the rose walk. At the end of the walk, turn (first) right in front of the terrace*: this was part of the remodelling of the garden by W F G Farmer, who also laid out the pinetum that lies behind it, and may have planted some of the existing trees such as the deodar cedar and giant sequoiadendron. *Continue along the main path*, passing the site of the glasshouses where W F G Farmer's head gardener, S M Carson, produced orchids and azaleas that brought the name of Nonsuch to the attention of the horticultural world. This area was, until recently, the home of Nonsuch Park's collection of peacocks, later housed behind the Nursery Lodge opposite the entrance to the gardens. As we round the corner to the right, the house comes into view again, and we can see the windows of the principal reception rooms. From the left, they are the drawing-room, ante-room, dining-room, lobby, library (originally a conservatory) and smoking-room.[141]

*The Mansion House in the mid 19th century*
*[Edward Walford, Greater London]*

These rooms, together with the morning-room at the front of the house, are connected by a series of double doors, and the suite would thus have been ideal for accommodating large parties. A visitors book survives from the time of Capt. William Robert Gamul Farmer, who inherited Nonsuch in 1860; this worn volume bears testimony to the Derby Week house parties attended by guests from the highest echelons of society. Mr F R Fielder, who served as footman in the Edwardian period, recalled "The house at Nonsuch was full of life at its most gracious: a constant stream of visitors taking tea on the lawn, dances, music and dinner by candlelight... in winter a great log fire added its flickering light. Later, the butler stood in the hall handing out silver candlesticks to light the way to bed."[142]

Captain Farmer died in 1910, and Nonsuch passed to his daughter Alice, the wife of Col the Hon. Francis Colborne, a veteran of several campaigns and equerry to Princess Henry of Battenburg (Queen Victoria's youngest daughter Beatrice). This led to a number of visits by members of the Royal family: Queen Mary visited in July 1919, and a letter was sent expressing her thanks for "the delightful afternoon spent at beautiful Nonsuch." Mrs Colborne continued the tradition of gardening at Nonsuch: it was said that she grew every variety of lilac. In 1920 Princess Louise wrote to thank her for a gift of lilacs.[143] The gardens also had a practical function. The Friends of Nonsuch newsletter quotes the recollections of Mr Telling, whose father was Head Gardener from 1910, becoming Bailiff in 1914: "The kitchen garden extended twice as far as it does now and behind this was an orchard... The local grocer Teddy Lovell bought fruit from the gardeners... However, most of the excess produce was sold to Hilliard & Co."[144]

After Mrs Colborne's death in 1936, the local authorities took swift action to safeguard Nonsuch Park as an open space. In the following year, the London and Surrey County Councils, with the corporations of Sutton and Cheam and Epsom and Ewell, provided £118,000 to purchase 263 acres of the park. The official opening took place on 29 September 1937, the day on which Epsom and Ewell received its charter of incorporation as a borough. The ceremony was performed, at 5.16 pm if the programme was followed precisely, by Lord Snell the LCC Chairman. During the afternoon, entertainment was provided by the band of the 9th Queen's Royal Lancers, ranging from music from Edward German's opera *Merrie England* (in tribute to the Park's Tudor origins) to accordion and piccolo solos.

*On reaching the Mansion House, take the small path to the left of the house to return to the forecourt. Bear slightly left and immediately right, to take the drive towards the Sparrow Farm Gate. To the left is Herald Copse, planted to commemorate the centenary of the Sutton & Cheam Herald and Epsom & Ewell Herald in 1978. Go through the gateway over the ha-ha into the open space of...*

# Nonsuch Park

Although the public had previously been allowed to walk through the park, its opening as a public park made it more generally accessible. The playwright John Osborne, growing up in Stoneleigh in the late 1930s, found that "The glory of Nonsuch Park then was that there were hardly any amenities. There were a few park-keepers, presumably there to see that small boys didn't chop down the oaks. I don't know how large it was, but to an eight-year-old boy it seemed the size of a county."[145]

To Osborne, Nonsuch Park became Sherwood Forest and the park-keepers the Sheriff's men. Nonsuch, however, was about to play its role in a very different war. Frank Tait, writing in the Nonsuch Watch newsletter, recalls "During the war, quite large acres of Nonsuch were farmed. Len Rowland was the farm foreman and Alf, his brother, drove the Fordson tractor. Wheat, barley and oats were grown, and at harvest Alf drove the tractor while Len sat on the binder which cut the corn and tied it into sheaves. A motley gang, including us boys, would follow on behind, collecting the sheaves and standing them in stooks to dry out. Occasionally there would be odd jobs to do at neighbouring Cherry Orchard Farm – really a market garden with a herd of pigs. In 1942, we picked beans and peas and did some hoeing. Sheep were brought in to graze the parkland during the war. I think they were only there in winter and spring, as the grassland was used for hay in the summer."[146]

The Park continued to be farmed after the war. Fiona Blackburn (née Fraser), whose father was Park Superintendent from 1947 to 1974, recalls "Sheep still grazed in the park... The kitchen garden produced quantities of vegetables for sale, both to individuals and to local greengrocers... The Nursery Gardens provided a brilliant place to play, being large and safe, and also providing opportunities for pinching fruit to eat – even grapes in hot summers... Growing fields of wheat and hay provided a means to make dens."[147]

Nonsuch Park, together with the adjacent Cherry Orchard Farm and Warren Farm, supports a diverse flora and fauna. Surveys in and around 1993 produced lists of nearly 80 species of fungi, from wood woolly foot to candle snuff, 41 lichen species, 30 mosses and liverworts in the Park itself and 41 in Cherry Orchard Farm at the old brickearth workings, and 264 species of higher plants (104 in the Park, where the soil is mainly sand or clay, and 201 on the chalk of Warren Farm). Common lizards and slow-worms are found at Warren Farm, and common frogs and toads in ponds in the Park. Birds believed to have bred in the Nonsuch estate in the preceding 5 years include kestrels, stock and collared doves, tawny owls, green and great and lesser spotted woodpeckers, skylarks (for which Warren Farm is a major site), blackcaps, mistle and song thrushes, coal tits and tree creepers.[148]

We have already investigated the fortunes of the Great Park and Little Park after the demolition of the Palace. Now, as we walk across the Park, remembering its previous uses as medieval arable field and royal deer park, we should tie up one loose end, the later history of...

## Cuddington Manor

The demolition of the manor house and the village which housed its tenants might be thought to have brought an end to Cuddington's status as a manor. However, it is possible to trace the history of the Cuddington title, although it must be admitted that the later manor courts were held jointly for Ewell and Cuddington.

After Henry VIII acquired the manor, it passed with the Palace to his son Edward VI and daughter Mary I, and to the Earl of Arundel, who bought the Palace from Mary, and his son-in-law Lord Lumley. Curiously, when Lumley transferred the Palace to Elizabeth I, the manor was not included. He died childless in 1609 and the manor passed to his nephew Splandian Lloyd (whose father Humphrey Lloyd had been Lumley's brother-in-law, household physician and fellow bibliophile).

The manor remained in the Lumley family until the death in 1730 of Dr Robert Lumley Lloyd, rector of St. Paul's, Covent Garden, owner and (at least in name) headmaster of Cheam School, and unsuccessful claimant to the Lumley barony. He bequeathed the manor, and his house at Cheam, to Lord John Russell, who brought his bride Lady Diana Spencer there the following year, only to inherit the title of Duke of Bedford, and the accompanying seat of Woburn Abbey, on the death of his brother a year later.[149] The bequest (subject to an annuity to Dr Lloyd's sister) was made in recognition of the favours shown him by Lord John's father, the 2nd Duke, and his "noble and honourable family."[150] The Duke retained the manor and the right to receive tithe payments, until 1755, when the tithes of the Great and Little Parks were bringing him £110 per year.[151]

In 1755 the Duke sold the manors of "Nonesuch alias Cuddington", Ewell, and West and East Cheam, to Edward Northey of Woodcote House, Epsom, whose father had been Attorney-General in Queen Anne's reign. The family retained the manors for six generations, until in 1993 Mr E Martin Northey sold the Cuddington and Cheam titles to John Adrian Connolly, an insurance consultant and vice-president of Cheam Cricket Club.[152]

*Our walk through Nonsuch Park should now have brought us to the car park at the Sparrow Farm Gate. Turn right onto the London Road and, after a few yards, cross at the pedestrian crossing and turn left into…*

## Sparrow Farm Road

We are now back in the 1930s development of Stoneleigh. The name of the road, however, reminds us that we are walking on the line of the driveway to Sparrow Farm, one of the farms into which the Great Park was divided after the destruction of the Palace. The name, indeed, probably derives from the Sparrow Field or Sparwefeld of the medieval manor. For most of the early 20th century it was leased to R White & Son.

A report produced in 1839 for the Tithe Commissioners gives an indication of the farming practices in the farms in Cuddington: the soil was described as "a light turnip land, in parts kind and free working and well cultivated, but in others a thin skin of sandy grit on a chalk subsoil… I observed some good Turnips and the tilth was clean, well-mannered and looking healthy. The four and five courses are followed – Wheat Turnips Barley and Seeds – or Wheat, Oats, Turnips, Barley and Seeds – according as the manures should be abundant or circumstances vary. Manure is obtained from London in lieu of Straw, which is sent thither rather than consumed on the Premises by feeding of Cattle etc."[153]

On our left, we pass the complex of schools opened in the 1930s under the name Stoneleigh East. Surrey County Council bought this irregular six-acre site in 1933 for £5000 from Clandon Trust Ltd, the developers of this part of Stoneleigh. The main part of the site, facing Sparrow Farm Road and Waverley Road, was occupied by the County Secondary and Infants' Schools, while the smaller portion of the site, fronting Chadacre Road, was used by the Junior Mixed School.

The first step in the development of the site was the installation of three temporary classrooms. In the autumn of 1934 a permanent school was opened in Chadacre Road. Mrs Laird, chairman of the Managers, stated that "The one they were opening would be for 'everybody' from five to fourteen years of age. Later there would be an infants'

*2nd Worcester Park Scouts near Sparrow Farm c.1930. Ron and Peter Kinton are at opposite ends; Donald Bradley, later succentor of Southwark Cathedral, is in the back row*

school, a junior mixed school for 384 and a central boys' and central girls' for 360 each."[154]

In the following April the school was divided. The Headteacher, Mr G Corner, retained responsibility for the Central (later Secondary) school, whilst Mr E W Stacey and Miss H M Robertson were appointed to head the Junior and Infants' departments. In 1937 Mr Corner was being assisted by Miss L E K Hall (Chief Woman Assistant), Messrs Jeal, Minty, Leach, Ritson and Shearman, and Misses Macartney and Ward, while Messrs Dallen and Blofield and Misses Helyar, Bird, Yeomans, Otway and Sparkes were the assistant teachers in the Junior department; their counterparts in the Infants' department were Mesdames Thomas and Wallwork, and Misses Hillard, Thurgood, Moore, Brickwood and Wylie.[155]

The log book for the Junior School, housed in the Chadacre Road premises, records a range of extra-curricular activities: an exhibition of children's handiwork in December 1935 raised sufficient funds for a radiogram to be purchased; the children won the cup for the most successful school at the Ewell Horticultural Society's exhibition in the following July, and weekly swimming lessons at Cheam Baths were instituted in April 1938.

The schools had not been open long before the outbreak of war brought changes. Thelma Jones, who started at the Junior School around this time, recalls "We didn't go to school for two terms because they were digging the trenches and we had school at home – we had about six or eight children came and used to sit round our dining-room table, and the teacher came about twice a week, and then they'd give you work, and

you had to do that before she came; Dad made a little blackboard easel to put up."
Back at the school, discipline could be strict: one teacher would begin the term with
brand-new rulers, but within a short time there wasn't a whole ruler in the class.

In December 1939 shelters were provided on the Sparrow Farm Road part of the site,
closer to the Central and Infants' schools, and some rooms in these schools were made
available for the Junior School in the mornings. In January 1940 the Juniors returned
to Chadacre Road, but found the Head Teacher's room and staff room occupied by
ARP personnel. Mr Stacey retired in 1941, and was succeeded by F R Burston, who
remained Head Teacher until 1961. His early years were dominated by the war: in
September 1941 air-raid practices were held, and the time taken to get the children
into the shelters was reduced to three minutes; school lunches were introduced the next
month, making it unnecessary for children to go home for lunch. The summer of 1944
brought the flying bomb attacks and attendance dropped below 9%; after a bomb fell
without warning on 27 June it was decided all work should be done in the shelters. In
July groups of pupils were evacuated to Stockport, Cornwall and Cumberland, under
the charge of Miss Harding, Miss Yeomans, and Mrs Privett and Miss Otway
respectively.

The Junior School premises were taken over by builders repairing bomb-damaged
property in the area. In October 1944, when 236 children had returned, they had to be
accommodated in the Infants' School, Woodwork room and Central School. Two
classes were allowed back to Chadacre Road in November, and the rest of the Juniors
moved back in December. After the end of the war it became possible to participate in
local sports competitions: in June 1947 the boys won the Junior Schools cup at the
Leatherhead and District School Sports, and the girls came second in the girls' schools
events.

In the mid-40s, Terry Major-Ball was a pupil in the Secondary School. The
Headmaster, Mr Corner, "got the best out of his pupils with discipline, understanding,
humour and basic teaching skills. I remember him in the playground staring intently at
the sky until a group of young faces gathered around him looking upwards. 'What are
you looking at, Sir?' they screamed. 'Nothing,' he replied. 'I'm just trying to teach you
to do things for a good reason and not just blindly follow the example of others'."[156]

At the time these schools were opened, the whole of the surrounding area was
administered by Surrey County Council, but after the incorporation of Sutton and
Cheam into Greater London part of the catchment area lay within the London
Borough of Sutton, whilst the remainder was in Epsom and Ewell, where the Council
retained independence from the County for education purposes until 1974.

In 1969 Stoneleigh County Secondary School (itself a merger of the senior provision at
Stoneleigh West and Stoneleigh East) was combined with Ruxley and Ewell Secondary
Schools, although the various sites continued to be used until the early 1970s when the
buildings at Ruxley Lane were extended to accommodate all the pupils.[157]

Since then, the Stoneleigh East premises have all been used for the under-12s: the
Chadacre Road site was leased to the London Borough of Sutton and became
Nonsuch Primary School, and the Junior School joined the Infants in Sparrow Farm
Road, where they now operate as Stoneleigh First and Sparrow Farm Community
Junior.

*At the junction with St. Clair Drive and Bradstock Road, Sparrow Farm Road bends left and right*, following the course of the old driveway which skirted the farmyard. Shortly after that junction, *go through the gateway on the right into…*

## Cuddington Recreation Ground

*Walk down the Recreation Ground* to the right of the Beverley Brook which we see here at the beginning of its journey to the Thames at Putney, and which we shall encounter again at Green Lane.

*When the brook disappears into a culvert, continue across the grass to the right of the play area and pavilion to the Sandringham Road gate.* In very wet weather you may prefer to go down St. Clair Drive, turning right into Dalmeny Road at its foot. Plants which may be found growing beside the brook include Good-King-Henry, pendulous sedge and stone parsley.[158]

When this part of Worcester Park was transferred to Sutton and Cheam Urban District in 1933, the Urban District Council took over the running of the Recreation Ground, and lost no time in drawing up plans for the allocation of different areas for football, cricket, and so on. By October, estimates had been approved for draining the land (£1990) and providing six hard tennis courts (£1200).

On 30 August 1934 the *Epsom Advertiser* reported that a children's sports afternoon had been held in the ground, organised by the Stoneleigh Park Residents' Association. As well as boys' and girls' races over 50, 75 and 100 yards, there were skipping and sack races, and mothers' and fathers' races. The occasion was also used for the presentation of prizes in the Association's front garden competition. In 1935, the programme included a ladies' egg-and-spoon race, a gentlemen's sack race, and the intriguing "Gentlemen's Catch-the-Train race."

*On leaving the Recreation Ground, turn right into Sandringham Road.* The 1933 Ordnance Survey map, produced soon after the road was constructed, shows it as Park Road. It was perhaps renamed in order to avoid confusion with Park Avenue and Park Terrace, and the name Sandringham would have been chosen to continue the theme of royal residences set by Windsor Road and Hampton Road.

*At the end of the road, turn (first) left into Dalmeny Road.* The most likely explanation of this name is that Dalmeny House, near Edinburgh, is the seat of the Earl of Rosebery, and the 5th Earl also lived at The Durdans in Epsom and owned three Derby winners.

To our right is Tudor Avenue: in 1933 one could buy one of R H Hewitt & Son's "magnificent well-built houses, fitted with every labour-saving convenience" for £750, in a location where "the residents can claim to live under ideal and unrivalled conditions in an atmosphere of beauty."[159]

Dalmeny Road lies on the boundary between Worcester Park Farm, based in Central Road, and (to the right) a smaller holding farmed in the mid-19th century by the Pennington family of the Drill Inn. Kingsmead Avenue (a continuation of Hampton Road and originally known by that name) was the first road to be constructed in this area, and in 1927 the annual parish meeting for Cuddington discussed complaints about cattle straying in Kingsmead Avenue.

In April 1943 the parish magazine reported that Major Cyril A J Martin, a resident of Kingsmead Avenue, had been awarded the George Cross "for conspicuous bravery in circumstances not yet publicly on record." Major Martin had been involved in bomb disposal work in London since the beginning of the Blitz in 1940. In January 1943 he was called to the Victoria Haulage Company's warehouse at Battersea, which was filled with new machine tools from the USA. A large calibre bomb had fallen on the warehouse containing a new anti-handling fuse, and it was necessary to remove the base-plate and extract the explosive. This was found to consist of solid cast TNT, which had to be removed by high pressure steam. Major Martin and another officer worked from the afternoon of 20 January to 8.30 the following morning, lying alongside the bomb in a cramped hole applying the steam through a hand-held nozzle. He was to perform this painstaking operation on two further occasions during the war.[160]

A hundred yards before the end of the road, we step outside the Great Park for the first time since we entered Sparrow Farm Road; we also leave the ancient parish of Cuddington and cross into Cheam. A comparison of the 1894 and 1933 maps reproduced opposite shows that the old boundary is still reflected in the street pattern: to the south-west, inside the Park, is the planned development of Kingsmead Avenue and its parallel neighbours; to the north-east the strip of land between the boundary and the main road was divided into about a dozen allotments under the 1810 Cheam Common enclosure, and was subsequently developed gradually, first with small groups of cottages and business premises, and later with half-a-dozen culs-de-sac.

*We now reach…*

## Cheam Common Road

*Our route now lies to the left, but first walk a little way to the right, and stop at the junction with Woodbine Lane.* The modern houses here date from the 1950s and replace the late-nineteenth-century cottages originally known as Poplar Place.

As we look at the gradual rise of Cheam Common Road, leading to its junction with the London Road at the Queen Victoria crossroads, a number of features are worthy of mention. On the corner of Shrubland Grove, the next turning on the right, is the Old Crown, formerly the Drill Inn. The name of this public house was presumably chosen because of the agricultural character of the area at the time, as were The Harrow and The Plough in Cheam. In the 1980s, however, the inn sign was changed from a drill of an agricultural kind to the military sort, before being given its present name in the 1990s.

There was a Drill Inn on this site by 1841, when it was owned by Francis Pennington, who also had a small farm covering the area occupied by Shrubland Grove and extending to the access road that is now Woodbine Lane. The property included several cottages of which two survive (nos. 119-121), bearing the date 1828 and the name Poplar Place, which by the 1890s applied to eight cottages facing the main road and four facing the access road. The farm also extended into the part of Cuddington parish now bordered by Dalmeny Road, Oaks Avenue and the London Road. Ten years later, possibly after the death of Francis Pennington, his children Harriet and Francis appear to have been running the inn and farm respectively. In 1861 Francis was running the Jolly Farmer beerhouse, possibly from one of the cottages in the Poplar Place area, but by 1871 he had taken over the Drill, where he remained for at least 20 years.

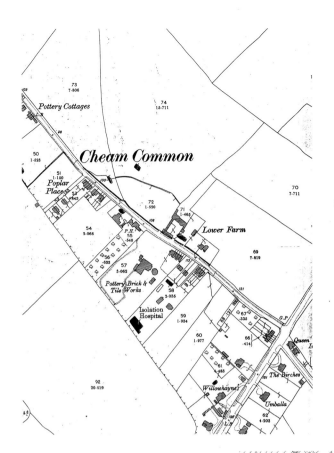

*Ordnance Survey map, 1894. At the bottom left, the former lands of the Great Park are still farmland; the former Cheam Common is being developed piecemeal.*

*By 1933 Kingsmead Avenue has been built through the Great Park land, development is spreading across the sites of brick works in Cheam Common Road, and housing development on the lands of Lower Farm on the north-east side of the road is largely complete*

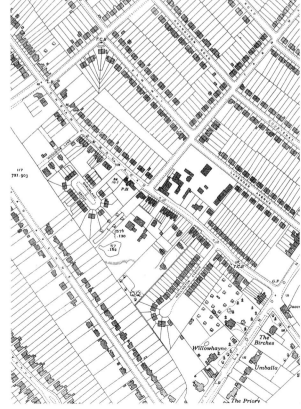

By 1906 the premises included a bar, tap room, shop, public room and large stable. In that year plans were drawn up by Yetts, Sturdy and Usher on behalf of Hodgson's Kingston Brewery Company for minor alterations, apparently involving the division of the bar into small public and private bars.[161] The present building, constructed in a neo-Georgian style with handmade bricks, dates from around 1938. Inside are two French glass panels engraved with designs of flowers and birds, which were moved here from a London public house.[162]

Shortly after the pub is the turning to Huntingdon Gardens. As the 1894 map shows, this road was built on the site of a pottery and brick works, which was the third brick works to have been established in Cheam Common Road. The 1841 tithe map and award show a brick field and complex of associated buildings, owned by James Waghorn, which lay immediately to the north-west of Dalmeny Road. (James Waghorn was probably related to William Waghorn, who owned the Queen Victoria public house, and also had a lease of some land at the southern tip of the Little Park of Nonsuch roughly where Springfield Road meets the Cheam Road, described in 1839 as sandpits and an old brick yard.) James Waghorn also owned the land where Lingfield Road now stands, and in 1861 William Jesse Baker was apparently running a brick and tile works here, as well as operating the Drill Inn. In 1871 Frederick Down was living close to the site and was described as the foreman; by 1874 Down & Medlock were listed as brick and tile makers, potters, and makers of garden and rustic pots. At some stage the works moved to the Huntingdon Gardens site, and about a dozen cottages (which still stand) were built facing the main road for the employees. The Pottery continued to produce bricks and tiles into the Edwardian period.

Next comes Lingfield Road. In the early to mid-1890s, after the brick works had left the site, this was the drive to a temporary Isolation Hospital run by the Epsom Rural Sanitary Authority.[163] It was probably the forerunner of Cuddington Hospital, built at the southern tip of Cuddington parish (off Banstead Road) in 1897.

On the opposite side of the road, the dark roof tiles of the large office building known as Macmillan House are just visible. This building stands on the site of the farmhouse of Lower Farm, part of the Northey family's Cheam manor estates.

By 1806 the fields belonging to the farm extended from the North Cheam crossroads over most of the area now covered by Farm Way, most of Colborne Way, and Burnham Drive. After the enclosure of Lower Cheam Common in that year, a large part of the common, now occupied by Ruskin Drive, Dorchester Road and the south-western portion of the sewage works, was added to the farm in lieu of common rights.

In 1925 Major-General Sir Edward Northey sold part of the farm to William J Lavender, whose father Arthur had rented it since 1896. 'W J' had begun a haulage business after serving in the RAF in the First World War. When his father decided to retire, 'W J' saw the possibility of combining building development on the farm fields with the production and transport of building materials, and he bought sand and gravel pits in the Thames valley.[164] He paid £7,000 for an area extending from the crossroads to the junction of Colborne Way and Grandison Road. As part of the agreement Mr Lavender undertook to construct a number of roads in order to open up the estate for development.[165]

The farmhouse survived for some years, and was used as a base for the Lavenders' fleet of sand and gravel lorries. David Blake recalls that, during the Second World War, the Home Guard used the outbuildings at the back of the plot for training in crawling into buildings under gas or fire.

The present boundary of the postal district of Worcester Park extends well beyond Lower Farm to include much of Park Farm. The latter, which belonged to John Hilbert in 1806, covered the Langley Avenue and Clarkes Avenue area, and under the enclosure was enlarged to cover Boscombe Road and the north-eastern side of the sewage works. Nowadays, however, the "Park Farm" label is used as estate agents' shorthand for the other half of the farm centred on Brocks Drive. By 1933 Langley Avenue was being developed by E Adams, who advertised bungalows at £550 in a promotional publication which announced "North Cheam... is a district that... is decidedly healthy, with invigorating and fresh breezes... One of the most picturesque parts of the district is probably Langley Avenue."[166]

*We now retrace our steps as far as Dalmeny Road, and continue north-westwards along Cheam Common Road.*

A hundred yards later on the right, notice the single storey house, number 154. This was originally built as a classroom for the private school run by Miss Mabel Box, who lived in the adjacent house, around the time of the First World War. Some years later, the developments of the 1930s brought large numbers of young families to the area, and scope for more private schools. David Blake was a pupil in the late 1930s at Waverley House Preparatory School, on the corner of Ruskin Drive and Beverley Road, where Mr Archibald Rough taught about 15 children in a schoolroom built at the back of the house. He remembers "standing in a line doing tables, and if you got the answer right you went up the line, and if you got the answer wrong you went down the line, which sharpened your mind quite considerably."

*On our left, we now come to...*

# St. Matthias' Church

The first Roman Catholic Church in Worcester Park was a simple brick structure in Brinkley Road, built in 1906 to a design by B Williamson and later extended to provide 250 seats. It was established by the Convent of the Daughters of the Cross which had opened St. Anthony's Hospital in the London Road in 1904. The Revd Bernard Kelly combined the roles of parish priest and chaplain to St. Anthony's, and the church's construction was financed by Frances Ellis, a benefactress of the Catholic Church.[167] Miss Ellis came from Ramsgate, and her connection with the Daughters of the Cross began through their Sanatorium in Margate. Between 1903 and 1930 she helped the order to purchase a number of houses for their work in health care and education, as well as financing the building of a number of churches in the Diocese of Southwark.[168]

Originally the parish covered a large area. The Revd Bernard Smoker, Parish Priest from 1937 to 1942, opened a new hall in Ewell, later St. Clement's, and the school of St. Cecilia in the London Road. There were Sunday services at the original church, the Ewell hall, St. Cecilia's, and the school in Sheephouse Way, Malden. He also perceived the need for improved facilities in Worcester Park: a site in Cheam Common Road was selected for a new church, and the present hall and presbytery were built alongside.

The Revd Laurence Duprez became Parish Priest in 1946. In 1961 the parish was divided: he took responsibility for the new parish of St. Cecilia, and the Revd Cornelius Beausang was appointed to St. Matthias'.

Canon Beausang recalls "Long before I came there were plans for a new church, but as development was needed elsewhere, the new church had to be put on the long finger." By 1961, however, with around 800 or 900 attending services in Brinkley Road, a new church was required. The designs were drawn up by Tonei and Maxwell, but the original inspiration came from a church which Canon Beausang saw in Ballyphehane in his native Cork "which I liked very much, because I liked the proportion of it; it was Romanesque in style." Certain changes were made to this design, including the substitution of transepts for side aisles, and an alteration to the shape of the window over the main door, which at St. Matthias' shows the Blessed Virgin Mary as depicted in the statue at Lourdes.

"The idea was that when you came into the church the thing that would stand out was the great crucifix over the altar which represents the crucified, risen Christ, who is both Priest and King; and then below that is the small altar where the Blessed Sacrament is reserved." Whilst the church was being planned and built, the Second Vatican Council was engaged in the discussions that would bring many changes to Catholic liturgical practices. As a result the designs were altered so that the priest could say Mass facing the people, in line with the revised practice.

It is well worth stepping inside to appreciate the spacious cruciform church. Notice the stained glass windows in the transepts, that on the left showing St. Matthias taking hold of the blade of a sword, symbolising his acceptance of martyrdom, and that on the right containing "a motif of the Blessed Eucharist, the host and the chalice, and underneath written 'He would give them the uttermost proof of his love', John's words describing the gift of the Eucharist by our Blessed Lord on the Holy Thursday night." When the new church was ready, Canon Beausang brought the reserved Sacrament from Brinkley Road before saying Mass for the first time in the new building. The church was taken into use in June 1965. It was officially opened by Archbishop Cowderoy in the following February, and consecrated by Bishop Henderson in 1977.[169]

*On leaving St. Matthias' Church continue to the left, crossing The Retreat to reach Griffiths Close.* This sheltered housing scheme was built in 1972 by Sutton Housing Society, and named after Frank Griffiths, one of the founders of the Society.[170]

*Cross Cheam Common Road using the pedestrian crossing, and continue leftwards over Ruskin Drive as far as...*

# Christ Church with St. Philip

The services in this church are held jointly for Anglicans and Methodists. In order to explain this situation, we must begin with the Methodist congregation which had built the church in 1931.

The congregation was formed in 1872 by James Amos, in Longfellow Road, who suggested to some of his neighbours that they should rent a room at 2s per week to supply the lack of a dissenting place of worship in Worcester Park, and to make provision for the children who had nothing to occupy them on Sundays.

On 4 February about six people met at Amos's house. He spoke on Psalm 103, and prayers were said for the undertaking. Soon afterwards, Amos drew up a memorandum: "A few Christian brethren agree to take a room to meet in for prayer & praise... and to open a Sunday School in the afternoon." George Snashall of Epsom was persuaded by Amos to join them; he moved to Longfellow Road that summer, and lent his large room as a venue for services. Amos recorded "On removing into Mr Snashall's house we had a grand tea meeting when every room in his house was filled, about 70 persons took tea."

In August 1872 the Superintendent Minister of the Primitive Methodist Mission in Kingston invited the new congregation to affiliate to their Mission. The Primitive Methodists had broken away from mainstream Wesleyan Methodism, and placed a particular emphasis on mission work to reach those who did not come into contact with the church. The invitation was accepted, and the Worcester Park congregation remained Primitive Methodists until the reunion of the Methodist churches nationwide in 1932.

Fund-raising was soon begun towards the provision of a permanent chapel. The site in Longfellow Road was obtained, and the foundation stone was laid on 25 May 1874. The Chapel was opened on 16 August, and on the 24th about a hundred people sat down to tea there. James Amos concluded his retrospective account of the previous four years, written in the trustees' minute book, "Dear brethren, a few of us have worked hard to get this much needed dissenting place of Worship in this neighbourhood... Be united, do all things in order and from principles of love."

The Chapel cost £425, of which £300 was raised by the opening, and the remainder paid off by 1896. In 1878 £9 was raised for the purchase of a harmonium. Over the subsequent years, various special types of service were instituted. Temperance meetings began in 1879: on 3 December a hundred people assembled for a meeting at which Mr Rogers, manager of the Coffee Tavern in Ewell, presided; the meeting included a temperance hymn, address, and tea provided in the school-room at a penny a cup. In February 1882 Mr Carter, a Baptist from Clapham, "conducted 14 Mission Services, well attended each evening, about 18 profess to find Christ through these services, men and women came to these services who had never attended a place of Worship, some confess they had never prayed in their life."[171]

In 1905 outdoor mission work was begun. By 1912, a year before James Amos's death, membership had reached 40, while in 1916 the numbers appear to have increased when the remaining members of a Wesleyan Methodist meeting in Lindsay Road joined them, most of their members having been called up. The congregation celebrated its 50th anniversary in February 1923 with a concert given by the Kingston Primitive Methodist Church choir, including selections from the oratorio *Captives of Babylon*, and a public meeting at which the minister was joined on a united platform by the Rector of Cheam, the Vicar of St. Philip's, and a minister from New Malden Congregational Church.

By 1927 the membership of the church had almost equalled the seating capacity of the Longfellow Road premises, and the decision was made to buy the present site on the corner of Cheam Common Road and Ruskin Drive, at a cost of £800. Plans were drawn up for a new church complex, the architect being H Kelsall Armitage, and it was decided that the first priority should be the construction of a Lecture Hall at the back of the site, leaving room at the front for a permanent church when circumstances demanded and permitted it.

In July 1928 the local minister and church treasurer and secretary sent out a circular letter appealing for contributions to the building fund. They drew attention to the negotiations (successfully completed in 1932) for the reunion of the Wesleyan, Primitive and United branches of the Methodist Church, and suggested that the new church would be "a pioneer of the Union"; it would be named "after the one Lord and Master of us all, 'Christ Church (Methodist)'."

*Architect's design for the new Christ Church complex, 1928*
*[Copyright of Surrey History Service, 6349/13/1]*

The Lecture Hall was opened in September 1928, with space for 200 seats, and in the following year the first full-time resident minister, Revd William Pickering, was appointed. It proved possible to begin construction of the permanent church sooner than expected, after a gift of £1000 by "a friend of Methodist Union", subsequently found to be Joseph Rank. The stone-laying ceremony was held in September 1930, the foundation stone being laid by Mrs J T Barkby, wife of the Secretary of the London Forward Movement of the Primitive Methodist Church, which had also contributed funds for the project. The new church was opened in May 1931.

By 1936 the membership had grown from 100 in the late 1920s to over 230, and the debt on the building project had been reduced from £3,750 to £2,800. It was time to begin the next phase, the construction of Sunday School premises, and the stone-laying ceremony was held on 28 May 1938. Stones were laid by representatives of various organisations within the congregation and in memory of former members, while bricks were laid by a number of young people from the congregation.

The new buildings were dedicated on 15 October 1938. The central feature was a main hall, to be called Wesley Hall (because the stone-laying ceremony had coincided with the bicentenary of John Wesley's conversion), with a superintendent's room and classroom flanking the platform. An Upper Room was included for prayer meetings, and the Lecture Hall was improved and incorporated into the scheme. At the opening ceremony, the key was handed over by the architect Hubert Lidbetter, and the main door was unlocked by Mrs F Wimble on behalf of Mrs Barkby.

Girls' Brigade and Boys' Brigade companies were founded in 1934 and 1936. Katherine Pollock recalls the flourishing work among young people in the post-war years, when the Girls' Brigade company had around 100 members: "The programme used to be built on the Latin word for hope, SPES, so our activities were Spiritual, Physical, Educational and Social, and it was a balanced programme: Bible study, crafts and literature, first aid and home nursing."

The final stage in the development of the church complex came in 1976, with the opening on 8 May of the Epworth Hall, a replacement for the 1928 Lecture Hall at the back of the site, designed by Alick Gavin of Mauger, Gavin and Pinfold.[172]

Four years later the Methodist congregation began to share the premises with their Anglican neighbours, who had been forced to demolish St. Philip's Church because of subsidence (see St. Philip's Church, page 117). A formal sharing agreement was signed in 1981. As the two congregations grew into a closer relationship, it was decided to seek a formal ecumenical agreement, and the Bishop of Southwark signed the ecumenical instruments on 30 November 1990.[173]

The integration of services has given the members the chance to learn from each other's traditions, with the result that many who originate from the Methodist congregation have accepted such practices as ashing on Ash Wednesday, while Anglicans have welcomed the strength of preaching in the Methodist tradition. Joint services are held at which new members receive the Anglican sacrament of Confirmation and are made full Methodist members, receiving laying-on of hands by the Anglican bishop and Methodist District Chairman together, witnessing to their dual membership of the two denominations.

The church itself looks on the outside much as H Kelsall Armitage intended in 1928. Inside, there have been a number of improvements. An organ, originally built in 1905 by Alfred Hunter for Dorking Methodist Church, was installed in 1975, and its dedication on 7 June was followed by a recital by Dr W S Lloyd Webber. In 1986 a legacy received by the Anglican parish enabled the two congregations to proceed with a jointly-funded scheme for the re-ordering of the front of the church, which was completed by Palm Sunday 1991.

*Leaving the church and continuing along Cheam Common Road,* we pass on the left the surviving members of the group of cottages shown on nineteenth-century maps as...

# North End Place

This place-name, still used as the name of the adjoining public-house, has become somewhat illogical, as we are actually at the *south* end of the main shopping area.

Presumably the cottages were the northernmost habitations in Cheam parish, before the development of what is now Central Road had begun.

At no. 225 a front extension was added to form a shop. This was for many years a sweetshop, which was taken over in 1923 by Mrs May Featherstone. Her daughter Joyce Fellgett recalls that, in the early days, all the sweets were weighed out from jars:

"Before the place grew, when it was country, you sold a lot of two-ounces of stuff, and it was sold in one of those little three-corner bags. Cadbury's chocolate used to come in twopenny bars in a wooden box, and it wasn't wrapped at all, and the counter was laden with comics that the children bought." Four years later, with the pace of development speeding up, Mrs Featherstone applied to be registered as a newsagent. The shop was found to be exactly half a mile from Lock's at the foot of Central Road, and the application was approved. "The great criterion was to be first with the papers, because the people buying the new houses went to work in the City, and they caught the workmen's train. One went at seven, so you can guess how early we had to be."

One Monday afternoon, early in the Second World War, "the warning went, and my mother continued calmly writing the names on her paper rounds for the evening papers. Suddenly it started and they had a dog fight overhead… Our shop had a flat roof, and everywhere was machine gun bullets and shrapnel… One of our most disturbed nights was when they had a mobile gun running up and down Central Road. We were issued with ear plugs, but it didn't work out, and they gave it up as a bad job."

The North End Tavern was originally housed in one of the cottages, and was operating by 1871, when James Cuff, whose family had lived at North End since the early 1840s, was combining the trades of builder and beerhouse keeper. In 1890 it was leased to Walter and John Flint East, brewers in Kingston. A year later they transferred their lease to the brewers Charrington & Co, who bought the freehold in 1903.[174]

The present fine Tudor-style building dates from the early 1930s, the central porch having been added in 1997 to replace two small entrances at opposite ends of the façade.

The strip of land behind North End Place, including Rose Cottage which faced down Central Road, was until the mid-1930s a nursery known as H Dare and Son. Henry Dare, who came from Cambridgeshire, had established the nursery in the mid-1890s; together with members of his family, he continued the business until his death in 1934.

Mr Dare's grand-daughter Olive Dare remembers the long front garden of Rose Cottage, filled with penstemons in beds edged with box. There was a greenhouse beside the cottage, and flowers were grown for sale on the land behind. Lucy Bell-Chambers recalls "My relatives used to come down at weekends, and we used to go up there and buy a bunch of flowers. Miss Dare had every kind of flower you could think of. You could walk up and down and pick what you wanted, sixpence a bunch."

Around 1910, Fred Dare, one of Henry's sons, had a fruiterer's and florist's shop in Alexandra Parade, Central Road, but he moved to Detroit soon afterwards. By 1926, in addition to "Rose Nursery" as it was called, the family had the "Bungalow Nursery" behind The Worcester, where Orchard Court now stands. Nearby, at 1A Park Terrace, they had a florist's shop run by Henry's daughter Lizzie (see photograph on page 11), and in the early 1930s they had a florist's shop at 202 Cheam Common Road.

112

*Frederick Dare, fruiterer and florist, of Alexandra Parade, c.1910*

On the right, meanwhile, we pass the showrooms of Barn Glass Works. This company was established in the mid-1940s by Reginald Clacy Delaiche in some of the former buildings of Worcester Park Farm between Stone Place and Windsor Road. Initially he concentrated on selling glass, cut to customers' requirements, from these premises. The business expanded into the premises on the corner of Lindsay Road, selling mirrors and picture frames. The company is now run by his son, and two members of the third generation have joined the business. Barn Glass is now based in Sutton, where other areas of work such as skylight units have been developed, but the Worcester Park connection has been maintained even though most of the Stone Place premises disappeared in the recent redevelopment.[175]

*We now reach...*

## Lindsay Road

The development of Lindsay Road is closely connected with the Blake family. Andrew Blake was a Suffolk man who came to Worcester Park around 1860 and took over Malden Green Farm. By the end of the decade he had also begun speculative development in Longfellow Road. At various periods he was a builder and contractor, hay and feed merchant and coal merchant. By 1901 he had turned his attention to Lindsay Road, and the terrace on the right-hand side bears the inscription "AB 1901".

Andrew Blake died in 1910, but his eldest son William continued the land, hay and feed concerns from the stables on the corner of Lindsay Road (where the Barn Glass premises now stand). His nephew David Blake recalls "He had carthorses and carts and so on, and when I was a small boy I used to go down on the cart to fields that he had by the gasometers at Motspur Park and he used to collect hay, and we'd bring the hay back, and I'd sit on this big horse and cart coming up Worcester Park High Street in the middle Thirties."

In the previous decade, the Blakes were still growing corn in one of the fields at the end of Lindsay Road. As Horace Shrubb recalls, "On a given day the traction engine would arrive with the machine for extracting the corn... they would have enough sheaves to justify this business of them turning up on a Saturday; we used to be down there watching it all – that was a great event, and you'd see mice coming out as they worked down."

The 1930 Kelly's Directory shows that, of seventeen houses in Lindsay Road, four were occupied by members of the Blake family – Andrew's widow at no. 4, the eldest son William at no. 16 and his brother Herbert (David Blake's father) at no. 18, while no. 32 was the home of Frederick Blake, one of the co-founders (with Edwin Shrubb, no. 12, and Ernie Styles, no. 14) of the Worcester Park Athletic Club.

Next door, at no. 30, was (Walter) Charlie Dare, who married Andrew Blake's daughter Ethel. He continued the horticultural tradition of his father Henry, and had a large plot of land beside the house: initially he used this for growing roses which he exhibited successfully at Kingston, and after the first World War he set up in business in his own right. His daughter Olive recalls "He used to grow masses of tomato plants, and it was my job when I was about 12 to clean all the pots. He filled two greenhouses with them, and then sold the tomatoes for ninepence a pound; then he had chrysanthemums: they were grown out in the open ground in pots all the summer, and then they were transferred to the two greenhouses. He had a lean-to attached to the house, but he kept that for begonias – that was his hobby."

The Cemetery on the opposite side of the road was laid out by Cuddington Parish Council, to remedy the situation that the parish had not had a graveyard since 1538. It was consecrated in 1902; in 1933 the cemetery, together with the eastern part of the civil parish, was transferred to Sutton and Cheam Urban District.

Until the mid-1930s Lindsay Road was almost surrounded by open fields, which provided a stimulus to the sporting interests of adults and children in the road. The field behind the houses on the right of the road, where Christ Church and Ruskin Drive now stand, was the home of the Cheam Common Cricket Club. The field belonged to the Blake family, who kept cart-horses there, so there were posts and chains to keep the horses off the cricket square. As Horace Shrubb recalls, this once led to a memorable incident:

"Charlie Dare who lived in Lindsay Road and played cricket for the Club used to prepare the pitches on Saturday mornings. He was out there on this particular Saturday, and Jacky Styles, a boy who also lived in the road, was out there with him. We had back gates leading out into the cricket field, and I thought I would wander over to join them. I had gone part of the way over, and suddenly they were laying flat on their stomachs, signalling me to get down. Eventually they got up and I went over to them, and they explained that a swarm of bees were flying round one of the posts."

Cheam Common Cricket Club had originally been established in 1872. The inaugural match was held on 26 August in a field belonging to Mr Pennington (probably near the Drill Inn), between the single and married members. The bachelors won with scores of 78 and 78 against 34 and 28 for 8. There appears to have been a separate Worcester Park cricket team at this time, against whom Cheam Common were victorious in the summer of 1874.[176]

114

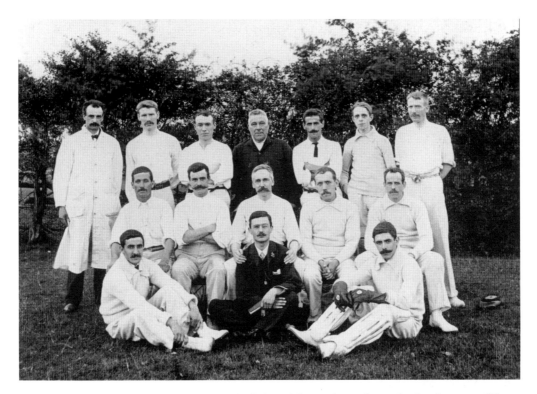

*Cheam Common Cricket Club in 1913. Second from the right in the back row is Oliver Foden, later first Secretary of the Worcester Park Athletic Club (see page 134)*

The Cricket Club was approached in 1919 by the Worcester Park Volunteer Company with a view to the amalgamation of the local sports clubs into a Worcester Park Athletic Club. This was agreed, and the new Athletic Club moved in 1921 to its present ground, Skinner's Field between Green Lane and the railway line (see Green Lane, page 149).

At the point where Lindsay Road stopped at that time, near the bend in the present road, was another field, known as the Football Field, and used by the Cheam Common Football Club. Like the Cricket Club, the footballers moved to Green Lane in 1921. However, initially there were no washing facilities and, as Bob Blake recalls, "We used to walk home to Lindsay Road in our football boots, and the state of the ground in mid-winter was terrible."

The Lindsay Road field continued to be used for both football and cricket by the boys in the area. Horace Shrubb recalls that his father "got up the idea of us getting together to buy some cricket stumps, and I think we paid sixpence each, and we got a lovely set of stumps which we used for quite a long time at the end of Lindsay Road. It was quite something for us to have full-sized stumps."

Beyond this field was the 'Pond Field', so called after a pond at the top end (in the angle where the present Ruskin Drive bends). The older children used to punt a home-made raft across the pond with a pole. "There was an occasion when Bob Blake was on the raft, several yards from the bank. It so happened that this coincided with Bob's mother bringing her Airedale dog Keeper into the field for a run, and it bounded up to the pond, jumped in and swam to the raft. The dog then tried to clamber on to the raft and in doing so tipped up the raft and Bob ended up in the pond."

115

*Ordnance Survey map, 1933: on the right, Lavender & Farrell's development has covered the Lower Farm land; in the centre, Wates's Ruskin Park estate is nearing completion, but has not yet extended to Dorchester Road, whilst in the top left Young's houses are appearing in Browning Avenue. Further south, the new Cheam Common Infants' School can be seen next to its corrugated iron predecessor, and the old Girls' school is still shown on the northern side of the road*

116

The further section of Lindsay Road, together with St. Philip's Avenue North, part of Brinkley Road, and the adjacent section of Browning Avenue, was developed by Wates in 1933 as the "Ruskin Park Estate". Later that year, they extended northwards to lay out the Dorchester Road and Buckland Way development. Katherine Pollock, whose parents moved to Buckland Way in 1935, recalls "They came out to Worcester Park one day, on the bus, just for an afternoon out, and they saw the houses in Buckland Way being built three bricks high, £50 deposit, and bought a house."

A site in Dorchester Road was earmarked for a school at this time, but the outbreak of war forestalled this. The land was used for wartime allotments (Thelma Jones remembers her father cycling over from Stoneleigh Avenue with his spades on the handlebars), and it was only in September 1974 that Dorchester Primary School was opened, the first headteacher being Georgina Ray.

*Continue past the parade of shops, and turn right at the War Memorial into the churchyard of...*

# St. Philip's Church

A line of stones around a grassy mound now marks the site of the church which stood here for just over a hundred years. When the development of this part of Worcester Park was begun in the 1860s, all the land to the right of Central Road was in the parish of Cheam. The parish church of St. Dunstan's, 1½ miles away in Cheam village, was hardly convenient for the new residents of Longfellow and Washington Roads, and the Revd Charles Hobbes Rice, who was appointed Rector in August 1867, quickly took action to provide a place of worship.

In April 1868 a room in one of the cottages at North End Place was licensed to be used for services. Mr Rice, who was running the parish single-handed at this time, began with a weekday lecture, soon followed by a service each Sunday at 7 pm. By 6 October a temporary Church Room had been put up on a field belonging to the churchwardens, probably on the Dalmeny Road side of Woodbine Lane. The average attendance soon reached 70. In the following year, Mr Rice was able to appoint a curate, and from 18 July it was possible to hold morning and evening services in the Church Room. The sermons at the morning services were aimed particularly at children, and by December there were 62 children on the Sunday School register, and an average of 50 children at the service.[177]

In 1871 a house was built to provide permanent accommodation for the curate in charge of the Church Room.[178] Curates during the early years included Henry Atwool MD (1869-70), Frederic Rose, who had previously been curate of two Nottingham parishes and the deprived Clare Market district near Lincoln's Inn Fields (1870-71), and Reginald Bigg-Wither (1871-74).

The Rector took a broad view of his ministry to the people of Cheam Common. By 1870 an Infants' School had been set up in the Church Room, a soup kitchen was opened in Thorn Cottage (close to the site of Balmoral Court), and there were "penny readings" at which a programme of extracts from authors such as Dickens and Hans Christian Andersen was read.

By 1872 the time had come to provide a permanent church, and on 1 June a meeting was held at which the decision was taken to build a chapel-of-ease which would contain 150 seats in the first instance, and be designed to allow expansion. The cost

*Postcard of St. Philip's Church, postmarked 1906*

was estimated at £1,000, and the architects Slater and Carpenter were invited to draw up a design. This partnership had been founded by Richard Cromwell Carpenter, who has been described as "the Anglican Pugin" as a tribute to his pioneering work in reviving the medieval style of church architecture. After his death in 1855, the practice was continued by his colleague William Slater and his son Richard Herbert Carpenter, the man responsible for the design of St. Philip's, who combined his father's preference for medieval Gothic with touches drawn from his observations in the Mediterranean and the Middle East.[179] The site was donated by Mr H Lindsay Antrobus of Lower Cheam.

Four months later, the building fund had raised £1,039, and the Rector's printed letter of 2 November, inserted in the parish magazine, shows that the rising population was exacerbating the problems of space in the church room; consideration was already being given to the possibility of building a larger church in one stage. Early next year, a tender was received of £2,394 10s for constructing a church seating 300 people; alternatively, if the aisles and ancillary rooms were omitted, the cost would be reduced by £578 5s.

The parish magazine reported the laying of the foundation stone in June 1873 in some detail: at 5.30 pm "a long procession set out from the Church Room at Cheam Common, consisting of the choirs from both divisions of the parish, the Cheam Common school children, the Building Committee, and a body of surpliced Clergy twenty in number.... On arriving at the ground, where a temporary platform had been erected and decorated for the occasion, the Special Service appointed to be used in Winchester diocese was intoned by the Rector, and chorally rendered throughout – the choirs conducted by Mr Leaver performing their part very creditably."

Tea was served afterwards in three large tents: "The tents decorated outside with pendant wreaths of wistaria and laburnum and inside with a profusion of flags and flowers, had a most inviting appearance, and to judge from the length of time before the guests quitted them, they found the entertainment itself equally to its taste."

It was decided that, if two-thirds of the £850 deficiency in the building fund had been raised by Midsummer Day, orders would be given to build the complete church, and this was achieved after some last-minute guarantees by members of the building committee. In his circular letter to parishioners that November, the Rector recorded "Within a year of our opening a fund for the purpose, we had laid the foundation stone, and entered into a contract for the erection of the whole church."

The church was opened for worship on 10 January 1875. At 11 am Morning Prayer was read by the Revd T G Browne, the curate in charge of the new church, and the Rector celebrated Holy Communion and preached on Psalm 122 v 1 ("I was glad when they said unto me: We will go into the house of the Lord"); at 3 pm the Litany was read, and a sermon preached by the Revd W Chetwynd Stapleton of Malden. Finally, at 7 pm Evening Prayer was read, and a sermon was preached by the former curate, the Revd R F Bigg-Wither. This set the pattern of services on the second and fourth Sundays of each month, except that the 3 pm service was generally to be the Litany with catechising. On other Sundays there would also be three services: Holy Communion at 8 am, Morning Prayer with the Litany and a sermon at 11 am, and Evening Prayer and sermon at 7 pm.[180]

The church remained for some time a chapelry of St. Dunstan's, served by curates-in-charge. Thirlwall Gore Browne, curate at the time of the opening, was one of the three sons of the Bishop of Winchester. He was succeeded by Alfred Sharpe (1877-78), followed by Frederick Goldsmith (1881-85), who moved to Western Australia in 1888 and in 1904 became the first bishop of the new Diocese of Bunbury, where he organised new parishes as the region was opened up by the railways and established a Bush Brotherhood.[181] James Sparrow served from 1885 to 1895, followed by George Dowling (1900-05), and Leonard Woolley (from 1905).

*Members of St. Philip's choir with the Revd William Birch, curate from 1932 to 34*

119

In 1906 St. Philip's was assigned a definite 'consolidated chapelry', later made a separate parish. The area stretched from the Beverley Brook to the Pyl Brook, and from the railway line and Sparrow Farm to the London Road. Mr Woolley became the first Perpetual Curate, remaining until 1914. Since then there have been eight vicars or priests-in-charge: Albert Shewring (1914-21), who had spent much of his earlier ministry in South Africa, exchanged livings with his successor Raymond Ravenscroft (1921-25), of Dalham near Newmarket; he was followed by Frederick Pegg (1925-32).

The Sunday School excursions at this time were a rare treat for local children. The September 1905 parish magazine records a trip to Hampton Court and Bushy Park, beginning with a noisy game of cricket for the boys, "and then the boys and girls [had] a noisier game together. The latter broke up prematurely. The girls said the boys could not play, or something of the sort. Then there were expeditions to the Palace... Lastly there was the boating on the river. Some of us had our hair turned grey by the sight of the boys' crews struggling with the mysteries of managing a boat."

As Horace Shrubb recalls, Hampton Court was still a popular destination in the 1920s. They walked to New Malden, and had "special trams to take us from New Malden to Hampton Court, and we trundled off all excited, all wanting to be on the top deck... Everybody dived in the Maze as soon as we got there, that started the excitement. You'd spend a lot of time down by the river, and we had our lunch there, and then we'd go to Bushy Park, where our tea was laid on."

Mary Samuda recalls that, as a girl in the 1910s, she went to church wearing "black patent shoes and white socks and white gloves, and you daren't take them off, and a hat."

The War Memorial at the entrance to the churchyard commemorates those members of the parish who gave their lives in the First World War. Among them are Sgt Arthur Wilfred Golden and his brother Pte H V Golden, whose family kept a sweet shop at 33 Longfellow Road. Sgt Golden joined up in November 1914 and went over to France with the 11th Battalion of the Royal Sussex Regiment in March 1916. He was awarded the Military Medal at the Somme in that year, and the Distinguished Conduct Medal in the Flanders offensive the following year; he died of wounds received in action on 25 April 1918. His brother, in the 18th Battalion, Canadian Infantry (West Ontario Regiment), who won the MM at Vimy Ridge, was killed in action in October 1917.[182]

In 1910 plans were drawn up for a hall in Lindsay Road, to be built in two stages. The whole scheme included a large hall to seat 300, a billiard room, two classrooms, a kitchen and cloakrooms. Ron Kinton, whose father Walter was the secretary of the Worcester Park Horticultural Society in the 1930s, recalls the society's shows of flowers and vegetables in the hall. Produce was donated to St. Anthony's Hospital after the show. He also recalls meetings of the 2nd Worcester Park Scout Group in the hall. Mr Kinton himself was later to become District Commissioner for Scouts in Sutton and Cheam, and his twin brother Peter became Group Scout leader of the 4th Worcester Park Scouts, founded in 1934. This group held its early meetings in the garage of Wilfrid Chittenden's house in Colborne Way but, with the assistance of Sir Sidney Marshall, Charter Mayor of Sutton and Cheam, acquired the site of the present hall in Balmoral Road.

*Design for proposed church hall for St Philip's, 1910*
*[Ecclesiastical Commissioners' file 82365 (Cheam Common augmentation),*
*now held at the Church of England Record Centre]*

From 1932 to 1951 the Vicar was the Revd S Guy Brockington. The Revd Leslie Jolly, his curate from 1942 to 1950, recalls that he was lively and energetic; as a preacher he had the gift of the gab, and tended to be dramatic.

The churchmanship at this time, as Mr Jolly recalls, was described as "Prayer Book Catholic", incorporating some features which would then have been regarded as high-church practices, such as incense, servers, the daily Eucharist, Christmas Midnight Mass, and Maundy Thursday vigils. It was based, however, on English pre-Reformation rites rather than on contemporary Roman worship: "We had a very knowledgeable sacristan, Mr Huggett, who had made a study of the liturgy and the Sarum rite [one of the most widespread pre-Reformation service books], so everything that was of the Roman variety was out – we had albs, not cottas, and we called the people who carried candles taperers, not acolytes – it was very English." Similarly, there were only two candles on the High Altar, although there were four candles on the ridell posts supporting the altar curtains.

The general pattern of services at this time was 8 am Holy Communion, the main sung Communion service at 9.45, and evensong at 4 pm. At 11.15 am there was a Children's Eucharist and Catechism, using an abbreviated form of the Book of Common Prayer service: the priest who was not on duty to take the service would stand "in the body of the Church instructing the children, as the service was proceeding, as to what was going on, and what was next."

Mr Jolly's particular contribution was to establish a branch of the C. of E. Men's Society and a Religious Drama Society. The latter began with a series of Passiontide tableaux, based on readings published by S.P.C.K., performed on the evening of Good Friday in 1943. In subsequent years, he organised productions of plays published by the national Religious Drama Society to mark the church's festivals, such as the nativity play *The Light Shineth in Darkness*, performed in December 1946.

Mr Brockington was succeeded in 1952 by Herbert Trundle (like his predecessor, a former curate of Cheam), who served until 1976. By this time, the structure of St. Philip's was giving serious cause for concern. The clay soil made subsidence a risk, and the church had to be underpinned as early as 1923. The vicarage was found to be unsound in 1927, and a new one was built in 1929-30.

In the 1970s, however, the problems became worse. The church hall in Lindsay Road was declared unsound in 1973, and was closed for over a year until it had been repaired. On Mr Trundle's retirement, the vicarage was found to be unsafe. The new vicar, Henry Burgin, arrived in 1977; at his induction service the Bishop challenged him to "disturb the comfortable and comfort the disturbed", but he can hardly have had in mind the degree of disturbance that the congregation was soon to face.[183]

Later that year, serious movement was observed in the fabric of the church. Reports were commissioned, and it was found that it would be impractical to repair the vicarage, and that the hall was unlikely to last for many more years. In April 1978, after pieces of stone had fallen from two of the arches, the congregation left St Philip's and services were held in the hall. It was decided that the cost of repairing the church would be too high, and it was demolished that autumn. A year later, after exploring various possibilities, it was decided to approach Christ Church with a view to sharing their premises, thus beginning the process that led to the present ecumenical agreement which has already been described. During this time the congregation has been served by Canon Martin Goodlad (1983-97) and the Revd Charlotte Elvey (since 1998).

*Leave the churchyard and turn right.* The curving row of shops on the right, The Broadway Market, was built in 1934 on the site of the former...

## Cheam Common Elementary School

The original Cheam Common Infants' School was opened on 1 Nov 1869 in the Church Room which probably stood between Dalmeny Road and Woodbine Lane. Parents were required to make contributions from 1d to 9d per week for each child, according to their means and the number of members of the family. Within a month there were 29 children on the roll; the schoolmistress was Miss Harriet Starr.

The school's first log book provides us with glimpses of life in the classroom. There was a succession of visitors: Miss Smith (presumably Rose Emma Smith – see Washington Road) came twice most weeks and took a class, usually for reading. On 14 November 1870 she brought toys for the children to play with in the dinner hour, and on 27 March 1872 she distributed buns and prizes. Miss Beck visited most weeks, and there were regular visits from the curate, the rector and their families.

Miss Starr was succeeded in 1872 by Katharine Bassett and in 1874 by Mary Jane Topley. Although we do not have a timetable surviving from this period, it is clear that, in addition to reading, writing and arithmetic, the curriculum included poetry, religious knowledge and needlework (including hemming, darning and patchwork). On Wednesdays Miss Topley introduced 'kinder garten', probably a teaching method using object-lessons devised by Friedrich Fröbel, but this was discontinued in 1877 because her successor Laura Pook "did not understand it." Much of the children's work was done on slates, but in May 1874 copy-books were given to the 3rd Class for the first time. From 1874 a succession of monitresses taught Class IV, the youngest children: in 1876 Miss Topley examined the class's progress "in letters, figures, form and colour."

In March 1878 a purpose-built school was opened close to the new church beside the parsonage. It was a brick, slate-roofed building, a little over 50ft by 20ft, divided by means of a wooden partition to provide accommodation for 51 infants and also 77 older girls (who would previously have travelled to the Girls' School in the Parochial Rooms in Cheam Village). The total cost of the building was just over £1300: much of this was raised through donations from Cheam and Cuddington residents, including Mr and Mrs Antrobus, who donated the site, and gave £200 and a further £110 for the construction of a lobby. Collections at St. Dunstan's and St. Philip's, and grants from the National Society and Surrey Church Association, made up the balance.[184]

A third classroom, just under 18ft square, was added at the back in 1892, bringing the total accommodation to 156. A schoolhouse was added on the north end at the same time. All the classrooms had a cement dado, with painted and whitened walls, and desks designed to seat 3 or 6 children. The entrance was at the back of the building, and led into a small cloakroom with 74 pegs and one sink; the lavatories were across the playground. A surveyor's report of 1904 found several aspects in need of improvement, from the smoky open stove in one of the classrooms to the loose gravel in the playground, which found its way into the building on pupils' feet.[185] By this time more space was required: in February 1904 the Infants' classes had moved to temporary premises in the Mission Hall in Longfellow Road.[186] At the end of June these classes were made into a separate school, which continues to be known as...

## Cheam Common Infants School

After two years in Longfellow Road, the school moved on 3 September 1906 to a corrugated iron building just across Cheam Common Road from the old school, on the corner of Balmoral Road. For the first few days the school must have seemed almost as

*Miss Harper with her pupils outside the "Tin-Tack" on Empire Day, c.1930*

crowded as the Mission, since only one room was ready and lessons were accompanied by a "great noise of hammering." Once the problems had been overcome, the corrugated iron building housed the Infants' School until the present building was built alongside it in Balmoral Road in 1932. After about three years here, the girls would move across the road to the 1878 building while the boys had to travel to Cheam or Malden to continue their education.

The "Tin-Tack" (originally "Tin Tab", short for Tabernacle) is remembered by many former pupils from the Infants' department. Maurice Upperton, who started at the school in 1916, recalls "The boys and girls were all taught together – there were only three rooms for three years... and a long cloakroom that ran the length of the three for hats and coats, and there was also a little gas-ring perched on a corner bracket, and the teachers made a cup of tea there – there was no staff room.

"The one memory I have of the school that will never leave me is that on Armistice Day the news came through that the War had ended, and Miss Young, the headmistress, said 'You can all go home today', and we were sent home at midday. We all went off down the hill whooping and shouting for joy: we didn't know much about the end of the War because we hadn't known much of the War."

Behind the school, where the present schools now stand, "there was a big field and an oak tree. We played our own games – hopscotch, and the boys had tops which you had to spin, peg-tops we called them; the girls had tops, but theirs were funny little things, and they had to whip them, so they were called whip-tops.

"In those days the village had a big day once a year, the village flower show, held on the school field. There were big marquees with all the exhibits – flowers, vegetables, craft work, knitting, handwriting, all sorts of things that could be expected of children to do. There was a pleasure area, and then in the evening there was dancing to a brass band."

Joyce Fellgett (née Featherstone), a pupil in the 1920s, also remembers the annual fête: "The schoolchildren entered their sewing, writing, modelling (Plasticine) etc., and the locals entered their garden produce." The field was also used for a fair, which might stay several weeks "with swings, cake walk, roundabouts, chairoplanes, galloping horses, etc."

"We had three teachers," recalls Mrs Fellgett, "Miss Jefferies, first class, and Miss Stone, a teacher I loved, very strict and north-country, where one was promoted to at the age of six – we all had to read, write and knit, and if a child could not do this she was given extra tuition after school. When we were seven we went into Miss Coles' class (the head teacher) and, joy of joy, we were given pens and ink and rulers to write with. We had to write compositions which were drawn from a box, and each one was different (no copying). I remember one boy drawing a composition to be written on 'A Thunderstorm'. He wrote 'In a thunderstorm I ran home to my mother' – much to the teacher's surprise: she didn't expect one sentence, and no mention of the lightning etc.

"In 'break', which was called 'playtime', we skipped and played 'he' and hide-and-seek. There was no milk – we were allowed to bring a piece of cake, biscuit, apple or orange, or a bar of chocolate, to be placed on the teacher's desk for 'elevenses', but if we were thirsty we had to drink water."

*A class outside the Infants' School, c.1930. Jean Everett, now Mrs Harrison-Smith,
is fifth from the left*

On 3 February 1930 Miss Robina Harper began duties as Headmistress. Her first weeks seem to have been dogged by infectious diseases: a case of scarlet fever was reported on her first day, and two cases of diphtheria later that week. One child developed mumps a fortnight later, and at the end of March it was decided to spray the school with formalin. This did not prevent outbreaks of measles in April and whooping cough in July, when attendance fell to 152 out of 233.

In 1931 overcrowding became a problem. On 13 April about fifty children had to be refused entry for lack of space, and no transfers to junior schools could take place because of a lack of space elsewhere. On 4 May, however, additional temporary rooms were ready for use, and 61 new children were admitted in three days. In September, Miss Harper was directed to allow the numbers to reach 404.

The new building in Balmoral Road was handed over for use on 4 April 1932. On 7 April Miss Harper recorded "12 kindergarten tables arrived this morning. No chairs, so far, have come, so the children have had to use the tables, today, for seats. For three days they have had to sit on the floor." Next day: "No more furniture, so far... Numbers of new children admitted this week is 50, making a total on the register of 431." Fortunately, on 14 April, "Kindergarten chairs (48) and teachers' chairs (24) arrived this morning." In 1936 the temporary buildings were in use again, as two additional classes had to be accommodated.

Life in the Infants' School in the 1930s followed an annual pattern. In late May, Empire Day was celebrated. In 1933, for example, each teacher gave a talk to her class; the pupils then gathered in the hall to listen to a broadcast by Admiral Jellicoe and a talk by Mr Rides (one of the managers), followed by Empire Day songs and the National

Anthem; a half-holiday was then granted. Derby week in June caused a slight alteration to the timetable, as afternoon school finished early so that children living beyond the North Cheam crossroads could go home before the traffic became heavy. Armistice Day was also marked, a wireless being obtained so that the children could listen to the Cenotaph ceremony. Christmas might be marked by a children's party and puppet show, as in 1931, or a display to parents, as in 1936.

Frequent visits were made by health visitors and nurses. School milk was introduced in 1930, and when the charge was reduced in 1934 to ½d per one-third of a pint the numbers taking it almost tripled to 340. It was recognised, however, that local health problems were less than those of the depressed North, and in November 1934 £2 5s was collected towards a scheme for helping Jarrow. Closer to home, a "Pound Day" for the Sutton and Cheam Hospital in 1936 produced 408 packages or lbs, with 8 marrows, 3 eggs and 2s 9½d in cash.

Unusual events sometimes occurred: in March 1931 "a North American Negro visited school... [to] talk to children on 'Life on a cotton plantation'... A great number of the children listened and thoroughly enjoyed his stories and songs." Excursions were made to the Aldershot Tattoo in 1932 and 1934.

A school inspection was carried out in October 1938. The inspector praised the standard of teaching for both abler and less able pupils, adding that "The teachers have solved the problem of combining the definite instruction that is necessary with encouragement of the children's spontaneity." He also noted that due care was given "to handwork, nature study, music and rhythmic work."

In 1939 the approach of war necessitated precautions. Gas mask drills were held before the end of the summer term, and in September the beginning of the new term was delayed. Entries in the log book over the following weeks continue the story:

30 Oct:    "All members of the Staff are now doing work in various homes of the children. Work begins at 9.30 till 12; and from 2 till 3 pm."

20 Nov:    "Top class children are in school today as is also a group in another classroom. One trench being ready in case of necessity."

23 Nov:    "The two Top Classes are working in school, also a small group, as from today, two trenches being available in case of emergency. The Teachers working in school are Miss Elphick, Mrs Buckley and Mrs Eadie. The rest of the staff are still working in homes near school."

28 Nov:    "School started today on half time – the older children in the morning and the younger ones in the afternoon – times being 8.55 to 12 noon, 12.30 to 2.30. The afternoon time is so as to enable me to have the younger children away from the Juniors as much as possible."

15 Dec:    "The Junior School moved to their own building today. School begins on Monday on full times i.e. 8.50 to 11.45 am; and 1.15 to 2.45 pm."

A year later, the threat of air raids had become reality. On 27 August 1940 only thirty children came to school after a long raid the previous evening. Daytime raids disrupted lessons on over 50 days between September and December. On 16 September alone there were four alerts, covering 9.55 am-10.40, 10.55-11.35, 12.10-12.45 and 2.10-6 pm. On 17 October the Headmistress recorded, "Time tables, as near as possible to the original, have been made out by the Staff. Essential lessons, lost in the morning through 'Alerts' will be taken in the second half of the session in place of Handwork."

After January 1941, raids became much less frequent, until the onslaught of V1 'buzz-bombs' in the summer of 1944. Once again, the log book gives an indication of the difficulties facing the school:

22 June:   "'Alert' has been on for the greater part of the day so the few children who have been to school have been in the shelters or working quite near."

29 June:   "Children (only 20 in school) working in the open near the shelters as the sirens are repeatedly sounding."

30 June:   "Alert sounded 8.55 – Clear 9.30 – Alert 9.35 – Clear 1.15 – Alert 1.23 – Clear 2.30. Dinners have had to be served in shelters and the children have spent most of their time there."

3 July:   "All day spent in shelters. Only 10 children in school."

10 July:   "Only 5 children in school. Evacuation lists being filled in."

11 July:   "Miss Elphick left this morning with children for Evacuation. She is to stay one month. Mrs Buckley left as Escort for a party going for Evacuation."

14 Aug:   "School re-opened today. Numbers are very small: 10. Miss Elphick and Mrs Bowles are continuing with Evacuation duties in Lancashire."

*Cheam Common School; Maypole dancing, c.1935*

Katherine Pollock, who entered the Infants' school in 1942, recalls learning tables in the shelters in 1944: "They were very dark with little slatted forms. There was not an awful lot we could be taught down there, but at least we could chant tables, and those of course are in my head for life."

On 29 and 31 August there were nine alerts in total. Thereafter no further alerts are listed in the log book, and by 29 September attendance had reached over 130. More problems arose in October, when the Infants' premises were taken over by building operatives, and most of the classes moved to the Junior building only to find that the heating failed there shortly afterwards. 1945 brought more welcome news:

20 June: "Mrs Buckley has gone to Cardiff... to bring back home children who were evacuated a year ago."

25 June: "Mrs Lethbridge and Miss Hughes will be absent for 3 days – 'doing return of Evacuees duty' – from Oldham."

26 June: "A consignment of sweets was received from the Mayor of Sutton and Cheam – these having been sent from Melbourne – Australia – for blitzed areas. Each child was given a packet of these sweets."

Fuel shortages were still a problem after the war: on 23 Jan 1946 the school dinners failed to arrive from the canteen at St. Katherine's, London Road. Miss Harper "went to see why, and found the Van could not run owing to being short of Petrol. I gave the man a coupon for 2 gallons and paid for it. Dinners arrived at 1.25 pm." In May, the old British Restaurant in Central Road (behind 23-31) was taken over as a school canteen. The school itself was short of fuel in March 1947, and closed for eight days, the children only attending for milk and dinners. On 19 December, Miss Harper retired, after 18 years' service which had seen immense change in the school and community which it served.

Her successor, Miss Marjorie Berry, served from 1948 to 1970. She introduced a number of activities which became annual events. Spring Festivals were held in March or April: in 1952 "the children brought flowers and Easter eggs; a service was held in the morning when the children sang hymns and recited poems... Later the gifts were taken to Children's Homes and to an Old Folks Home." On 27 June 1953 the Parents & Teachers Association held a Coronation Fête at which the children gave a performance of 'The Crowning of the Rose Queen' and a demonstration on the agility apparatus. This Rose Queen Festival became a regular occurrence each July. Visiting theatre companies entertained the school, and the top classes put on plays for the younger ones, such as *Peter Rabbit* in 1963 and *The Clockwork Clown* in 1968. A swimming pool was added to the school's facilities in 1970, and a new play area in 1971.

In September 1987 a new nursery class was opened. Initially this was housed in a spare classroom, but in July 1994 work began on clearing a site for purpose-built premises. Around the same time, a competition was held to design a garden for the school with the aim of promoting environmental education. The new nursery building was taken into use on 1 May 1995: the last of the iron classrooms, of which the first had been installed as a temporary measure in 1904, was taken to the Chalk Pits Museum in Amberley.[187]

*Standing opposite the entrance to Balmoral Road* and looking beyond the Infants' School playground, we can see the cream-rendered building of...

## Cheam Common Junior School

Until March 1932 the girls' school had remained as a Church of England school. Olive Dare, a pupil in the early 1920s when Miss Carette was headmistress recalls that sewing lessons, in addition to needlework and knitting, included instruction in the use of a sewing machine: "We had a concert, and saved enough money from that to buy the machine." Although the school only had a hard playground, they were able to use the field behind the Infants' School for netball games. Although there were new developments in school life – the netball team began to play against other schools at Banstead and Sutton in the late 1920s, and a gramophone was purchased in 1928 – the school was still housed in the 1878 building close to St. Philip's.

The premises were now in need of replacement, and the site was required for road widening. In April the school opened as a Council school in the corrugated iron building in Balmoral Road which the Infants' School had just vacated. Girls aged 11 and over, numbering over 100, were transferred to the new Cheam Central School at the end of the year, and in March 1933 the school completed its transformation into a Junior Mixed school.

The new school soon began to enjoy success in local competitions: in May 1933 Cheam Common won both the Boys' and Girls' Junior Shields at the Sutton and District Schools Sports Association sports day. This success was followed in the autumn of 1934 at the Sutton schools swimming gala, at which the boys' team won the first prize, and the girls came first equal. The range of activities open to pupils continued to grow: in March 1935 a party travelled to Kingston for one of the Robert Mayer children's concerts and, later in the year, 43 went on a Port of London Authority Docks and River Cruise.

In 1934 work began on the construction of the present school building in Kingsmead Avenue which was ready in time for the beginning of the summer term in 1935. By this time there were 375 pupils on the roll.[188]

Dorothy Payne (née Soley), a pupil in the Junior School in the late 1940s, remembers the headmistress Mrs Wood, and another teacher of the same surname who, because she collected savings contributions each week, was differentiated as "Savings Mrs Wood". Miss Batchelor "used to take us out on the nature walks into the park in Sandringham Road, collecting leaves", where they also played rounders.

One of her favourite lessons was sewing, including embroidery, hemming and smocking gingham: "once we got started on our work, Mrs Wood used to read to us, things like *What Katy Did, Little Women, Little Men*... once she'd got us started she never seemed to need to help anyone – everyone was so interested in doing their sewing, and listening."

*Continue around the right-hand bend to reach the top of...*

## Central Road

This is the principal shopping street in Worcester Park. Before we continue down the hill, it is time for a few words about its development.

The properties on the left (south-western) side of Cheam Common Road all occupy the strip of land between the road and the boundary of the Great Park, and of Cuddington and Cheam parishes. The double bend we have just passed has brought us back to the boundary, which ran along the south-western side of what is now Central Road. If we could picture the view from here, as it was in 1800, on our left we would see the lands of Worcester Park Farm, which had been part of the Great Park, whilst to the right would be Lower Cheam Common, formerly part of Sparrow Field.

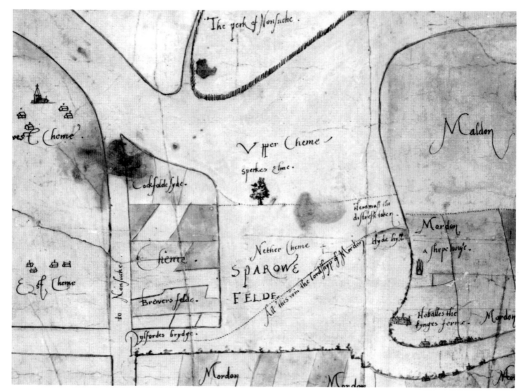

*Map of Sparrow Field, c.1540. South is at the top, where a rather narrow London Road can be seen leading between the two parks of Nonsuch; at the left hand side is the northern part of the London Road leading to Pylford Bridge. The open common of Sparrow Field occupies most of the area between Colborne Way and Green Lane*
*[Public Record Office, MPB 1/25]*

As a result of the Cheam Common enclosure of 1810, the land between Green Lane and the sites of Lindsay Road and Browning Avenue was divided into a dozen strips, each allotted to a different owner of common rights. This division, and the slow pace of development in the area, dictated the pattern of roads in the area today.

On the right-hand side of Central Road itself, the first development was the group of ten shops, known as Cheamside, centred on the junction with Longfellow Road, and built in around 1870. By 1913 twelve shops had been constructed between St. Philip's Avenue and Brinkley Road, the upper and lower parts being known as Percival Parade and Alexandra Parade respectively. In the early 1930s the shopping area grew considerably, as a result of the rapid residential development: by the time of the 1933 Ordnance Survey revision, the imposing Tudor-style parade between Green Lane and Cheamside, Caldbeck Parade to either side of Caldbeck Avenue, and another group of shops below Brinkley Road, had all been added.

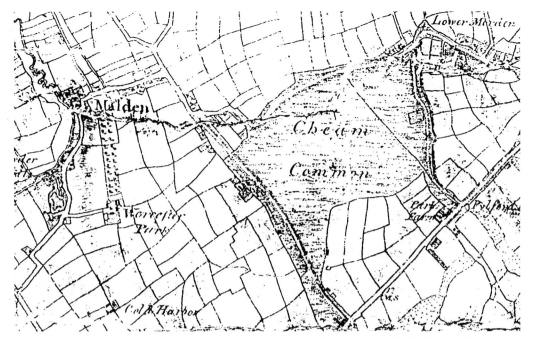

*Preliminary two-inch drawing for the first edition of the one-inch Ordnance Survey map, c.1800, showing Cheam Common before it was enclosed*
[By permission of The British Library, OS Map Drawings 127]

On the left-hand side of the road, development proceeded in a rather different way. The 1897 Ordnance Survey map shows the buildings of Worcester Park Farm occupying most of the land between Windsor Road and what is now Stone Place, whilst Windsor, Hampton and Balmoral Roads had been laid out but were standing empty. By 1913 the farm buildings were sharing this side of the road with semi-detached villas, which extended from Balmoral Road to Windsor Road, and also covered part of the area above Lynwood Drive (then Stoneleigh Drive). As development continued across the farmland, the buildings of Worcester Park Farm became available for redevelopment, and during the mid-1930s the villas were also replaced by further shopping parades, as the prime sites presumably became too valuable to remain in residential use.

At this time Central Road was still part of Cheam Common Road. In 1933 and 1934 the Worcester Park Chamber of Trade repeatedly suggested that the shopping area should be renamed High Street, but this was opposed by the Cheam and Worcester Park Ratepayers' Association,[189] and refused by the Sutton and Cheam Urban District Council. The vehemence of the Chamber of Trade's reaction, including a suggestion that they should adopt the name unofficially, led the *Sutton and Cheam Advertiser* to observe "there is greater need to change their manners than the name in Worcester Park."[190] In December 1934 the name Central Road was agreed upon, and the change came into effect on 1 April 1935.

*Continue past the turning to St. Philip's Avenue.* Most of the top half of that road was built by 1910, but it was made into a cul-de-sac by the construction of the Meadow Lawn Tennis Club's courts on the piece of ground at the end of the road. The 1933 map shows that the remaining portion of this strip of land was regarded as too valuable to be left empty, with the result that "St. Philip's Avenue North" was constructed running from Browning Avenue to the edge of the tennis ground. In due course the two sections were connected, but even then a piece of land was left which was occupied by an Army Cadet Force Hall and later by Dalewood Gardens.

On our right, we now pass the shops originally known as Percival Parade (triple windows and brick surrounds on the first floor façades) and Alexandra Parade (bay windows and gables). The fourth on the right, no. 42, was a sub-post office by 1913, and remained so into the 1990s. The tobacconist's / newsagent's shop which it occupied extended into the next shop up, which is still a newsagent's. No. 44, where Model Road and Rail now attracts model-makers from a wide area, was a baker's shop by 1926, run by Henry Chitty. Mary Samuda remembers Worcester Park Cycle Club trips organised by Mr Chitty in about 1920. One Easter, a group, including his son Archie and Len Hughes, went to Weybridge. She had no lamp, having expected to be back by ten: "We spent the afternoon there, then we started coming home. Well, we had two punctures, and we had to wait for them. I passed Surbiton Police Station with Hughes' hand on this shoulder, and Chitty's hand on that one, and they said 'Go it, Mary! Cycle!'."

Chitty's shop was later taken over by John Morley, and run as a branch of his main shop on the corner of Longfellow Road. Bob Blake recalls that a two-wheeled truck with shaft handles was used to take bread and cakes to the top shop. To get the truck to the top of the hill, Mr Morley "employed a well-known local character always referred to as Manny Turner, who was only about five feet tall. John Morley hitched the truck to his old Jowett car with Manny Turner in the shafts to hold it down. Most of the time Manny's feet weren't touching the ground because he was a little short man. I always imagined the saying, 'His feet didn't touch the ground' as very appropriate." Two doors down was a motor engineer's workshop (Percival Beale in 1926, Charles Rusby in 1930, and Charles White in 1938). As Horace Shrubb recalls, there was a petrol pump in front of the building: "They used to swing it out into the road – you pulled into the kerb and then they'd swing it out."

The premises on the corner of Brinkley Road, now occupied by D G Coles, were originally owned by George William Young. As his daughter Mary Samuda recalls, he set up in business as a builder in 1908 in the lowest shop of Alexandra Parade. The business prospered and he built a new office on the corner site, with living accommodation above and workshops behind. In addition to undertaking building and decorating work, he built some new property, including the shops below Brinkley Road.

*Cross Brinkley Road.* On the right, between nos. 30 and 32 Brinkley Road is the former St. Matthias' R.C. church.

Meanwhile, on the left-hand side of Central Road, we are passing nos. 55-59, which during the Second World War were occupied by two factories engaged in war work, Benwin & Co, aeronautical engineers (whose output included Spitfire fuel tanks) and Wilsons.[191]

A few doors down, at no. 81, is Camera Continental, a well-established camera specialist shop opened by Ken Wilkins in 1966. In the late 1930s and 1940s no. 81 housed the local branch of the commercially-run Chain Library. The librarian, Gwen Major-Ball, was the mother of John Major, and the future Prime Minister spent much of the first year of his life in his pram inside the shop.[192]

Joyce Fellgett remembers visiting the Chain Library, which was lent a touch of glamour by Mrs Major-Ball's fur coat: "During the War I was called up: I had 24 hours on and 24 hours off and I used to go and get a book to read. For general fiction it had newer stuff coming in all the time… and my father used to go on a Saturday and get Western books out."

*Two views down Central Road past Worcester Park Farm, c.1920 and c.1970. The modern view shows the Macfisheries Supermarket in the old Odeon*

*On the right, we now reach Washington Road.* The development of this road is a good example of the results of the division of Cheam Common into strips of land under the 1810 Enclosure. With the exception of the furthest quarter, the whole of Washington Road, its houses and gardens, occupied an allotment made under the Enclosure to Thomas Harris, in exchange for other pieces of land, and known as The Eight Acres. In 1815 Harris sold it to Sir Henry Bridges of Beddington who, as we shall see, already owned the site of Longfellow and Lincoln Roads. Together with that land, it was sold to John Waite, a seedsman, in 1859, and in 1865 to the British Land Company Ltd. The company seems to have made more rapid progress with the development of Longfellow Road, but by 1894 there were about twenty houses in Washington Road, which had increased to nearly one hundred by 1910. The development was carried out piecemeal by individual builders, who tended to rent out the houses rather than sell them. For instance, nos. 17-27 were, in the 1920s, owned by Pastor Baldwin, who ran services at the Mission Hall in Longfellow Road and gave the houses the name "Wycliffe Terrace", no doubt after the fourteenth-century Bible translator. Gerald Woods, who grew up in the terrace at this time, recalls that one of his relatives once met Mr Baldwin "hurrying down the road with his two index fingers sticking out in front of him about a foot apart, and on starting to speak to him, he said 'Don't stop me, I'm on my way to get a piece of glass cut'."

Mrs Jean Harrison-Smith (née Everett), who moved to Washington Road as a child with her parents in 1928, recalls that there was a cottage at the end of the road known simply as 'Eamer's' (no. 139, subsequently rebuilt), where Mrs Eamer sold ice cream, sweets and drinks. "You went in an old wooden door, and there was one room, and then you went through another room, and it seemed very dark, and there were sweets in boxes – you could get a farthing's worth of something. She used to make ice cream, and I remember Mother sending me down with a pudding-basin for ice cream."

The large house on the right, no. 22 or Bennett House, was the home of Miss Rose Emma Smith, until her death in 1927. In the later years of the 19th century Miss Smith had lived in The Avenue, in the house called The Oaks where Badgers Court now stands. She moved to Washington Road to be nearer to the children she taught in the Sunday School at St. Philip's.

*Opposite Washington Road is Windsor Road.* Worcester Park's first purpose-built public library, situated on the left-hand side of the road at the end of the parade of shops, was opened in July 1936.

The first branch library in Worcester Park was opened in the old iron buildings of Cheam Common Infants' School in June 1932. The *Epsom Advertiser* announced "It… will be opened each Thursday from 7.30 pm to 9.30 pm. It is hoped that in the near future another branch will be opened… on a different evening and also in the afternoon for the convenience of housewives who may find the evening times inconvenient." The branch was staffed by volunteers, a leading role being played by Mr O C Foden (who had commanded the Worcester Park Volunteer Training Corps in 1914-16 and was the original secretary of the Worcester Park Athletic Club). It was the only public library in the Sutton and Cheam area until the Sutton branch in Manor Park opened in January 1933.

A year later, the branch already had 1600 members. The accommodation, however, was inadequate and the County Education Committee was seeking to resume use of the classrooms. By October 1933, the children's section, with 300 members, had been closed, and afternoon opening suspended. With book issues reaching 800 per week, the demand for the service was clear, and a site in Windsor Road was purchased in 1934.[193] Once the new building was opened two years later, membership figures rose quickly to 3357 adults and 987 juniors.

This building remained in use until 1996, when it was found to be structurally unsound and was demolished. A new library on the opposite side of Windsor Road was opened to the public on 25 January 2000, and is believed to be the first UK library to be opened in the 21st century.

The name of Worcester Park Farm, whose buildings stood between Windsor Road and Stone Place, appears to have been transferred from the farm at the top of The Avenue in the late 1860s, but there had been a farm on this site much longer. On the 1839 Cuddington tithe map it is named Isteds Farm, probably after Richard Isted who had been the tenant farmer in the late 18th and early 19th centuries. This farm was included in the estate bought by John Jeffries Stone in 1860, and its fields extended almost as far as Salisbury Road in the west and Dalmeny Road in the east. The property was cut roughly in half by the railway line, so the Cattle Arch (now in Dewsbury Gardens) was provided to enable livestock to be moved between the two parts.

*Left: Worcester Park Farm House, on the site of Superdrug, with its tennis court. Right: Joseph Scott, bailiff to the Stone family, with his daughter Irene at Worcester Park Farm*

Joseph Scott lived at the farm as bailiff to the Stone family from c.1907 until about 1917, after which he moved to Longfellow Road and set up a haulage business. In the 1920s the farm was occupied by William Beer, and was sometimes known as Beer's or Stoneleigh Farm. By then the farm was increasingly hemmed in by houses. Gerald Woods, Joseph Scott's grandson, recalls "All I ever saw on the fields was grass and some scruffy cows." The farm's orchard occupied the lower corner of Windsor Road. On this site, in 1934, the Odeon Cinema was opened.

Oscar Deutsch had begun his chain of Odeons in the Midlands in 1930. His first London cinema was opened at Kingston in July 1933. Its counterpart in Worcester Park was opened on 8 January 1934, with the film *I was a Spy*. The cinema, designed by Yates, Cook & Darbyshire had a seating capacity of 894 (543 in the stalls and 351 in the circle). The projection equipment consisted of two British Thomson Houston Kalee 8s. (I am grateful to Terry Aves, himself a former projectionist with the Rank Organisation, for this information.)

The cinema was opened by Cllr S H Marshall, Chairman of the Sutton and Cheam Urban District Council, assisted by the Gaumont-British junior star Joyce Kirby. The *Sutton and Cheam Advertiser* reported "The interior walls of the theatre are treated in a warm shade of amber, with a series of silver bands... The cornice is green and lends a toneful appearance which, on meeting the sloping ceiling, is finished off with an original design reminiscent of eagles outlined in red." Reference was made to the grey silk velour screen curtain, the green tableaux curtain, and the 800 yards of carpet in various shades of red.

The Odeon closed on 29 September 1956 with *Reach for the Sky* and *We Found a Valley*. It was converted into a supermarket, known successively as Macfisheries, MacMarket, International, Gateway and Somerfield. It remained a feature of the Worcester Park skyline until its demolition in 1998, after the opening of a new Somerfield store in Stone Place.

A few doors down from the Odeon, no. 99 (now When Saturdays Come and previously Plus Two Sports) was a grocery run by Cater Bros. Jenny Dore remembers shopping here in the early 1950s: "You would go and buy your eggs at one counter and biscuits at another counter, and bacon at another counter. Eggs were in paper bags, so invariably by the time you got home you'd broken an egg."

Worcester Park farmhouse itself stood a little further down the hill, roughly on the site now occupied by Superdrug, and formerly by Woolworth's. The next shop down, Peppers' delicatessen, housed a branch of the butcher's T Kingston (formerly George Kingston) for over fifty years. Margaret Trickett (née Davies) recalls that, when her parents moved to Woodlands Avenue in 1938, Kingston's delivered to the door if required, and at Christmas presented their regular customers with an earthenware breakfast set, cream with narrow stripes of grey and orange.

Four doors down is Fowler's the stationer, one of only a handful of shops still trading under the name listed in the 1938 Kelly's Directory, albeit not under the same management. In the Cheam Common parish magazine for 1941 Fowler's were advertising "stationery, framing, toys, fancy goods; library consisting of up-to-date novels at 2d per vol. No Deposit." Margaret Rymill recalls that the library was housed in a room at the back: "All the books had green paper covers and they all looked exactly alike." G R Fowler's son, Acting Flt Lt Leslie Gordon Fowler, was awarded the DFC in 1943 for his "fine fighting spirit which had inspired confidence in his crew."

Before the construction of these shops, a ditch ran along the side of the road, running into the Beverley Brook near Stone Place. Lucy Bell-Chambers recalls that, around 1920, "We used to play 'dags' on it [jumping across the ditch] going up to school in the morning." When they reached Windsor Road, they would see Mrs Buckle's parrot in the window of the house on the upper corner "and we used to say 'What's the time Poll? What's the time Polly?' and he always answered you back 'Nine o'clock' and you'd think, 'Oh no, nine o'clock, we're late'."

Turning our attention to the right-hand side once again, *we pass Caldbeck Parade and continue across Caldbeck Avenue*, developed by H H Hartfree in 1932 on the site of two of the 1810 enclosure strips. Gerald Woods recalls that, in the 1920s, the lower strip was the smallholding of a Mr Tilbury, while the upper was farmed by Tommy Waite, who ran the corn chandlery further down the hill: "Tommy Waite was a sharp faced man who always seemed in need of a shave. Wanting to grow a crop of wheat on this ground and not knowing how to set about it he approached my Grandfather Scott for his advice. My grandfather said he would do it for him and did so using the old fashioned method of taking seed from a bag strapped on to his stomach area and alternately with left and right hands throwing it over his opposite shoulders. Apparently Tommy Waite witnessed the procedure with mouth agape but was delighted with the heavy and even crop that resulted."

Among the shops that have occupied the units in Caldbeck Parade is Marigold's Cake Shop, situated at no. 100 (seven doors up from Caldbeck Avenue) until the late 1980s, and in earlier years also known for its tea room. Below Caldbeck Avenue, at no. 118, was Edgar Thomas, whose advertisement in the Jan 1941 parish magazine described him as a "Specialist in Ladies' and Children's Wear… a splendid selection in Children's Outfitting and Baby Linen." To the younger residents of the time, his supplies of corsets with metal stays already appeared old-fashioned.

*Continuing beyond Caldbeck Parade,* we reach some of the oldest shops in Worcester Park, in a parade originally known as…

## Cheamside

Cheamside consisted of five shops on each side of Longfellow Road, probably built soon after the development of that road began in the late 1860s. Gerald Woods vividly recalls the shopkeepers here in the 1920s. No. 10 Cheamside, now no. 128, was Tom Mearing's cycle shop. He took a full-page advertisement in the 1930 Kelly's Directory of Epsom, describing his Imperial Cycle and Gramophone Works as "Agents for all the leading makes of Cycles", "Makers of the all-British Imperial Cycles", "Authorised Dealer in H.M.V. and Columbia Gramophones, Records and Radio Sets", also indicating "Prams Repaired and Re-Tyred". He later moved next door to no. 126, later Firmin's and now The Conservatory florist and garden centre, where part of the name Mearing is still visible on the parapet. On 8 September 1934, under the headline "An eventful week for Mr Tom Mearing", the *Worcester Park Times* reported that his new premises were nearing completion, he had won the singles final in the Worcester Park Athletic Club bowls section, and a presentation had been made to him recognising his twelve years' service as treasurer of the Worcester Park Choral and Dramatic Society.

*Postcard showing Cheamside, the group of shops at the junction of Central Road and Longfellow Road. The backs of some of the houses in Washington Road can be seen further up the hill. Postmarked 1920*

No. 9, now Ross's Fruiterers, has been a greengrocer's for many years, but was once Mrs Glanville's wool shop, succeeded by 1926 by George Crockford, a draper, and by 1930 by Frederick Howell, a fishmonger. Next door at no. 8 (now William Hill) was Francis Lock's newsagency: he was succeeded by 1926 by Archie Lock and before 1932 by Arno's Library (which in turn became Preedy's, before moving across the road to no. 153 where it has since been taken over by W H Smith). The premises were later occupied by the furniture dealers W J Combley & Son.

No. 7 until 1999 had a consistent use as a wine merchant's. In the 1920s-30s it was owned by J T Smith; Gerald Woods recalls his method of sorting a pocketful of assorted coins: "He fished out a good handful from a trouser pocket and gently held them between thumb and fingers of one hand and let those that weren't being gripped drop through into his other hand. The half crowns, the largest, he then put aside and repeated the process…" On the corner, no. 6 (now Summers Insurance Services) "was a grocery shop run by a Mr Randall when we first knew it. He was succeeded [in about 1930] by Mr Frost who had big ideas about expanding the business. He blended his own brand of tea which he named 'Whisperit'." Maurice Upperton recalls "being sent to Randall's at the very end of the Great War with a jug, and Mr Randall went to a big wooden barrel and drew off a pint of treacle – that was a wonderful find in wartime, which he let good customers have, and I carried this treacle all down Longfellow Road to Lincoln Road with great joy."

*Delivery cart for W H Randall, 'baker and grocer' according to the nameboard above the Hovis sign*

Before investigating Longfellow Road, let us complete our survey of Cheamside. On the opposite corner, no.5 (now the Halifax) was occupied for over 65 years by the Morley family's bakery. John Morley bought the business in 1909. His son John William, who began helping his father at the age of twelve, succeeded him and ran the business until his retirement in about 1977. Flour was brought from a mill at Ewell, and later by horse and cart from London, in twelve different grades, to be used in the bakery buildings that ran alongside Longfellow Road behind the shop.[194]

The shop is well-remembered by many residents. One, speaking of the early 1930s, remembers "cakes seven for 6d in Mr Morley's... a well-made cake for 2d and his bread was beautiful – a white loaf was 4d." Margaret Rymill recalls that, on the way home from school around 1950, "we used to buy bread rolls, two for a penny if they were getting stale at the end of the day, and walk home eating them." Mr Morley junior still delivered bread using a hand-cart at this time, despite having lost part of one of his arms.

Next door at no. 4 (now Casual) was the Newell family's shop. In 1926 James John Newell was trading as a boot dealer. Gerald Woods remembers his "black irregular teeth caused by the standard practice in those days of holding the steel tacks in his mouth." By 1932 Laurence Newell was operating a wireless shop here. An earlier occupant of this shop, around 1910, was Arthur Rides, a draper and milliner. Mr Rides was a notable member of the Methodist Church, as was another shopkeeper, H C Harriss, who ran an ironmongery at 169 Central Road. Members of the Rides and Harriss families served the church as senior stewards, secretaries, treasurers and Sunday School Superintendents for much of the period 1905-34.

No. 3 (now Clarks) was for many years a butcher's shop. By 1899 it was being run as a branch of Alan Woods's shop in Park Terrace (see page 8), managed successively by his brothers Harry and Edgar. The latter's son Gerald recalls that it "was really one room and not a very big one at that. ... The shop had a marble slab across the inside of the window; a wooden bench which was used for cutting up the meat. This bench had a fat-drawer in it where the offcuts went, later to be converted into dripping in a big copper at the main shop. Many a breast of lamb was rescued from this drawer and went instead into some poor person's bag for their dinner for an odd copper or nothing at all... The ice safe where the meat was kept... had two compartments, one for the meat and one for the ice... These blocks of ice melted away of course and had to be replaced at regular intervals."

The first two shops in the terrace have subsequently been rebuilt. No. 2 was a sweet shop and tobacconist. By 1935 the proprietor was G R Barelli. One resident recalls "Sweets fascinated all children, because we could get a whole handful of sweets for a farthing – jellies, or liquorice rolls, sherbet fountains. If you had a farthing you could have a real treat – a ha'penny was wonderful." A door at the back of the shop led to the premises of Harold Stanton the barber, behind the Woods's shop. Horace Shrubb recalls that, in the 1920s, "if you went there on a Saturday you'd find all these old boys from the farms and so on round about, they would come in there for their weekly shave." By 1938 Mr Stanton had taken premises in Park Terrace. The post-war years brought alternatives to his traditional short back and sides: David Blake remembers his father "getting his hair cut at Meaker, the tailor opposite the Odeon on the corner of Washington Road: they had a back room which was a barber's inset into the tailor's... they used to have a steel steam cabinet in the corner and they brought hot towels, and everybody had their hair cut with a new pair of scissors that came out of this steam cabinet, I mean we'd gone up-market a great deal by then."

Finally, the first shop in Cheamside was a corn chandler's, whose owners included the Pennington, Parker and Waite families. In 1924 Tommy Waite was succeeded by

James Pearson, who had previously owned a corn chandlery at New Malden which he had expanded to include a plant nursery. Mr Pearson later moved his business to the opposite side of the road, at no. 157 (now John James Gardening), where he continued to sell seeds, plants and pet and poultry food. After his death in 1941 the shop was run by his son Stanley, until his retirement in 1976.[195]

At this point we should notice one more shop on the left-hand side of Central Road. The premises now occupied by W H Smith (no. 153) bring back memories for many former customers of J E Freeman.

Ada Batt recalls "Mr Freeman's was like a miniature Bentall's [high praise, from a former book-keeper in the Kingston department store]: he had all his separate little departments, ladies' hats and ladies' corsets upstairs all nice and private, and later on he opened two shops up the top of the High Street; he opened a carpet and linoleum shop on one side, which of course he did very well at with all the new houses coming around, and later on he opened up a bedding shop, so Mr Freeman did us very well."

*This view up Central Road c.1960, shows Freeman's and Pearson's shops (on either side of A Hall's butcher's shop)*
[Courtesy The Francis Frith collection]

Opposite Longfellow Road is Stone Place, the access road to the supermarket, opened as Somerfield in 1998 and twice the size of their previous store in the former Odeon.

*At this point you may like to take a detour down Longfellow Road, and back up Green Lane (about 1½ miles). The alternative is to continue down Central Road to the junction with Green Lane.*

*If you choose to take the detour, turn right into...*

## Longfellow Road

Longfellow Road was one of the first roads to be laid out in Worcester Park after the opening of the railway station. It occupies another of the long, narrow fields dating from the 1810 enclosure of Lower Cheam Common, and was one of the larger allotments, broadening at the far end to include the site of Lincoln Road. It was allotted to Sir Henry Bridges of Beddington, in lieu of his rights in the common fields and common, and in exchange for other properties, and became known as The Long Six and Ten Acres (it actually measured just over 17 acres).

Sir Henry enlarged his landholding in the area in 1815 by buying the site of Washington Road, called the Eight Acres (which really did measure just over eight acres) from Thomas Harris of Cheam. In 1859 he sold them both to John George Waite, a seedsman from High Holborn in London. He died within four years, and in 1865 his executors sold the properties to the British Land Company Ltd, which had been set up in 1856 to purchase lands and improve them "by draining and by laying out and making thereon such roads and other ways and parks gardens pleasure grounds playgrounds and other places for promoting health or convenience as should be deemed expedient... and the erecting suitable buildings thereon and the selling or letting of same before or after erection of buildings."

The Ordnance Survey map compiled in 1865-66 shows that the company swiftly laid out Longfellow, Lincoln and Washington Roads, perhaps choosing the names of American heroes in commemoration of the forthcoming centenary of the War of Independence, or out of respect for President Lincoln, who had been assassinated early in 1865. In June 1866 they offered the estate for sale at auction in 66 lots.

This arrangement, under which independent builders bought a few plots, meant that development proceeded piecemeal. For instance, Andrew Blake (who had previously farmed Malden Green Farm and went on to develop part of Lindsay Road) bought six plots, and built eight cottages,[196] nos. 13 – 27, which stood opposite Albany Mews (built by Linden Homes in 1997), but were demolished to make way for an extension to the Telephone Exchange.

It has been suggested that the first houses in Longfellow Road were built for the men constructing, or working on, the railway. This seems implausible, however, as development did not begin until six years after the line was opened. The census returns for 1871 list one railway porter living in the road, but most of the thirty houses were occupied by agricultural labourers, gardeners or craftsmen (including bricklayers, bootmakers, a wheelwright and an engraver).

As we walk down Longfellow Road, we pass on the right the site of the original Baptist mission room, between nos. 6 and 8, which was used until 1951, when the congregation moved to The Avenue (see page 11).

Although Longfellow Road is now almost entirely residential, a number of the earlier occupants opened small shops in their front parlours, and in 1926 Kelly's Directory was still listing sixteen business premises. Gerald Woods recalls visits to "Dippy Baker's" shop, perhaps Mrs Ellen Baker's shop at no. 33, which received its nickname from a bran tub containing "a variety of small items something like one gets out of Christmas crackers these days but probably better... wrapped up in coloured paper so that one couldn't feel for anything specific"; the shop also sold sweets of all kinds.

Two doors down, at no. 37, George Crockford opened a fish-and-chip shop in about 1920. Lucy Bell-Chambers recalls "We'd never tasted fried fish ever, and Mr Crockford opened this shop on a Saturday, and I remember my little brother Cyril coming home this Saturday night and saying to Mum 'We're going to have some fish and chips, Mum'." A little further down, on the left, is the former Methodist chapel, replaced in 1932 by the new buildings in Cheam Common Road (see Christ Church with St. Philip, page 108).

Shortly after the old chapel is a playground. Lucy Bell-Chambers recalls that this land was purchased, probably in the early 1920s, by Miss Rose Smith (see Washington

Road, page 133). "Miss Smith came into my mother's kitchen one day, and she said 'Now, Mrs Colley, I've bought the piece of land over there for the children, to keep them safe'."

Mrs Bell-Chambers recalls the routine of daily life in Longfellow Road at this time: "The kitchen table had to be scrubbed, and my mother was a stickler, she wouldn't let anything go. Two days a week we had washing: on Saturdays we used to go up The Avenue and all round the fields to get a barrowful of wood to light the copper. You had to boil all the whites [on Mondays] and then on Tuesday it was colours day." She also remembers the concern shown by the better-off for others in the community. On one occasion when her mother was ill, Mrs Clarke (who lived in St. Andrews near the foot of The Avenue) "made an egg custard and brought it down to Longfellow Road. She was a dainty lady with a big black hat and high-heeled shoes, and she came upstairs and said 'Now Mrs Colley, you've got a lot of looking after of children to do, you've got to get better. Now I've made you this custard, and you eat it up'. She really was a lady, and a lovely person."

*Mr T B Lane of Longfellow Road; the name-board on the cart advertises the family business as an agency for Watney Combe Reid & Co, brewers, as well as a grocer's*

No. 105 was, until the 1950s, occupied by a grocery shop established by Henry Lane in the 1890s, and later continued as Lane Bros. by his sons Tom and George, and grandson Ron. Maurice Upperton, whose family regularly shopped there in the years between the wars, recalls "There were two mahogany counters, one on each side. On the left hand side he weighed up the butter; bacon was sliced in the shop by hand. I used to love to go in there to see the way he packed up sugar: he took a sheet of paper, twisted it into a cone and fastened the end, and he'd pour sugar in there without spilling it."

*Continue down Longfellow Road, as far as the turning to Browning Avenue.* This road was laid out for Sutton and Cheam Urban District Council early in 1933. G W Young, the Worcester Park builder, was selected to build the first 72 houses. By January 1934, when the first houses were nearing completion, there had been 400 applicants for them.

*Follow Longfellow Road round to the left.* The bungalow on the right at no. 260 is the boyhood home of John Major, Prime Minister from 1990 to 1997. John Major's father, (Abraham) Thomas Ball, spent most of his formative years in the 1880s-90s in Pennsylvania; he taught himself acrobatics, practising in the cellar of his father's building business premises, and by his teens was appearing on the flying trapeze. The family returned to England in the closing years of the century, and he soon developed a career as a character actor and comedian.

By 1902 he had formed a music-hall double act with Kitty Grant, who later became his first wife, appearing under the name Drum and Major, or occasionally in pantomime as Tom Drum and Kitty Major. The choice of stage-name perhaps resulted from his having performed as a drum major in a Pennsylvania band before President Cleveland; an unexpected consequence occurred in 1903-04 when he was in Uruguay during a civil war, was mistaken for an officer and put in charge of a group of men. The Drum and Major revue included sketches, songs and dances; contemporary notices describe Kitty as "a red-haired 'slavey' with a penchant for speaking her mind, investing the part with an abundance of funny eccentric comedy" and Tom as "a policeman of distinctly unusual appearance and attainments."

In about 1930, after Kitty had died and Tom Major had married his speciality dancer Gwen Coates, he retired from show business. Around this time they settled in the bungalow in Longfellow Road. Soon afterwards, he began making cement garden ornaments. Major's Garden Ornaments flourished in the 1930s, and he expanded into sand and cement supply and landscaping.

John Major was born in St. Helier Hospital in March 1943. He began his schooling at Cheam Common, where his sister Pat and brother Terry had also been pupils after the decline in their father's business during the war caused them to leave Kingsley High School in The Avenue. From an early age he showed that he had inherited his father's entrepreneurial streak, which was perhaps the cause of his strong words in support of small businessmen during his time in office. His sister Pat Dessoy, interviewed in *The Daily Telegraph*, recalls "We used to breed dozens of mice at home, and he would sell them off. Suddenly, there was a new surge of customers and we found tied to a lamp-post outside the house, a notice saying 'Buy two and get a free slice of cake'."[197]

His interest in cricket was encouraged by visits to Worcester Park Athletic Club, and he spent hours practising, chalking up stumps on the garage door to bowl at.[198] Maurice Upperton recalls a similar spirit of improvisation 30 years earlier, when a long and a short piece of wood were used instead of a bat and ball, for games of 'tip-cat'.

Major's Garden Ornaments, which had been suspended during the war, was resumed and Terry Major-Ball joined his father in the business, which had diversified into decorative tiles and floral baskets as well as cement animals ranging from ducks and squirrels to herons and crocodiles. Their customers included department stores such as Bentall's, and Mark Tapley, the garden ornament shop at 54 Central Road. The business, however, fell into difficulties when a widow and her sister put a substantial amount of capital into the firm, and then withdrew it. In 1955, in order to repay the money, the Major-Balls sold the Worcester Park bungalow, and moved to rented rooms in Brixton. Thomas Major-Ball's eyesight and general health were declining, and the move did nothing to help Gwen's asthma. The garden ornament business continued until 1962, from premises closer to Brixton. Although John spent some time assisting in the workshop, it was clear that the business did not offer long-term security, and he moved into banking, a career which would give him the opportunity to develop the political ambitions he had felt since his early teens.[199]

*At the end of Longfellow Road, turn right into Green Lane alongside the...*

# Beverley Brook

Two streams, one running down Cuddington Recreation Ground and one coming from the Woodlands Avenue area, meet in a culvert at the south end of Green Lane. The brook emerges to run beside Green Lane, and flows between Motspur Park and New Malden, and through Coombe Hill, Richmond Park and Barnes, to join the Thames at Putney. The present spelling of the name dates back at least to the 1660s; in the previous century the name was 'Beverey', and the derivation 'beaver rithe (streamlet)' suggests that it dates from before 1200, when beavers became extinct in England. The stream may well be the 'Beferithe' found in medieval copies of documents dating from 693 and 957.

The brook has, inevitably, been an attraction to children across the generations. Maurice Upperton remembers that, around 1920, local boys would wait by the mouth of the culvert "and there we used to lie in wait for the fish, and as they emerged into the light we would grab them with our nets...We dug clay from the sides of the brook and made models which we baked in our ovens at home." One resident, who lived in Green Lane as a girl, recalls that, around the end of the 1920s, "that was our playing-ground... it was only shallow, safe for us to play in, which we did... in the summer holidays my mother would give us a packed lunch... and we'd go off in a gang of three or four, climbing trees, play ball or chase each other."

A decade later, some parents had a different view. Dorothy Payne recalls "There used to be trees with nice handy branches that hung over, and one day I went to swing over and the branch broke, and I sat down in Beverley Brook. I had to get my shoes and socks dry before I got home, so that I wasn't found out – only the naughty children went down to the brook." Terry Major-Ball, John Major's brother, also mentions that the brook was forbidden territory: "Naturally this made it an even more attractive proposition to try jumping it. Whenever I got wet Pat would take me home and push me into the goldfish pond in the garden." A few years later, the future Prime Minister's pedal car took an unscheduled diversion down the bank of the brook.[200]

*Walk along Green Lane past the Joint Computer Centre.* This was opened in 1969 to provide a joint computer service for the Royal Borough of Kingston-upon-Thames and the London Borough of Sutton. The original installation was an English Electric System 4 model 30, consisting of a central processing unit with 65,000 positions of core storage and the ability to handle four programs at once, two paper tape readers capable of reading 1500 characters per second from punched tapes, three magnetic tape units able to read or write information at 30,000 characters per second, three magnetic disk units and two line printers.

The spur to the introduction of computer services in local government in the London area was provided by the 1965 reorganisation of the borough structure. Both Kingston and Sutton were formed by the amalgamation of a number of smaller authorities with a range of mechanical and electro-mechanical accounting machines. It was decided that the system would initially be used for the payrolls, and would soon be extended to other financial procedures. It was realised from the start, however, that it might be possible to use the computer for a range of tasks from electoral registration to traffic surveys.[201]

Stephen Church, the original head of the Joint Computer Department who ran the Centre for its first quarter-century, recalls that the two borough councils had very advanced ideas about the ways in which computing could change local government administration. They had already decided that, by setting up a joint service, they would be able to afford a system capable of being linked to terminals in the respective council offices, which was then a highly innovative objective. Initially, however, data was recorded on paper tape at the Civic Offices in Sutton and Kingston Guildhall, collected by a van twice a day, and entered onto the computer at Worcester Park. Once the opportunity presented itself, the operation was transferred to Worcester Park so that re-usable magnetic tape could be used.

By 1972 it had become clear that the original installation was not suitable for use with a large number of terminals, and in order to meet this objective it was replaced with an IBM 370/145 system, which used similar programming and data structures. It now became possible to put terminals into the various council departments, so that data could be entered by the staff concerned, and up-to-date information could be retrieved instantly. The Department wrote software to meet the data processing requirements of many sections of the two councils, and the systems were interlocked, so that, for instance, the information from the time sheets of one department's employees could be transferred to the personnel, payroll and accounting departments, without the need to store the data in several separate places.

The JCD's constant aim was "trailblazing cautiously", providing systems that were innovative but cost-effective and delivered on time. The terminal-based cash receipting system, for instance, which was developed by IBM in collaboration with the Department, paid for itself because running balances were maintained throughout the day and the total sum available for investment was known immediately the cash offices closed; it could therefore be placed on deposit immediately, instead of on the following morning, thus earning an extra day's interest. Another idea developed by the JCD and subsequently widely adopted was the use of barcodes and light-pens to record book issues in libraries: this system was based on the barcode system used by Sainsbury's to control stocks, and was inspired by a lunchtime supermarket trip by Mr Church and the Borough Librarian Roy Smith. The designers, Plessey, were persuaded to adapt the system for library use in connection with the opening of the new Central Library in Sutton, making it possible to ascertain instantly whether a particular book was available at any of the branch libraries.

This level of innovation brought the Centre to notice nationally and internationally. The chance to be part of the experiment attracted high-calibre staff, and many of those who received their initial training in programming and other aspects of computing at Worcester Park went on to senior positions elsewhere. The Centre was visited by delegations from other countries including Israel and the newly-independent countries of Africa, who wanted to follow the example of linking together local authorities.

Terry Moore, who succeeded Mr Church in the early 1990s, comments on the changing pattern of computer provision. The Centre was extended twice in the 1970s, and expenditure on the mainframe probably reached a peak around 1980. In the 1980s, some systems were transferred to mid-range processors, and in the late 80s the spread of personal computers in Council departments began. The last mainframe installed at Green Lane was an IBM-compatible Amdahl, used from 1993 to 1996. In 1995, as a result of compulsory competitive tendering legislation, the service was contracted out to CFM, now part of ICL, and since 1996 the mainframe services have been obtained from an ICL server in Salford. This is used primarily for financial applications, whilst a number of separate mid-range processors at Green Lane are used for systems such as electoral registration and personnel records. There has, at the same time, been a decline in the number of programs written in-house, as software packages have become more widely available: the last major program written at the JCD was the council tax system introduced in 1993.

Next on the right, we pass the entrance to the Worcester Park Sewage Disposal Works. Epsom Rural District Council constructed a Low Level outfall works here in 1927-28, originally to deal with sewage from Banstead, but later converted for use by northern and western Cheam. In 1930-31 High Level works were added, designed to deal with a dry-weather daily flow of 600,000 gallons from parts of Cheam, Banstead, Cuddington, Ewell, Tadworth and Walton-on-the-Hill; the sedimentation tanks were provided with Dorr Clarifier Mechanism, and four centrifugal pumps assisted the flow to the works.

In 1933 the works were transferred to Sutton and Cheam Urban District Council. Plans were soon drawn up for improvements, including a sludge digestion scheme and additional filter beds, and major reconstruction took place in the 1950s.

In the later 20th century the works were run by Thames Water. Stephen Church recalls that the manager Bill Oliver took pride in the purity of the water discharged after treatment, and demonstrated this "by drinking a glass of the finished product which was invariably crystal clear… As a test / monitoring facility he had a magnificent tank of Tropical Guppies through which a trickle of the end product ran continuously, Guppies being very susceptible to the slightest contamination. He very rarely lost any, other than through old age." The large lakes in which the water was left to stand gave rise to rumours in the Huntsman's Hall that the Computer Centre was a front entrance to a labyrinth of underground offices under the lakes, to which the government would be moved in the event of nuclear war. Mr Church never disillusioned "the story tellers as to who I really was when, as an occasional and therefore relatively unknown customer, I was informed, in the strictest confidence of course, that I was actually a secret government mandarin." Another innovative feature was the use of the methane produced by treatment processes to power other parts of the operation, surplus power being fed into the National Grid.

The works attract a range of birds: sedge warblers and wrens breed on the banks of the sludge lagoons, and snipe and meadow pipits over-winter on the lagoons. The sludge-drying beds attract seed-eating birds such as finches; wagtails and jackdaws feed on worms and larvae in the sprinkler beds, and wheatears and flocks of swallows are occasional visitors.[202]

146

In 1996 it was decided to replace the Worcester Park works with a new facility on Thames Water's Hogsmill site at Berrylands. Work began in October 1997 on the construction of a tunnel, 20 metres deep, connecting the Worcester Park and Hogsmill sites.

*Continue along Green Lane as far as the T-junction.* Green Lane continues to the right towards Lower Morden. This is part of the ancient lane, but most of it remains unsurfaced. The boundary of Worcester Park postal district comes about 300 yards further on, just before the track passes between the Battersea New Cemetery and the Carshalton, Merton and Morden Cemetery. (The former, incidentally, had made many Londoners familiar with Worcester Park even before large-scale development began.) Across the road is Green Lane School, opened in 1950 to relieve the pressure of numbers at Cheam Common.

In the 1930s-40s, gypsies sometimes camped on land near the school site. Dorothy Payne recalls that they brought their horse-drawn caravans over the fields, and came round selling pegs, and chrysanthemums made of wood shavings dyed yellow or orange. A resident from Green Lane remembers "On occasions when we were in the front garden, they would stop and Mother used to get a bucket of water for the horse."

*Turn left, taking the road over the Beverley Brook, into...*

# Kingshill Avenue

We are now entering the Station Estate development, built in the late 1930s by Wates Brothers. This firm had been built up by four brothers out of a company founded by their father in 1901. By 1939 they were selling houses on twenty estates.

The site which they developed between Green Lane and the railway line had previously been occupied by the Wimbledon, later Albemarle, Shooting Grounds. By 1906 Mr Claude Brooking was providing practice in pheasant shooting, partridge driving and grouse driving, charging 7s 6d for practice and attendance, and 8s 4d per thousand clay birds. The sixty-acre ground boasted three pheasant-shooting towers up to 105ft high.[203] The facilities attracted the Prince of Wales, later Edward VIII, and Earl Mountbatten of Burma. Horace Shrubb recalls "My brother Norman who was in the RAF was out in India for four years during the War... they were all out on parade... and Mountbatten asked my brother where he came from, and he said 'Worcester Park'. He said, 'Oh, I know Worcester Park, I used to go shooting down there'." Maurice Upperton, who grew up in Lincoln Road in the years after the First World War, recalls "The gentry would come down from London learning to shoot, and they would go out and practise in these fields. They had a huge steel tower with machines that threw the clay pigeons into the air, and later they fitted up these fields with machines that were hidden in the long grass, and they could be operated from a distance to fire a clay pigeon. The boys would go up after the shooting-party had left, gathering the ends of the cartridges which were made of brass, and if you got a few hundred and took them along to the scrap metal merchant you could get some money for them." The business was run from Malden Green Farm by Edgar Little, who used to "send men out here keeping an eye on us." Years later, the residents of Station Estate were regularly finding black, ridged fragments of clay pigeons in their gardens.

The estate laid out by Wates effectively consisted of two crescents, Kingshill Avenue and Pembury Avenue / Caverleigh Way, with various linking roads. In the centre, a strip of land was left vacant, as the site for an intended by-pass road, which was to have been built from Malden, near Manor Park, over the railway, and along the unmade portion of Green Lane to Morden.

During the Second World War, large amounts of rubble from bomb-damaged buildings were dumped on this land. Margaret Rymill, who grew up in Kingshill Avenue, recalls

*Advertisement from the Homefinder Small Property Guide, 25 August 1934*

the potential of "The Dump" for children: "If one climbed over or wriggled under [the fence] one could get up onto it... if it was dry and slippery you could slide down." After the War, nothing came of the road scheme, and eventually the land was grassed and landscaped, providing the residents with the pleasant open space we see in front of us.

The houses follow the vernacular English style that was so popular in Worcester Park, and many of them display half-timbering or tile-hanging. Ada Batt, who moved to a newly-built house in Kingshill Avenue on her wedding day in 1937, recalls:

"The builders had left it beautiful... Wates were very good; they said 'If you find anything at all that isn't quite right or quite to your liking, come down to the office [near the site of Green Lane School] and tell us, and we'll soon send up a man to do it." The kitchen was a particular delight to those who had been used to a coal-fired range: "There was a cooker, and quite nice dresser-cupboards... It was painted cream and green; when you saw people's back doors open you could look down from your back door and see all the green and cream doors – and what happened? Within the year if you looked down every one was blue and white... The water was heated by an immersion heater upstairs, and also there was a little open fire both in the front room and the dining-room: in the dining-room there was a boiler at the back – if you just had it going all day you had a nice boiler full by evening; and in the kitchen there was an immersion heater." The Electricity Board invited the new residents to demonstrations of cooking on electric stoves at their New Malden showroom. "They were very nice little houses; in fact they were beautiful little houses, really."

*Turn left immediately into Caverleigh Way and walk to the end of the road. Turn left into Pembury Avenue, cross the bridge and turn right to rejoin...*

# Green Lane

Two maps dating from the mid-16th century suggest that Green Lane was already in use then as a track, lying between the enclosed fields of Malden and the open grazing of the portion of Sparwefeld which became Cheam Common, and joining Lower Morden Lane just as it does today.[204] Green Lane is thought to have continued across Malden Road through Cuddington until it was sealed off by the imparking of the Great Park around 1538. It is tempting to believe that Green Lane was the route called "Fishers Way" which was said to be one of the boundaries of Sparwefeld, although it is possible that this was actually the footpath beside the Pyl Brook.

Until the 1920s there were no houses on the opposite side of Green Lane from Central Road almost as far as Longfellow Road, except for one cottage on the nearer corner of Lincoln Road. Kingston Cottage, now 64, was the home of a dressmaker, Miss Thompson whose customers included the Misses Wheeler (see Worcester Park House, page 58). Maurice Upperton recalls "I came out of my house one day and saw the carriage and pair of the Misses Wheeler parked in Lincoln Road, because Green Lane in those days was just a dirt track. The coachman was dozing on the box, and my brother and I crept behind the coach, and we wrote with our fingers in the dust on the back of their coach."

*Continue along Green Lane, past the bridge to Back Green,* to A F Tann's car showroom which stands on the site of the kennels of the Worcester Park Beagles, which were formed in 1886 (perhaps in succession to the Morden Harriers, which dated back to 1834). One of the members was W G Grace, who occasionally arranged cricket matches for the hunt against his usual club, London County. In 1901 he scored 114 for the Beagles team.[205] Although the pack often hunted locally, especially in the early years, by the end of the First World War they covered a stretch of the Downs from Epsom to Oxted. In 1922 they combined with the Buckland Beagles, but continued to use the Green Lane kennels until about the end of the decade. Maurice Upperton recalls that the dogs were exercised daily in Green Lane: residents got used to hearing their names such as Major, Dan or Jack being called out. The pack was merged with the West Surrey and Horsell Beagles in 1970, under the title Surrey and North Sussex Beagles.[206]

The houses adjoining the showroom occupy the site of a cottage called Tattle Arbour (sometimes Harbour), which together with the kennels stood in a bend of the brook. Tattle Arbour was, by 1891, the home of William Saitch, a greengrocer, and his family. His sons Jack and William J Saitch are well-remembered. Jack remained at Tattle Arbour; as Maurice Upperton recalls, "He made a living by horse and cart; he was a keen businessman, and he laid the first track along to the main road out of old brick bats to make his cartage easier."

His brother William moved to 210 Longfellow Road; he was a greengrocer. Joyce Fellgett recalls that William Saitch "came round with greengrocery, all the week if you wanted anything. Old Mr Saitch, the father, used to come round selling winkles and shrimps at Sunday teatime." Maurice Upperton recalls that William Saitch "had a business head on him. His son Fred was adept at catching small creatures. I remember him having a moleskin waistcoat, and he showed me a mole that he'd caught and skinned." Horace Shrubb adds that Mr Saitch owned a roundabout and some other fairground equipment, and would set it up on Plough Green "from time to time, perhaps some holiday weekend." The greengrocery business was continued by William J's sons, especially Will who took responsibility for a shop at 1 Longfellow Road (and later relocated to a shop opposite Plough Green), and Arthur who continued the delivery round. The latter, as his son W Arthur Saitch recalls, obtained produce from the Borough Market in Southwark two or three times weekly, and delivered in many of the roads between The Avenue and Kingsmead Avenue until his retirement in the mid-1960s.

After the lane rejoins the river, we reach the entrance to the Worcester Park Athletic Club. We have already seen that the Club began in the fields around Lindsay Road. The present premises were leased to the Club in 1921, and facilities were laid out for cricket, football, tennis and bowling, although David Blake recalls that, just after the war, the cricket field still showed sufficient remnants of furrows to make the balls take unpredictable routes in the deep. In the 1930s the Club, together with the Malden Institute, arranged annual fêtes on the field, which included races, stalls, sideshows and dancing.

At this period there was a pavilion on the corner of Green Lane and Central Road. By the end of the 1930s a new pavilion had been built on the site of the present facilities, and the old one relocated alongside it for use as changing-rooms. The club continued to function during the war, despite the inevitable absence of many members, and played matches against service and civil defence teams. On 1 August 1943 there was even a baseball match between the Canadian and US servicemen stationed locally.[207] The game, part of the International League series, resulted in a 24-5 victory for the US army team.[208]

150

*Worcester Park F.C. 1921-22. The players shown are*
*back: B Herbert, ? , Ernest Styles;*
*centre: Edgar Hayes, Frederick Blake, Clifford Hughes, ? , Wally Harrington;*
*front: Charles Taylor, ? , Leslie Carey[209]*

The decades since the war have seen many improvements to the ground, including the installation of an all-weather cricket pitch, a new bowls pavilion, and a grandstand for the football pitch. Its origins in the fields at the other end of Central Road have not, however, been forgotten: members walking between the cricket field and bowling green pass through a gate commemorating Fred Blake, one of the founders in the 1920s.

On the opposite side of Green Lane, after passing Brookside Crescent and Beverley Gardens, we reach the neo-Georgian former Post Office, opened in 1939 to replace the office in Park Terrace. By 1934, Worcester Park residents could expect four deliveries per day, the last commencing at 7 pm, and letters could be posted at the Worcester Park Sorting Office at 4.15 pm for delivery in London the same evening, or at 10 pm for first delivery in London the next morning.[210] The Post Office was replaced by an agency in Central Road in c.1992.

The field between Green Lane and Longfellow Road, including the site of the post office, was formerly a corn field. Lucy Bell-Chambers remembers seeing German prisoners of war working there during the First World War: "I used to go and bring them dry bits of bread."

For a few years about 1930, as one resident recalls, gypsies set up a fair close to the site of the post office: "They used to have the grease pole, and the local lads used to try and get up this thing because at the top was a nice big joint of beef. My father used to take me and we used to stand and watch these lads, and I think on one occasion I remember the fellow getting there. They used to put sand on their hands, do anything to get up to the top."

Behind the old post office is the Telephone Exchange. The subscribers in Worcester Park, who had previously been connected to the Malden exchange, were given their own exchange on 15 January 1936. It was named DERwent, and was opened with 1250 lines, and capacity for 2000. A second exchange, GALleon, was opened hypothetically on Derwent level 5 in August 1965, and the physical exchange began operation in October 1966. When London exchanges were converted to numerical codes, Derwent retained its existing numerical equivalent as 337, while Galleon became 330.[211] More recently, a third exchange has been added under the number 332, which was the first of the Worcester Park exchanges to use digital equipment.

*At the end of Green Lane, we rejoin Central Road. The final section of our route lies to the right.* Before continuing, however, we should notice the Tudor-style parade of shops to the left, beyond Kingfish (formerly Lloyds Bank – see Park Terrace, page 8). These shops were built in the early 1930s, and provided the residents of the rapidly-growing district with an additional range of food, clothing and furniture shops. The South Suburban Co-operative Society had taken nos. 170-172 by 1935. Ada Batt recalls that the Co-op had "counters down both sides, and a chair you could sit on, and ask the young lady or gentleman behind the counter for all you wanted. They used to add it all up on the side of a 2lb of sugar, and they had an overhead wire, and they sent the bill and your money off to the cashier, and it came back with your change in." The grocery department occupied one shop, and a butcher's department was located in the adjacent premises; the two were subsequently knocked together to form a supermarket, which survived until the late 1980s.

There was another grocer, David Greig, at no. 156. Sugar was weighed out into blue paper bags. When Dorothy Payne took over the shop in 1969 as a delicatessen, she found hundreds of blue bags under the counter, and used them for coffee beans. As a child, when visiting her grandmother, she had also found an alternative use for the material bags in which flour was sold: "We used to stitch them onto a piece of wire, and the wire onto a stick, and fish in the canal with them."

*Opposite this parade of shops, easily visible from the corner of Green Lane, is…*

# Lynwood Drive

The first part of the road, originally called Stoneleigh Drive, was laid out around 1910, and terminated at a white five-bar gate just beyond the junction with Donnington Road.

In 1931 the builder John Cronk, who specialised in value-for-money houses, bought the land to the south of this development. He was able to offer three-bedroomed terrace houses, with electricity and a choice of decorations, for £525. As his development was a continuation of Stoneleigh Drive, he advertised it under the same name, which provoked fierce indignation from residents who had paid twice as much for their semi-detached houses in the older part of the road. In December 1932 Epsom Rural District Council received a complaint on the matter. Their surveyor suggested that the new section could be named 'Stoneleigh Drive South', but this was rejected by the Parish Council. The Clerk to the RDC investigated the matter, and found that the Council had in fact already decided to call the new section Meadow Road, and this decision was accordingly confirmed.

*Houses in Stoneleigh Avenue seen in c.1935 and 1997, and an advertisement from the Epsom Advertiser of 27 July 1933, when the road was still called Stoneleigh Drive*

The residents of the new houses, doubtless dismayed at the inconvenience of altering their addresses again, presented a 110-signature petition against this decision in February 1933. The Council, no doubt with a sense of relief, informed them that, since this part of Cuddington was to be transferred to Sutton and Cheam Urban District in a few weeks' time, they should take the matter up with Sutton. In June, the Sutton and Cheam Council proposed that, as a compromise, the southern portion should be known as Stoneleigh Avenue, as it remains to this day. For the residents of Stoneleigh Drive, this was not enough, and they now suggested that their own part of the road be renamed. The Council rejected their first suggestion, Worcester Drive, but eventually agreed to call the road Lynwood Drive.[212]

To the right of the junction with Lynwood Drive is a group of three shops dating back to the Edwardian period. The left-hand one is still occupied by a branch of Barclays Bank, which opened here in February 1930.[213] The bank began negotiations for the premises in the summer of 1929. The Stone trustees were delighted by this development, one commenting "Banks don't open Branches until they see that the neighbourhood is going ahead."[214] It is said that Barclays was prompted to open a branch by the glowing report of the neighbourhood given by the Methodist Church Treasurer in his application for a loan to finance the building of Christ Church.[215]

In the 1920s W T Mills established an auctioneer's and estate agent's practice in the central shop. He was joined by Edgar Birtles shortly afterwards, and the firm, which took over Millward & Co from Park Terrace, continued to trade as Mills Birtles until the 1980s when it was incorporated into Gascoigne-Pees.[216]

Earlier in the 1920s, however, Mrs Purkis had catered for a younger clientele here. Maurice Upperton recalls buying sweets here: "They had jars all round the walls, and she used to sell for a penny one of each. She would go to each jar and take one out. You bought toffees by the slab, and they'd hit it with a hammer and break it up."

*View from the corner of Green Lane, c.1910. The shops on the corner of Lynwood Drive have changed little, but the Huntsman's Hall has lost the front extension shown here*

Looking further to the right, after the modern parade (built on the site of Ivy Cottage, the Tilbury family's farmhouse) is the Forge Garage. The forge provided an essential service when Worcester Park was reliant on horses for carts and carriages, but blacksmiths also made hoops for the local boys. Maurice Upperton recalls "Girls used wooden hoops, and the boys used iron hoops: it was a length of iron, turned into a circle and welded, and we used to run to school with a hook on the end of a handle, and by holding it round the perimeter you could make the hoop revolve as you walked. The hoop had to be bought, but what we used to do if we had no money was find an old pram wheel and put a spindle through it and run with that, and then we'd hide the wheel in the hedge near the school and gather it again at night or when we went home at dinner time." Further right again, we see the...

## Huntsman's Hall

The back corner of the Huntsman's Hall site, by the railway embankment, marks the meeting-point of the three parishes in which Worcester Park lies. The garden area to the right is part of Lower Green, in Malden parish, as is the sports field behind us. The three older shops on the corner of Lynwood Drive were in Cuddington parish and within the Great Park pale. The public house itself, and the garage and modern shops to the left of it, stand on the tip of the old parish of Cheam. Like the land on the opposite side of Central Road, where the shopping parades now stand, this was part of Lower Cheam Common. When the common was enclosed in 1810, the commissioners sold this site to William Griffin for £22. In 1856 there were three cottages on the land.[217]

The public house must have been built soon afterwards, as the 1861 census returns list it as the Railway Tavern. Seven years later, it was leased for 21 years by Thomas Wood, a publican, to Thomas Hunter Tricker, a Kingston brewer. By the time of the 1871 census it had been given its present name. In 1886 it was sold to the brewery company Nalder and Collyer, which was subsequently taken over by the present owners Ind Coope.[218]

Worcester Park. — The Huntsmans Hall.

*Postcard of the Huntsman's Hall, postmarked 1907. Notice the railway station and footbridge in the background*

The appearance of the pub changed several times over the following decades. Between the 1866 and 1894 Ordnance Survey maps, a front extension was added, as seen in the photograph above. By 1927 the premises included a public bar, behind the left half of the front extension, with a private bar and hotel bar to the right, all served from a central servery, and a "workmen's lunch room" to the left. In that year, plans were approved to add a rear extension, providing a "tea room and lounge" behind the hotel bar.[219] The subtle gradations in clientele between the various bars – as well as gradations between the Huntsman's Hall, North End Tavern, and The Worcester, continued for some decades, but the pub was modernised in the 1960s, and the widening of Central Road caused the removal of the front extension.

*Turn right into Malden Road, and walk towards the small parade of shops and the railway bridge.* The present bridge was installed in November 1962; its predecessor had provided a much narrower carriageway and less headroom. The plans produced in

1856 for the construction of the railway show that the arch was intended to be 16ft high, and that the road was to be lowered by 6ft.[220] Ada Batt recalls that, at the end of the 1930s, "The path was only about two foot wide, and it was right down on a level with the road, which was very dangerous for us young mums going under with a perambulator, because you had one wheel on the path and one wheel on the road." The low headroom made the bridge impassable to double-decker buses, so single-deckers were used for the 213 Kingston-Sutton route, while the 127 service to Morden used special smaller double-deckers.

And so we return to Malden Green. A few yards' walk under the railway bridge, and up the flight of steps to the right or around the office block, will lead us back to Worcester Park station. After a walk of, perhaps, three or four hours, we have returned to our starting point.

If, instead, we had waited on the green for those hours, what would we have seen? People of Worcester Park, from the boroughs of Epsom, Sutton and Kingston, converging on their station and shops, and going about their daily activities. If, though, we could have stood here for centuries, what sights would we remember?

Would we recall the first wisps of smoke, as Iron Age man began clearing trees before building a village below Malden? The last beaver swimming away down the Beverley Brook, or the solemn rogationtide processions around Sparrowfield? Perhaps we see a park pale being put up behind the green and deer herded inside; a man on horseback, breathless from a short ride, looks on and tells his infant son that he will be master not only of a park, but of an imperial nation.

Queens and earls flash past, never staying long; the sound of muskets drifts across the trees; a Roundhead colonel is followed by a Royalist secretary. The palings rot, the deer wander away across the green; Worcester Park is a park no longer.

Smoke again: a bridge straddles the green, and an LSWR locomotive brings visitors, men with trophies financial, archaeological or botanical, from Persia, Bengal or Newfoundland. Small boys hide behind the bushes in the hope of knocking off the hats of unwary travellers, a young novelist sneers at the quietness of their retirement, and a law stationer shakes his head as he contemplates the vacant building plots opposite his genteel villas. What is that sound of tapping? A princely polo stick or a makeshift cricket bat? A carpenter installing a bay window or a for-sale sign? There is no smoke now, but an electric train draws in, and a flutter of Ideal Home Exhibition brochures descends from Station Approach.

But perhaps, if we had waited this long on Malden Green, we would have seen, more clearly than these moments of excitement, the cattle wandering across the commons, ignorant of boundaries and lawsuits, the oaks and elms steadily growing in the park, the horses pulling the farmers' carts and the gentlemen's carriages. Finally, perhaps, we would have seen ourselves, on our way to school and to work, catching the train or running for the bus. We do not know the names of those who, day by day, have ploughed and reaped, herded, sawn and hammered, moved in and commuted: but we have seen the community they have built, and we know that we have a part in shaping the community we leave for those who follow us across the green.

# Practical points

Conveniences are available as follows:

Shadbolt Park: inside the doctors' surgery, available for use by the public during surgery hours

Stoneleigh Broadway: outside station entrance in main section of Broadway

Nonsuch Park: adjacent to Mansion House forecourt

Central Road: inside the supermarket in Stone Place car park, and the Public Library

Refreshments:

There are cafés or public houses at Vale Road, Stoneleigh Broadway and Central Road. Nonsuch Park is ideal for picnics, and refreshments are also available at the Mansion House.

Disabled / pushchair access:

Most of the route is on level pavements, with no steep climbs. There are gentle upward slopes in the Avenue and Auriol Park, and steeper descents at Grafton Road, Cuddington Recreation Ground and Central Road. A short diversion is necessary for wheelchairs and pushchairs at Stoneleigh Station, as mentioned in the text.

# Summary of Main Route

Walk down Station Approach. At its foot is Malden Green.

Using the pedestrian lights, cross over Malden Road and Park Terrace. Walk up Park Terrace for a few feet as far as the entrance to The Avenue. Walk up The Avenue.

Turn left into Woodlands Avenue. Continue as far as the roundabout. Turn right there into Edenfield Gardens.

Continue around a left bend as far as the point where Edenfield Gardens bends to the right and Fairford Gardens leads off straight ahead. At this junction, leave Edenfield Gardens and take the path to the right through the gates of Shadbolt Park.

Walk up the path, and continue in either a clockwise or anticlockwise direction around the Wood, the Tree Lawn and the Main Lawn until Shadbolt House comes into sight. Follow the main drive past the left-hand side of the house, go out through the ornamental gates, cross over Salisbury Road and turn right.

Continue past The Croft to regain The Avenue, and turn left.

Continue up the left-hand side of The Avenue until you are standing opposite the junction with Cleveland Road; continue past Copsemead, cross The Avenue and go through the wrought iron gates into the grounds of St. Mary's Church.

Turn left out of the church and walk round the outside. Leave the gardens by the small iron gate; turn left onto St. Mary's Road. At the end of the road turn left into Royal Avenue. At the junction with The Avenue continue to the right around the bend, and past the junction of Delta Road into Grafton Road.

Cross to the other side of Grafton Road and continue to the bottom of the hill. Turn left into Cromwell Road. Keep straight ahead across Salisbury Road into Timbercroft.

Turn left into Sterry Drive. Our route lies up the footpath in the angle of the road between nos. 24 and 26. At the group of pine trees, fork right with the green railings on the left to reach the top of Chestnut Avenue; turn left into Auriol Park.

Follow the path around the right-hand side of the Park. At the junction with the main drive turn right. Leaving by the Park gateway, turn left into Thorndon Gardens.

Walk up Thorndon Gardens as far as the school playing-field. Here our route continues to the right. Straight ahead is Cuda's Close. Turn right into Newbury Gardens beside the school field, and first left into Vale Road. Continuing past Cunliffe Parade, turn right into Cunliffe Road.

Walk to the end of Cunliffe Road, turn right into Stoneleigh Park Road. Take the first right into Stoneleigh Crescent. Rejoin Newbury Gardens and turn left.

Continue down Newbury Gardens, and cross Stoneleigh Park Road. Enter Station Approach, passing St. John's Church on the right. Cross the railway using the covered bridge.

Exit the station into The Broadway. Continue to the end of The Broadway, past the roundabout and straight ahead into The Glade. Turn right at the end of The Glade into Chadacre Road, and left into Briarwood Road, leaving the Stoneleigh Park Estate through the brick gateway.

Turn right onto the London Road, and continue a short distance as far as the right-hand bend. Cross the London Road with great care. Turn left into Nonsuch Park and walk along the avenue. (Follow the avenue round to the left if you wish to omit the Banqueting House site; then take the diagonal path on the left towards the gardens.)

Otherwise take the tarmac path to the right at the point where the avenue turns to the left, and immediately turn right into a narrow unsurfaced path, following the 'London Loop' waymark. Three hundred yards after leaving the avenue, we reach a fork in the path, marked with Bollard no. 4. Fork right into the Wilderness, and then keep on the higher path to the left.

After another hundred yards turn left in front of a dell and up a few steps on the left back into the enclosure to reach the Banqueting House.

Continue across the grass to the left of the Banqueting House platform, past bollard 6, and onto a narrow path ahead. Go straight across the footpath at bollard 5, and turn left onto a parallel footpath running behind the gardens of the houses in Castle Avenue. After 400 yards, we reach the tarmac path connecting the Palace site and Castle Avenue. Continue straight across it and over a concrete platform on to a path partly formed by an abandoned concrete road, running along the north-western boundary of Warren Farm.

158

Continue for 600 yards along the concrete road until a prominent footpath from Warren Farm (marked with a footpath sign) crosses it; turn left onto the footpath, and cross over the avenue onto the path nearly opposite (rejoining the short-cut route).

Follow the path as far as the hedge, and through the gateway into the gardens. Keep straight on to the forecourt in front of the main entrance to the Mansion House.

Continue along the drive around the service wing, around a sharp right turn. At the end of the service wing, turn right through the gate into the gardens.

Turn left into the formal flower garden. Walk alongside the wall, and take the first path on the right into the rose walk; turn first right in front of the terrace, and continue along the main path.

On reaching the Mansion House, take the small path to the left of the house to return to the forecourt. Bear slightly left and immediately right (passing Herald Copse on the left), to take the drive through the gateway over the ha-ha into the open space of Nonsuch Park. This drive leads to the Sparrow Farm Gate.

From the car park at the Sparrow Farm Gate turn right onto the London Road and, after a few yards, cross at the pedestrian crossing and turn left into Sparrow Farm Road.

At the junction with St. Clair Drive and Bradstock Road, Sparrow Farm Road bends left and right; shortly after that junction, go through the gateway on the right into Cuddington Recreation Ground, and walk down it on the right of the brook. Continue across the grass to the right of the play area and pavilion.

On leaving the Recreation Ground, turn right into Sandringham Road; at the end of the road, turn left into Dalmeny Road.

We now reach Cheam Common Road. Our route now lies to the left, but first walk a little way to the right, as far as Woodbine Lane.

Retrace your steps as far as Dalmeny Road, and continue north-westwards along Cheam Common Road. On your left is St. Matthias' Church.

On leaving the Church continue to the left, crossing The Retreat to reach Griffiths Close.

Cross Cheam Common Road using the pedestrian crossing, and continue leftwards over Ruskin Drive as far as Christ Church with St. Philip.

Leaving the church, continue along Cheam Common Road, and cross Lindsay Road.

Continue past the parade of shops, and turn right at the War Memorial into the churchyard of St. Philip's Church.

Leave the churchyard and turn right. Continue around the right-hand bend to reach the top of Central Road.

Continue past the turning to St. Philip's Avenue. Cross Brinkley Road. On the right, we reach Washington Road. Opposite is Windsor Road. Cross Caldbeck Avenue.

You may like to take a detour down Longfellow Road, and back up Green Lane (about 1½ miles). The alternative is to continue down Central Road to the junction with Green Lane.

If you choose to take the detour, turn right into Longfellow Road; passing the turning to Browning Avenue.

Follow Longfellow Road round to the left. At the end turn right into Green Lane alongside the Beverley Brook. Walk along Green Lane past the Joint Computer Centre. Continue as far as the T-junction.

Turn left, taking the road over the Beverley Brook, into Kingshill Avenue.

Turn left immediately into Caverleigh Way and walk to the end of the road. Turn left into Pembury Avenue, cross the bridge and turn right to rejoin Green Lane.

Continue along Green Lane, past the bridge to Back Green. At the end of Green Lane, rejoin Central Road.

Turn right into Malden Road, and walk towards the small parade of shops and the railway bridge.


# Alternative shorter walks

**Walk I: The Avenue and Cheam Common** (approximately 1¾ to 2½ hours)

Start at Worcester Park Station (page 3) and continue to Cunliffe Road (page 70). At the end of Cunliffe Road, turn left instead of right, and continue down Stoneleigh Park Road, which becomes Ardrossan Gardens, for 800 yards until you reach Dewsbury Gardens. Turn right through the Cattle Arch under the railway. At the junction with Lynwood Drive / Stoneleigh Avenue, cross over into Sandringham Road, rejoining the main route at the exit from Cuddington Recreation Ground (page 103).

**Walk II: Stoneleigh and Nonsuch** (approximately 1¼ to 2 hours)

Start at Stoneleigh Station (page 74) and follow the route through Stoneleigh and around Nonsuch Park, returning to Stoneleigh at Sparrow Farm Road (page 100). At the entrance to Cuddington Recreation Ground (page 103) continue along Sparrow Farm Road for about 250 yards. At the T-junction, turn left into Rosedale Road to return to Stoneleigh Station.

The reader may devise other short walks extracted from the main route, for example:

- From Worcester Park station, through Shadbolt Park to St. Mary's Cuddington

- Around Nonsuch Park: the Palace, Banqueting House and Mansion House

- Central Road Worcester Park, including Longfellow Road and Green Lane.

# Notes

Many of the details mentioned in the text are quoted from interviews with local residents. Except where indicated otherwise, the word "recalls" in the text should be taken to be followed by a note "in conversation with the present writer, 1997-2000." In the case of Gerald Woods the word "recalls" may indicate a quotation from the memoirs which he generously allowed me to read, and in the case of Joyce Fellgett, Canon Idwal Jones, Dr E H D Phillips and Roger Wilks it may refer to written communications.

Some books which I have drawn on repeatedly are mentioned in a shortened form in the notes. They are as follows:-

Charles Abdy, A Brief History of Cuddington (Nonsuch Antiquarian Society, 1995).

A J Crowe, Inns, Taverns & Pubs of the London Borough of Sutton (London Borough of Sutton Libraries and Art Services, 1980).

John Dent, The Quest for Nonsuch (Hutchinson, 1962; revised 1970 and republished by London Borough of Sutton Libraries and Arts Services, 1981).

Sir C Alexander Harris, Cuddington Parish Fifty Years Ago (1945).

Alan A Jackson, Semi-Detached London (Second edition, Wild Swan Publications Ltd, Didcot, Oxon, 1991).

F W Knight, The History of Cuddington Parish (1945).

Robert Leach, History of St. Mary's Church, Cuddington (St. Mary's PCC, 1995).

Kenneth N Ross, A History of Malden (1947).

The following record offices have also been referred to in a shortened form:-

CERC: Church of England Record Centre, 15 Galleywall Road, Bermondsey, London SE16 3PB.

HRO: Hampshire Record Office, Sussex Street, Winchester, Hants SO23 8TH.

LBSA: London Borough of Sutton Archives, Central Library, St. Nicholas Way, Sutton, Surrey SM1 1EA.

LMA: London Metropolitan Archives (formerly Greater London Record Office), 40 Northampton Road, London EC1R 0HB.

PRO: Public Record Office, Ruskin Avenue, Kew, Richmond, Surrey TW9 4DU.

SHC: Surrey History Centre (incorporating Surrey Record Office), 130 Goldsworth Road, Woking, Surrey GU21 1ND.

---

[1] House of Lords Record Office, Evidence, H.C., 1846, Vol. 25, London and South Western Railway
[2] I am grateful to the National Railway Museum, York, for supplying copies of the timetables on which this information is based
[3] Reprinted in The Courtier, June 1997, p. 36

[4] Jackson, Semi-Detached London, pp. 184, 197

[5] LBSA: Cuddington Vestry minute and account book, Acc 229

[6] LBSA: Cheam Ratepayers' Association minute book, 20/2/1

[7] I am grateful to Jim and Margaret Parker for this information

[8] Ross, History of Malden, pp. 76, 105

[9] Ross, History of Malden, pp. 106, 133

[10] Harris, Cuddington Parish Fifty Years Ago, p. 2

[11] Lloyds TSB Group Archives, 71 Lombard Street, London: Epsom branch manager's private memorandum book, ref 5196

[12] I am indebted to Gerald Woods for these recollections by Tom Parker

[13] SHC, 6017 bundle 1

[14] Worcester Park Road Extension Act 1871; House of Lords Record Office, Evidence, H.L., 1871, Vol. 3, 24 Mar 1871

[15] According to your Faith: being an account of the Life and Village Mission Work of F L Baldwin (1893). I am grateful to Robert Mills, Secretary of the Worcester Park Baptist Church, for providing a copy

[16] The Times, 11 Jul 1925

[17] By Tom Parker, according to Gerald Woods

[18] Homerton College Library, Cambridge: Brereton Collection: B5804-5, B5808, B5049, B5022, B5039, B5105. I am grateful to Geoff Mizen, the College Librarian, for facilitating my access to these papers

[19] SHC, 6018/Bundles 2, 6 and 8

[20] The Times, 18 Jun 1936; Guildhall Library Ms 11097/27

[21] I am grateful to Maurice Upperton for this information

[22] Reprinted in The Cuddingtonian, February 1986

[23] Knight, History of Cuddington Parish, p. 21

[24] The Times, 30 Jul 1917

[25] I am grateful to Dennis Turner for this information

[26] F.T. Grant Richards, Memories of a Misspent Youth (Heinemann, 1932), p. 329

[27] Servite Houses 1945-1989

[28] Sale particulars, 1920: SHC SP2/13

[29] The Times, 28 Oct 1976 p. 19g, The Daily Telegraph, 26 Oct 1976, p. 14f

[30] Harris, Cuddington Parish Fifty Years Ago, p.2

[31] SHC Papers of Frank Bateman, estate agent, 265/3/4/52

[32] HRO Act Book of Bishops Sumner, Wilberforce and Browne, 21M65/A2/7

[33] Surrey Comet, 19 Jan 1867

[34] Ross, History of Malden, p. 132

[35] HJ Wale, Sword and Surplice or Thirty Years' Reminiscences of the Army and the Church: an autobiography (1880); Crockford's Clerical Directory, 1877

[36] Sutton Borough Archives: Cuddington vestry minutes, LG2/14

[37] Sutton Borough Archives, LG2/14; Knight, History of Cuddington Parish, p. 21

[38] Harris, Cuddington Parish Fifty Years Ago, pp. 5-6

[39] SHC 2508/1/1

[40] CERC file on Cuddington, 55057

[41] HRO Act Book of Bishops Browne, Thorold and Davidson, 21M65/A2/9 p. 261

[42] The Daily Telegraph, 21 Mar 1989

[43] Leach, History of St. Mary's, p. 55

[44] Leach, History of St. Mary's, p. 108

[45] Sermon preached in St. Mary's, 1995

[46] I am grateful to Mrs Alison Brown, Secretary of the Drymen & District Local History Society, for this information.

[47] The Times 29 May 1917

[48] Nicholas Lovell, V.C.s of Bromsgrove School (Bromsgrove School Enterprises Ltd, 1996), pp. 11-14

[49] The Times, 3 Aug 1917 p. 4a

[50] Quoted in N Lovell, V.C.s of Bromsgrove School, p. 14

[51] I am grateful to Mr Nick Gaselee for showing me a pedigree containing this detail

[52] W Rowley Hall, The Parish Church of St. John the Baptist Old Malden, Surrey: a brief guide and history, 1979

[53] I have enjoyed several stimulating conversations with Barbara Webb about the orientation of Worcester House and the direction of the avenue of trees described in 1650. She has pointed out the lack of direct evidence proving a connection between this avenue and the line of Royal Avenue. Until any further evidence comes to light, I am following the traditional view that Worcester House faced towards Royal Avenue, and that two rows of trees stood on the line of Royal Avenue in 1650, as they certainly did by the mid-18th century.

[54] PRO PROB11/283 f. 213

[55] British Library Add MSS 37047 f 25

[56] British Library Add MSS 33596 f 21

[57] Basil Duke Henning, The History of Parliament: The House of Commons 1660-1690 (Secker & Warburg, 1983), Vol. II, pp. 758-759

[58] Dent, Quest for Nonsuch, pp. 200-201

[59] Henry B Wheatley (ed), The Diary of Samuel Pepys (G Bell & Sons, 1923) Vol. V, p. 148

[60] Basil Duke Henning, op cit, Vol. III, p. 28

[61] Dent, Quest for Nonsuch, p. 218

[62] Glenys & Alan Crocker, Gunpowder Mills of Surrey (Surrey History, Vol. 4 no. 3, pp. 134-158)

[63] PRO, will of William Taylor, proved in 1764

[64] SHC 6017 bundle 6

[65] Ann Clark Amor, William Holman Hunt, The True Pre-Raphaelite (Constable, 1989), p. 274; Angela Thirlwell (ed), The Pre-Raphaelites and their World (The Folio Society, 1995), pp. x-xi

[66] Barbara C L Webb, Millais and the Hogsmill River (Barbara C L Webb, 1997)

[67] Ann Clark Amor, William Holman Hunt, pp. 83-91

[68] Margaret Bellars, 'A Suburb that had not altogether come off', in Kingston Borough News 30 Apr 1976

[69] British Library, Layard papers: Add MSS 38975 ff 104-107 and 196-197

[70] John Sutherland, Longman Companion to Victorian Fiction (Longman, Harlow, 1988), pp. 16-17

[71] Judith Goodman, Merton and Morden: A Pictorial History (Phillimore, Chichester, 1995), figure 91. I am grateful to Joanna Tarbutt for this reference

[72] This information is taken from the Souvenir Programme for the opening of the new Headquarters in 1960. I am grateful to Tim Jones for providing a copy

[73] M Stenton & S Lees (eds), Who's Who of British Members of Parliament (The Harvester Press, Brighton, 1981), Vol. 4 p. 86; F W S Craig (ed), British Parliamentary Election Results (1969 and 1983)

[74] The Times, 19 Apr 1924 p. 6c

[75] J M A Tamplin and A F Flatow, The League of Mercy and its Order (The Orders and Medals Research Society: The Miscellany of Honours No. 1, 1979): I am grateful to Lesley Smurthwaite at the National Army Museum for this reference

[76] Gentleman's Magazine, March 1847, p. 319

[77] Hector Bolitho and Derek Peel, The Drummonds of Charing Cross (George Allen & Unwin Ltd, 1967)

[78] I am grateful to Lord Ironside for information about the Wheeler family

[79] Arthur Lloyd-Taylor, The Taylors of Kew (Southern Publishing Co. Ltd, 1973-1974)

[80] Surrey County Council Legal Information Centre, County Hall, Kingston-upon-Thames: deed packet 4794

[81] I am grateful to Mrs P Phillips (née Ratcliff) for this information

[82] Michael Davis, Purple Passages: Parkside 1879-1979 (East Horsley, 1979) p. 8

[83] Michael Davis, Purple Passages: pp. 13-20

[84] Michael Davis, Purple Passages: pp. 20-27

[85] Helena Barrett & John Phillips, Suburban Style: The British Home, 1940-1960 (2nd edition, Little, Brown & Co, 1993), pp. 130-134

[86] HRO, Wessex Film and Sound Archive, Tape/A55

[87] SHC Epsom and Ewell Borough Council deeds 6122/38; Harris, Cuddington Parish Fifty Years Ago, p. 7

[88] The Times, 12 Apr 1938 p. 16d

[89] Michael Davis, Purple Passages: p. 25

[90] I am grateful to Mr J W M Crisp, Secretary of the Hurlingham Polo Association, for this information

[91] Hartley Library, Highfield, University of Southampton: Mountbatten papers, MB1/A103

[92] SHC: Epsom and Ewell Borough Council deeds 6122/38

[93] SHC, Epsom & Ewell Borough Council Recreation Grounds & Allotment Committee minutes, 6000/2/84

[94] Les Gorham, The Birth of a Bowling Club, in The Cuddingtonian, Spring 1995

[95] King George's Fields Foundation, Interim Report 1936-46

[96] LMA, Bedford Estate Archives, E/BER/S/E/8/2/5; SHC, Land Tax returns, Worcester Park

[97] Charles Abdy, The Lost Farms of Ewell (Nonsuch Antiquarian Society Occasional Paper 25, 1995), pp. 23-24, 32

[98] Epsom Advertiser, 26 Sep 1935

[99] SHC C/EM/72/1

[100] I am grateful to Ms Walsh, the Head Teacher, for allowing me to consult the school's log book

[101] SHC 6116/1/20-23

[102] SHC 6122/24B(58)

[103] Leach, History of St. Mary's, p. 112

[104] This information is taken from the church's Golden Jubilee programme (1987). I am grateful to Denise Gould, one of the present stewards, for providing a copy

[105] John Osborne, A Better Class of Person: An Autobiography 1929-56 (Faber & Faber, 1981)

[106] Jackson, Semi-Detached London, p. 224

[107] Reprinted in The Courtier, June 1997, p. 36

[108] Jackson, Semi-Detached London, p. 233

[109] Jackson, Semi-Detached London, pp. 227-228, 234

[110] A photocopy of this brochure is available in Stoneleigh Library

[111] SHC 4253/2; LMA E/BER/S/E/8/2/5

[112] Epsom Advertiser, 26 Sep 1935, p. 7e

[113] Peterborough Advertiser, 30 Dec 1934. I am grateful to Richard Hillier of Peterborough Central Library for this reference

[114] I am grateful for permission to consult the Deacons' minute books

[115] John Morris (ed.) Domesday Book: Surrey (Phillimore, Chichester, 1975), section 5.19

[116] Dent, Quest for Nonsuch, pp. 280-281

[117] J S Roskell, Linda Clarke & Carole Rawcliffe: The History of Parliament: The House of Commons 1386-1421 (Alan Sutton Publishing, Stroud,1992), Vol. II, pp. 706-707

[118] Dent, Quest for Nonsuch, pp. 25-26; Ross, History of Malden, pp. 35-41

[119] PRO E315/414; extracts given in Dent, Quest for Nonsuch pp. 281-283

[120] PRO PROB11/12 f 122v

[121] LMA Archdeaconry of Surrey probate registers, DW/PA/7/2 ff. 20, 24 & 25

[122] LMA DW/PA/7/4 f. 42

[123] HRO, Register of William of Wykeham, 21M65/A1/11

[124] Ross, History of Malden, p. 38

[125] Simon Thurley, Tudor Royal Palaces, pp. 60-65

[126] Abdy, A Brief History of Cuddington (Nonsuch Antiquarian Society, 1995)

[127] Dent, Quest for Nonsuch, pp. 54-133

[128] George Braun and Frans Hogenburg, Civitates Orbis Terrarum (Cologne, 1572-1618), mentioned in Dent, pp. 56 & 78

[129] Dent, Quest for Nonsuch, pp. 134-216, 227-258

[130] Roy Strong, The Renaissance Garden in England (Thames and Hudson, 1979), pp. 25-39

[131] Roy Strong, The Renaissance Garden in England, pp. 63-69

[132] Dent, Quest for Nonsuch, pp. 59-64, 112-133, 290

[133] Dent, Quest for Nonsuch, pp. 123-130

[134] Cuddington tithe map and award

[135] Charles Abdy, The Lost Farms of Ewell (Nonsuch Antiquarian Society Occasional Paper 25, 1995), p. 24

[136] J E B Gover, The Place Names of Surrey (Cambridge University Press, 1934)

[137] Charles Abdy, The Lost Farms of Ewell (Nonsuch Antiquarian Society Occasional Paper 25, 1995), pp. 13-17

[138] Dent, Quest for Nonsuch, p. 292

[139] PRO PROB11/729 f 308

[140] Surrey Gardens Trust, A Walk round the Gardens of Nonsuch Mansion (1995)

[141] Gerald S H Smith, Nonsuch Mansion: A Modern Echo (Epsom and Ewell Borough Council, 1992)

[142] Dent, Quest for Nonsuch, p. 224

[143] The Friends of Nonsuch, Newsletter 26 (February 1998)

[144] The Friends of Nonsuch, Newsletter 21 (November 1996)

[145] John Osborne, A Better Class of Person: An Autobiography 1929-56 (Faber & Faber, 1981)

[146] Nonsuch Watch, Newsletter 23 (October 1997), abridged

[147] The Friends of Nonsuch, Newsletter 31 (December 1998)

[148] June Chatfield, Flora and Fauna of Nonsuch (The London Naturalist, November 1994, republished by Nonsuch Watch)

[149] Georgiana Blakiston. Woburn and the Russells (Constable, 1980), p. 97

[150] PRO, PROB11/643, sign. 95

[151] LMA: Bedford Estate papers: valuation, E/BER/S/E/8/2/5

[152] I am grateful to Mr Connolly for this information

[153] PRO IR18/10123

[154] Epsom Advertiser, 1 Nov 1934

[155] SHC, C/EM/72/1

[156] Terry Major-Ball, Major Major: Memories of an Older Brother (Duckworth, 1994), p. 55

[157] SHC, Report by the Borough Education Officer of Epsom and Ewell 1965-1974, Acc. 1385

[158] Ian Yarham, Richard Barnes & Bob Britton, Nature Conservation in Sutton (London Ecology Unit, 1993)

[159] Frank Green & Dr Sidney Wolff, London Suburbs Old and New: Useful Knowledge for Health and Home (Souvenir Magazines Ltd, 1933), pp. 188-189

[160] The Register of the George Cross (This England Books, Cheltenham, 1990), p. 90

[161] SHC 6116/1/7

[162] Crowe, Inns, Taverns & Pubs of the London Borough of Sutton, p. 72

[163] 1891 census returns; LBSA Cheam valuation list, 1896

[164] Worcester Park Times, 30 Dec 1933

[165] SHC Northey papers 4073

[166] Frank Green & Dr Sidney Wolff, London Suburbs Old and New: Useful Knowledge for Health and Home (Souvenir Magazines Ltd, 1933), pp. 194-195

[167] E A Western, The Daughters of the Cross at St. Anthony's 1904-1984

[168] I am grateful to Joan Bond of the Catholic Central Library for this information

[169] I am grateful to Canon Beausang, Parish Priest from 1961 to 1998, for this information

[170] Epsom and Banstead Guardian, 23 Oct 1997

[171] SHC, Christ Church Methodist Church records, 6349/3/1

[172] SHC 6349/13/1

[173] SHC 6349/14/6

[174] Crowe, Inns, Taverns and Pubs, p. 88

[175] I am grateful to Mr M Delaiche for this information

[176] LBSA, Cheam and Cuddington parish magazines, 2236/5/1,3

[177] HRO, Act Book of Bishops Sumner, Wilberforce & Browne, 21M65/A2/7; Sutton Borough Archives: Cheam Parish Magazines, 1869-70 and June 1904; Sutton Advertiser, 12 Jun 1873

[178] WR Church's Family and Advertising Almanack (Sutton), 1872

[179] John Elliott, 'The Anglican Pugin, his successors & the Digbys of Sherborne', in Ecclesiology Today, no. 14 (September 1997)

[180] LBSA: Cheam Common parish records: Cheam & Cuddington parish magazines, 2236/5

[181] Bede Nairn & Geoffrey Serle (gen. eds.), Australian Dictionary of Biography IX pp. 42-43

[182] West Sussex Gazette, 2 May 1918. I am grateful to A Readman of West Sussex Record Office for this information

[183] LBSA: Cheam Common parish magazines, 2236/5/29-34

[184] CERC: National Society file: Cheam Common

[185] SHC, surveyor's report, CC47/32

[186] Kelly's Directory of Surrey, 1905

[187] I am very grateful to Mrs Gregory, the Head Teacher, for allowing me to make use of the log books

[188] I am very grateful to Mr Easthope, the Head Teacher, for allowing me to make use of the logbooks of the Junior School and its predecessor the Girls' School

[189] LBSA 20/2/2

[190] Sutton and Cheam Advertiser, 11 Jan 1934

[191] Letter by E Clifton in the Epsom & Banstead Guardian, 9 Jun 1994

[192] Terry Major-Ball, Major Major: Memories of an Older Brother (Duckworth, 1994), p. 52

[193] Epsom Advertiser, 30 Jun 1932; 11 Jan 1934; LBSA: Sutton & Cheam Urban District Council minutes, 1932-34

[194] Margaret Bellars, Kingston Then and Now (Michael Lancet, Esher, 1977), p. 100

[195] Margaret Bellars, 'Business which sowed the seed of success...' in Kingston Borough News, 27 Aug 1976

[196] I am grateful to Mr David Blake for this information

[197] The Daily Telegraph, 24 Jun 1996

[198] John Major: The Autobiography (HarperCollins, 1999), p. 12

[199] Terry Major-Ball, Major Major: Memories of an Older Brother (Duckworth, 1994)

[200] Terry Major-Ball, Major Major: Memories of an Older Brother (Duckworth, 1994), p. 54

[201] Joint Computer Centre brochure, c.1968

[202] Ian Yarham, Richard Barnes and Bob Britton, Nature Conservation in Sutton (London Ecology Unit, 1993), p. 80

[203] Margaret Bellars, writing in Kingston Borough News, 26 Mar 1976, quoting a Country Life advertisement

[204] PRO: MPB 25

[205] Benny Green, Wisden Book of Obituaries (Queen Anne Press, 1986)

[206] Barry Kitts, The Worcester Park Jelly Dogs, Henry Williamson Society Journal, September 1994. I am grateful to Gerald Woods for providing a copy of this article

[207] Cyril W Southerby, The History of Worcester Park Athletic Club

[208] Sutton and Cheam Advertiser, 5 Aug 1943

[209] I am grateful to Arthur and Peggy Saitch for the illustration, and to Horace Shrubb for the identifications

[210] LBSA, Sutton & Cheam UDC minutes, 26 Feb 1934

[211] I am grateful to BT Archives for this information

[212] SHC, Epsom RDC minutes, 6070/3/35; Sutton Borough Archives, Sutton & Cheam UDC minutes 1933-1934

[213] Barclays Group Archives, Dallimore Road, Wythenshawe, Manchester: Premises Committee minute book, Acc 80/19

[214] SHC 4253/3

[215] Harold Lefevre, The Golden Chain: The Story of Christ Church Methodist 1872-1949, p. 14

[216] I am grateful to Mr Neil Birtles for this information

[217] SHC QS6/8/505

[218] Crowe, Inns, Taverns and Pubs, p. 80

[219] SHC 6116/1/19

[220] SHC QS6/8/505

# Index

170